I BELIEVE

I BELIEVE

SERMONS ON THE APOSTLES' CREED

HERMAN HOEKSEMA

Edited by Marco Barone

REFORMED
FREE PUBLISHING
ASSOCIATION
Jenison, Michigan

REFORMED WITNESSHOUR
FOR BY **GRACE** ARE YE SAVED

reformedwitnesshour.org
mail@reformedwitnesshour.org
First Protestant Reformed Church
2800 Michigan St NE
Grand Rapids, MI 49506.

Printed in the United States of America.

"He Lives" at page 147: words and music by Alfred Ackley, © 1933 Curb Word Music (ASCAP). All rights administered by WC Music Corp.

Scripture cited is taken from the King James (Authorized) Version.

Italics in Scripture quotations reflect the author's emphasis.

Cover design by Erika Kiel
Interior design by Katherine Lloyd, the DESK

Reformed Free Publishing Association
1894 Georgetown Center Drive
Jenison, Michigan 49428
616-457-5970
mail@rfpa.org
www.rfpa.org

ISBN 9781936054633
Ebook ISBN 9781936054671
LCCN 2023935039

CONTENTS

Article 1

I believe in God the Father, Almighty,
Maker of heaven and earth

Article 2

And in Jesus Christ, his only begotten Son, our Lord

Article 3

Who was conceived by the Holy Ghost, born of the Virgin Mary

Article 4

Suffered under Pontius Pilate; was crucified, dead,
and buried; he descended into hell

Article 5

The third day he rose again from the dead

Article 6

He ascended into heaven,
and sitteth at the right hand of God the Father Almighty

Article 7

From thence he shall come to judge the quick and the dead

Article 8

I believe in the Holy Ghost

Article 9
I believe an holy catholic church; the communion of saints

Article 10
The forgiveness of sins

Article 11
The resurrection of the body

Article 12
And the life everlasting

Appendices

INTRODUCTION

Why should we bother with the Apostles' Creed? The Creed is made up of about 110 words in the English language. The book by Herman Hoeksema (1886–1965) that the reader currently holds is a collection of thirty-eight sermons on the Creed, with a total count of almost 110,000 words. One might think that Hoeksema was perhaps overdoing it in delivering so many sermons on such a brief, old document. Why dedicate so much time and thought to the Creed?

There are at least three possible reasons that help us understand why Hoeksema considered it appropriate to dedicate so much time to an exposition of the Creed.

1. The historical importance of the Apostles' Creed

None of Christ's apostles had any role in the Creed's composition, since it was many years after the apostolic era that the creed had its origins.[1] Nevertheless, the Creed can be so named because it is a faithful summary of biblical teaching. The Creed has been used for many purposes,[2] and it is an ideal summary of the faith of the universal Christian church.[3] The Creed unites all believers through the ages in one faith.[4] To this day, the Creed is a tool toward a clear understanding of the Christian faith.[5]

Throughout the history of the church, many preachers and theologians produced commentaries or expositions of the Creed.[6] The Reformers

---

1   For a short history of the origin, development, and uses of the Creed see Philip Schaff, ed., *The Creeds of Christendom with a History and Critical Notes*, 6th ed., 3 vols. (New York: Harper and Row, 1931; repr., Grand Rapids, MI: Baker Books, 2007), 1:14–23.

2   Cf. Cornelis P. Venema, *What We Believe: An Exposition of the Apostles' Creed* (Grand Rapids, MI: Reformed Fellowship,1996), 9–10; J. I. Packer, *Affirming the Apostles' Creed* (Wheaton, IL: Crossway, 2008), 17–23.

3   Cf. Venema, *What We Believe*, 13.

4   Cf. R. Albert Mohler Jr., *The Apostles' Creed: Discovering Authentic Christianity in an Age of Counterfeits* (Nashville, TN: Nelson Books, 2019), xv.

5   Cf. C. E. B. Cranfield, *The Apostles' Creed: A Faith to Live By* (Grand Rapids, MI: Eerdmans, 1993), 6.

6   For instance: Rufinus of Aquileia, Augustine of Hippo, Quodvultdeus of Carthage, Thomas Aquinas, Peter Martyr Vermigli, Heinrich Bullinger, Caspar Olevianus, Herman Witsius, and William Perkins.

defended the value and role of the Creed for the church.[7] For his *Institutes*, Calvin followed the order of the Apostles' Creed.[8] Martin Luther included explanations of the Creed in his *Smaller Catechism* and *Larger Catechism*, both included in the authoritative source of Lutheran doctrine, *The Book of Concord* of 1580.

As a Reformed preacher and theologian, Hoeksema recognized the historical importance of the Creed. He subscribed to and loved the Heidelberg Catechism and its explanation of the Creed found in Lord's Days 7–22.[9] However, the Creed was not intended to be a full and systematic exposition on the Christian faith, and Hoeksema was aware of the importance as well as the limits of the Creed.

> It [the Creed] professes faith in the triune God; yet it does not expressly mention the Trinity, far less declare any specific doctrine concerning the relation of the persons of the Trinity to the divine essence. All the important doctrines of God the Father, God the Son, and God the Holy Spirit are expressed here. All the salient doctrines of salvation are professed in this *credo*...But they are all stated simply as so many facts of the gospel, without as much as suggesting their dogmatic implications. And the same is true of the article concerning the Holy Spirit, the church, and the benefits of Christ's work, such as the forgiveness of sin, the resurrection of the body, and life everlasting. (page 4)

Thus, "if men appeal to the Creed as a proof of their orthodoxy, they are of course bound to explain its meaning."[10] That is what Hoeksema does in the sermons found in this book. And that we can consider to be the first reason why our author dedicated significant time to the exposition of the Creed.

---

7 Cf. Michael Horton, *We Believe: Recovering the Essentials of the Apostles' Creed* (Nashville, TN: Word Publishing, 1998), 8.

8 Cf. John Calvin, *Institutes of the Christian Religion*, Henry Beveridge trans. (Peabody, MA: Hendrickson Publishers, 2008), 2.16.18.

9 Herman Hoeksema, *The Triple Knowledge: An Exposition of the Heidelberg Catechism: Volume 1* (Grand Rapids, MI: Reformed Free Publishing Association, 1970), 296–698; *The Triple Knowledge: An Exposition of the Heidelberg Catechism: Volume 2* (Grand Rapids, MI: Reformed Free Publishing Association, 1971), 3–315.

10 William Cunningham, *Historical Theology: Vol. 1*, in *The Works of William Cunningham: Vol. 2* (Edinburgh: T. and T. Clark, 1864), 89.

2. Subscribing to and reciting the Apostles' Creed

Subscribing to and reciting the Creed is a very serious act. On the one hand, the opening words are not "we believe" but "I believe," and each worshipper talks for himself or herself.[11] On the other hand, in corporate worship, the many *I believe* becomes *we believe*.[12] Moreover, subscribing to and reciting the Creed is "a solemn pledge of allegiance."[13] In fact, the Creed "boldly declares that there is truth that is foundational to life, a truth that cannot be compromised without the peril of falling into the abyss of meaninglessness."[14] Understandably, the Creed has been called "the extreme text of self-examination"[15] because it "presses the question of whether a person is willing to adopt *the* faith expressed in the Creed as *my* faith."[16]

Hoeksema also realized the intensely personal nature of the Creed.

> This confession is definitely personal. Faith is a personal matter, a matter of the heart. And therefore, from the outset I want to strike a personal note, and confront you with the question: "Do you? Do you know what you are saying, when you confess, 'I believe in God'? And giving yourselves account of the contents of your speech, can you repeat these words from the heart, 'I believe in God'?" (page 5)

Hoeksema was well aware of the importance of the Creed, not only for the body of Christ as a whole, but also for the life and calling of the individual Christian.

3. The contents and beauty of the Apostles' Creed

In the statements of the Creed, Hoeksema perceived a unique and simple beauty that cannot pass unnoticed.

---

11 Cf. Packer, *Affirming the Apostles' Creed*, 29.

12 Cf. Mohler, *The Apostles' Creed*, xxii.

13 Ben Myers, *The Apostles' Creed: A Guide to the Ancient Catechism* (Bellingham, WA: Lexham Press: 2018), 5.

14 R. C. Sproul, *What We Believe: Understanding and Confessing the Apostles' Creed* (Grand Rapids, MI: Baker Books, 2015), 10.

15 Helmut Thielicke, *I Believe: The Christian's Creed* (Philadelphia: PA: Fortress Press, 1968), xi.

16 Stanley D. Gale, *The Christian's Creed: Embracing the Apostolic Faith* (Grand Rapids, MI: Reformation Heritage Books, 2018), 4.

There is something charming about this simple and beautiful confession of faith to which the whole Christian church subscribes. It is very brief, yet quite comprehensive, expressing all the main truths of revelation that are necessary for a Christian to believe. Its form is wholly positive, and not controversial...It is a declaration of the historical facts of the gospel, rather than an abstract statement of doctrine. (page 4)

One could hardly disagree. The Creed is a product of the attempt of the ancient church to clearly declare what is "true, essential, and splendid—splendid because they allow the splendor of truth and the splendor of Christ to be fully seen."[17] Though the Creed "cannot be taken in itself as a complete expression of what we hold in regard to the facts of our Faith," it nevertheless "brings before us those facts in their simple majesty."[18]

Regarding the first article of the Creed, Hoeksema jubilantly exclaims: "How beautiful and rich is that first article of the apostolic confession: 'I believe in God the Father, Almighty, Maker of heaven and earth'" (page 9). The reader will regularly perceive Hoeksema's love for the truths he is expounding.

Conclusion

I hope that this introduction has explained some of the reasons why the Creed deserves the attention that Hoeksema gave to it.

Through his exposition of this important document, Hoeksema guides the reader to the life-changing contemplation of the triune God and his work in Christ. Hoeksema very often expresses awe at the beauty and spiritual glory of the divine truths conveyed by the Creed, sometimes in a contagious way. In fact, he has communicated that awe to this editor too, and it is my hope that his sermons may also be a blessing to the reader.

—Marco Barone

---

17 Mohler, *The Apostles' Creed*, xx.
18 Brooke Foss Westcott, *The Historic Faith: Short Lectures on the Apostles' Creed* (London: MacMillan and Co., 1890), vii.

EDITOR'S FOREWORD

I came across the sermons in this book while looking through the online sermon archive of the Reformed Witness Hour (RWH), a Protestant Reformed radio program founded in October 1941 and still broadcasting today. As I browsed the archive, my attention was quickly caught by a sermon series by Herman Hoeksema titled "The Apostles' Creed." I was able to find the transcripts of these sermons in the library of the Protestant Reformed Theological Seminary in Wyoming, Michigan. Knowing something about the theological and historical importance of the Apostles' Creed, I decided to photocopy the sermon transcripts and propose them for publication to the Reformed Free Publishing Association. This book is the result of that discovery, or, more correctly, rediscovery.

Hoeksema delivered the sermons collected in this book during the weeks he served as the radio pastor of the RWH in the years 1951, 1952, 1954, and 1955. In addition to the sermons belonging to that series, I have included in the appendices of this book two related RWH sermons by Hoeksema, which do not formally belong to his Apostles' Creed series. I have done this, first, because Hoeksema explicitly mentions and quotes the Apostles' Creed in these two sermons, and second, to offer readers more material by the same author on the "apostolic confession," as Hoeksema himself often calls it.

Regarding editorial changes, I as editor and the copyeditors involved with this book have fully respected both the wording and the meaning of the transcripts of Hoeksema's original sermons, even where the language or the syntax is archaic or where the terms used may sound awkward to contemporary readers. Only the following changes have been made:

1) Obvious typos and grammatical mistakes have been corrected;
2) Scripture references and references to other works have been added where Hoeksema does not provide them;
3) A few explanatory footnotes have been added (all footnotes are mine);

4) Occasional phrases related to the timeframe in which Hoeksema's sermons were delivered have been omitted (for example, "in this present radio season," "last year in our radio ministry," "Last year till the 20th of February, as some of you probably will remember," and similar). These have been omitted for two reasons:

   a. These phrases make the reading of the written text cumbersome and more difficult;

   b. They neither add to nor take anything away from the author's messages.

The above has resulted in no change whatsoever to the meaning the author wanted to convey. The reader can be assured that he is reading Hoeksema's own words as recorded in the original transcripts of RWH sermons. May the reader be blessed in his reading.

—Marco Barone

BROADCAST TIMELINE

1951

I Believe in God — 10/14
The Father Creator — 10/21
The Lord of All — 10/28
The Name Jesus — 11/04
Jesus the Christ — 11/11
The Only Begotten Son — 11/18
Christ Our Lord — 11/25
Born of a Virgin — 12/02
Christ in Our Nature — 12/09
God and Man — 12/16
Christ Bearing the Wrath of God — 12/30

1952

Active Suffering All His Life — 01/06
Suffered Under Pontius Pilate — 01/13
The Death of the Accursed Tree — 01/20
Dead and Buried — 01/27
Our Temporal Death — 02/03
Reconciled to God — 02/10
Everlasting Righteousness — 02/17
Crucified with Christ — 02/24
The Descension into Hell — 03/02
Christ Is Risen — 03/09
The Power of Christ's Resurrection — 03/16
The Wonder of the Resurrection — 03/23
The Meaning of the Resurrection of Christ — 03/30

Article 1

I believe in God the Father, Almighty,
Maker of heaven and earth

Chapter 1

I BELIEVE IN GOD

It is my purpose, the Lord willing, to discuss with you the main truths of the Christian faith, as they are expressed by the church from ancient times in what is known as the Apostles' Creed. This apostolic confession is well-known to all that call themselves Christians. Nevertheless, I will repeat it, and ask you to repeat it with me, and speak in your hearts as follows:

1. I believe in God the Father, Almighty, Maker of heaven and earth;
2. And in Jesus Christ, his only begotten Son, our Lord;
3. Who was conceived by the Holy Ghost, born of the Virgin Mary;
4. Suffered under Pontius Pilate; was crucified, dead, and buried; he descended into hell;
5. The third day he rose again from the dead;
6. He ascended into heaven, and sitteth at the right hand of God the Father Almighty;
7. From thence he shall come to judge the quick and the dead;
8. I believe in the Holy Ghost.
9. I believe an holy catholic church; the communion of saints;
10. The forgiveness of sins;
11. The resurrection of the body;
12. And the life everlasting. Amen.[1]

Before I enter into the contents of this confession, I wish to make a few general remarks. In the first place, this so-called Apostles' Creed is a

---

1   This and all the quotations of the Apostles' Creed that Hoeksema makes are from *The Psalter with Doctrinal Standards, Liturgy, Church Order, and added Chorale Section*, reprinted and revised edition of the 1912 United Presbyterian Psalter (Grand Rapids, MI: Wm. B. Eerdmans Publishing Co., 1927; rev. ed. 1995), 80.

very ancient confession of faith by the church. Although its origin lies in the dark, and although it cannot be determined who is the author of the creed, we know that it is one of the oldest confessions that was ever written. The report that it was composed by the twelve apostles, and even that each of the apostles wrote one of the articles, is, of course, a myth. And it is not even to be regarded as a beautiful myth. For it was not the calling of the apostles to compose creeds, but they were instruments of revelation and the inspired preachers of the gospel of Jesus Christ.

There is something charming about this simple and beautiful confession of faith to which the whole Christian church subscribes. It is very brief, yet quite comprehensive, expressing all the main truths of revelation that are necessary for a Christian to believe. Its form is wholly positive, and not controversial. In this creed the church professes her faith apparently without considering the possibility of its being gainsaid or the necessity of defending the truth over against heretics. It is a declaration of the historical facts of the gospel, rather than an abstract statement of doctrine.

It professes faith in the triune God; yet it does not expressly mention the Trinity, far less declare any specific doctrine concerning the relation of the persons of the Trinity to the divine essence. All the important doctrines of God the Father, God the Son, and God the Holy Spirit are expressed here. All the salient doctrines of salvation are professed in this *credo*, such as the divinity of Christ, his virgin birth, his humiliation and exaltation, and his expected return on the clouds of heaven. But they are all stated simply as so many facts of the gospel, without as much as suggesting their dogmatic implications. And the same is true of the article concerning the Holy Spirit, the church, and the benefits of Christ's work, such as the forgiveness of sin, the resurrection of the body, and life everlasting. Indeed, well may it be said that every Christian subscribes to this very ancient confession of the church, and that he who does not subscribe to the whole of it cannot be called a Christian.

These few remarks must suffice to introduce my series of sermons on the Apostles' Creed. And now I will pass at once into a discussion of its content.

The first of the twelve articles reads: "I believe in God the Father, Almighty, Maker of heaven and earth." In the present sermon I will call your attention only to the first four words of this article: "I believe in God."

Notice, in the first place, that this confession is definitely personal. Faith is a personal matter, a matter of the heart. And therefore, from the outset I want to strike a personal note, and confront you with the question: "Do you? Do you know what you are saying, when you confess, 'I believe in God'? And giving yourselves account of the contents of your speech, can you repeat these words from the heart, 'I believe in God'?" I do not hesitate to say that if this is true, you are a Christian.

Let me be permitted to explain this statement.

First of all, I wish to emphasize the fact that the confession, "I believe in God," is by no means the same as saying, "I believe that God is, or that God exists." The faith that God exists is common to all men, without exception. I say this advisedly and emphatically. There are no real atheists. I am well aware of the fact that there are men who profess to be atheists, that is, those who attempt to convince themselves that there is no God, and who make that purely negative profession theirs. Others, who are very closely related to the atheists, call themselves agnostics, and claim that if there be a God, we cannot possibly have any knowledge of him. Still others meet God and his knowledge with a shrug of the shoulders. They do not say that God is not. Neither do they positively aver that God is unknowable. But they are proud in expressing a doubt concerning the knowledge of God, and call themselves skeptics.

I am convinced, on the basis of Holy Writ, that all these attitudes of the atheists and agnostics and skeptics are nothing but the lie of fools. It is according to the Bible the fool says in his heart: "There is no God" (Ps. 14:1). But in this attempt he will never succeed. God does not permit man to deny him, no matter what proud philosophy he may imagine in his heart. And the only result is that they become the objects of God's fierce wrath:

18. For the wrath of God is revealed from heaven against all ungodliness and unrighteousness of men, who hold the truth in unrighteousness;
19. Because that which may be known of God is manifest in them; for God hath shewed it unto them.

20. For the invisible things of him from the creation of the world are clearly seen, being understood by the things that are made, even his eternal power and Godhead; so that they are without excuse. (Rom. 1:18–20)

No man will ever be able to rid himself of the conviction that God is.

Nor do I say that you are a Christian because you probably believe that there is a god. The sinner is inclined to make a god of his own, a god unto himself. This is true of paganism or polytheism, with its many gods. Romans 1:21–23,

21. Because that, when they knew God, they glorified him not as God, neither were thankful; but became vain in their imaginations, and their foolish heart was darkened.
22. Professing themselves to be wise, they became fools,
23. And changed the glory of the uncorruptible God into an image made like to corruptible man, and to birds, and four-footed beasts, and creeping things.

But it is not only the pagans that grope in the darkness of their polytheism that form a god unto their own image and according to their own imagination. The modern and civilized heathen commits the same error. One does not have to make images of silver and gold, or wood and stone, and bow before them in order to make his own god. Also the proud philosophy that is called pantheism commits the same error. Pantheism professes to believe that God is all, and all is God. And this proud philosophy culminates in the imagination that man is God, or that God reaches his highest consciousness in man. Nor is the god of the deist the true God, in whom we must believe in order to be a Christian. Deism professes a god that is far above the world, but is not in the world; a god indeed that has created the world, but after having created it made that world self-sufficient, running according to its own laws. The god of deism is really one with whom we can have no contact, no fellowship, whom we do not have to fear, because he is forever separated from us.

And so, even the modern heathen fashions many gods of his own imagination. Such, for instance, is a god that is only love, in the sentimental sense of the word: a god of love without holiness, and a god of mercy without righteousness and justice. Or we make a god of our own imagination when we think of him as depending upon the will of man. All these gods are creatures of our own imagination, and therefore lies.

But when I say that you are a Christian when you can say from the heart, "I believe in God," I imply two things.

First of all, I mean to emphasize that by this confession you state that God is God, and that you know him as the true God. Who is God? My answer is briefly: he is the one who has revealed himself in Jesus Christ, the revelation that is contained in the holy Scriptures, and in the light of which we hear and interpret the speech of God in all his works. We of ourselves can never say who and what God is. What we say of ourselves concerning God is always a lie. We can never approach him who is in an inaccessible light. If we are to know him, he must approach us. We can never speak of ourselves concerning him, but must be silent when he speaks. For he is the infinite one, and the finite can never approach the infinite.

But God revealed himself, that is, he spoke concerning himself to us in language which we could understand. He spoke to his people from the very beginning of history in the holy gospel, which was realized in the fullness of time in our Lord Jesus Christ. That holy gospel has been preserved for us in Holy Writ. Through that holy gospel we know him as God. He is the Infinite One, whom the heaven and the heaven of heavens can never contain. He is the Eternal One, in whom and for whom there do not exist the limits of time. He is the Immutable One, with whom there is no change or shadow of turning. He is the Immense One, the omnipresent God, who is transcendent above all creation, yet immanent in all things. He is the Almighty One, who does whatsoever he pleases. And he is the sovereign Lord of all, in heaven and on earth. Moreover, he is the Holy One, completely consecrated to himself, the God of absolute love, who loves himself above all and all creatures for his own name's sake. He is absolute righteousness, whose will is always in harmony with his own perfect goodness. And he is gracious and merciful, full of lovingkindness and truth to them that fear him. He is the Jehovah, the immutable I Am, the Rock in whom we may trust.

For that God, that has revealed himself in the holy gospel and in whom the Christian believes, is the God of our salvation. He has made himself known to us in Jesus Christ, the Son of God come into the flesh, God of God, Immanuel. In that holy gospel he has revealed himself as the reconciler, who in the cross of Christ was reconciling the world unto himself, not imputing their trespasses unto them. And in that same holy gospel he revealed all the glory of his power unto salvation, by raising our Lord Jesus Christ from the dead and exalting him above all that is named, not only in this world, but also in the world that is to come. He is our deliverer from the power of guilt and sin and death, who through his Holy Spirit applies all the blessings of salvation to us and makes us partakers of life eternal. And when the Christian says, "I believe in God," he refers to none other than the God that has thus revealed himself, in the holy gospel, as it is preserved for us in Holy Writ.

But, secondly, we must not overlook the fact that the confession does not say, "I believe that God is," but, "I believe *in* God." To be a Christian, it is certainly not sufficient to believe that God exists, not even that the God that has revealed himself in Scripture exists. But he must and does believe *in* God. And that means that by faith he stands in a very intimate personal relation with that God whom he knows from the holy gospel. He knows him, not as a matter purely of the intellect, not as a matter of doctrine only, but as a matter of the heart. He that professes that he believes in God thereby declares that God is *his* God; that he is *his* redeemer, who forgives all *his* sins; that he is his reconciler, who placed him in the state of perfect justification; that he is *his* deliverer from all the dominion of sin and death.

He knows him with a personal, spiritual knowledge of love. And so, by faith he trusts in him, relies on him for time and eternity, in life and in death, confident that even as God has forgiven all his sins, so in the day of our Lord Jesus Christ he will raise him into everlasting life and glory. And thus, knowing God with a spiritual knowledge of love, and trusting in him as the God of his salvation, he also loves him in principle, loves him with all his heart and mind and soul and strength, forsakes the world and sin, fights the good fight of faith, walks in the light, and declares the praises of him that called him out of darkness into his marvelous light, glorifying the God of his salvation. I believe in God. Do you? Then, and then only, are you a Christian.

Chapter 2

THE FATHER CREATOR

How beautiful and rich is that first article of the apostolic confession: "I believe in God the Father, Almighty, Maker of heaven and earth." Notice the various elements contained in this confession. I believe in God, that is, I believe that God is, and that he is as he revealed himself in his word. Secondly, I believe *in* God. I do not simply believe that God exists, nor that he exists as he has revealed himself merely; but I believe that he is *my* God, and that therefore he is the God of my salvation in Jesus Christ my Lord. Thirdly, according to the article, I believe that God is Father. He is Father, in the first place, in himself, for within the Trinity the first person is the Father of the second. He is Father of our Lord Jesus Christ. He is Father by virtue of creation. And finally, he is Father in a very special sense of the word of his own people in Christ Jesus our Lord. And that Father, we confess, is omnipotent, almighty, with power to do whatsoever he pleases. And this is revealed in the work of creation, for creation is the work of his omnipotent will.

We must not make the mistake, therefore, that is so frequently made, that in discussing this first article of the apostolic creed we lay all emphasis on the work of creation. It is not creation, but the Creator that is the chief subject of this first article of the apostolic confession. It is faith in God that is expressed here. And this God, as Father Almighty, is revealed first of all in the work of creation.

Creation is revelation, revelation of God. It does indeed reveal God to us as the omnipotent one. The act of creation is an act of omnipotent will. We must not define the act of creation as to make something out of nothing. Such a definition is indeed very defective. It may have value from a pedagogical viewpoint to teach our children that creation is to make something out of nothing. But as soon as they begin to reflect, they should be shown the inadequacy of such a definition or description of the act of creation. Such a definition does not even mention God. Besides, it is certainly not true that nothing is the source of creation. Nor is creation always out of nothing. The plants are called out of the ground; so are the animals; and man is formed out of the dust of the earth.

Nevertheless, that definition may serve to emphasize the fact that apart from God's creative act there is not and never was anything whatsoever. Outside of God there is nothing. God was not limited in his act of creation by some kind of material that existed and upon which he wrought creatively. All things are the product of his omnipotent will alone. He called the things that are not as if they were. And by faith we understand that the worlds were framed by the Word of God, so that the things which are seen are not made of things which do appear. And thus the act of creation reveals God as the absolute sovereign of all and as the Father omnipotent.

Indeed, through creation God speaks to us as the omnipotent one. Creation does not prove that God exists, as has often been alleged. We cannot and we need not prove the existence of God. A God that we could prove is exactly no God, for he would lie within the compass of our logical reasoning, and by our own mind we can never apprehend or attain to God. God lies exactly outside of the bounds of our comprehension.

But although creation does not prove God, through creation God nevertheless reveals himself and speaks to us as the omnipotent one. We must be totally blind not to see this, and we must be completely deaf not to hear this language of God speaking to us through creation. For in all the works of his hands God reveals himself to us as the one that is entirely other than the creature, as the omnipotent God that can do whatever he pleases, and whose acts are wonderful. Man can build a house, but God makes a tree, the living tree. And that is exactly what man is totally incapable of doing. Man can make an airplane and fly through space; but God makes a bird, and the bird mocks at the airplane. Man makes a machine; but God calls the bodies that fly in the firmament with unmistakable precision of time. And so all the works of God in creation loudly proclaim that he is the omnipotent God. We must not think of omnipotence merely in the vague sense of infinite power, but rather in the sense that there never was any power, that there is no power, and that there never will be any power, whether within God or in the universe, except the power of God. His is the power forevermore.

This is also the comfort of the Christian. For in and by that almighty power of God he is preserved unto salvation, even unto the end. The Christian is confident by faith in that power of God. He knows that nothing can betide him, but by that almighty power. Even the devil and all his hosts and all the world of wickedness cannot prevail against the church and against the believer, because even the power of the devil is ultimately God's power. And when God does not want the devil to rage anymore, he does not fight him—God never fights—but he simply drops him and thus makes him powerless. By the power of God the Christian knows that all things work together for good unto them that love him.

Besides, creation is the product of the will of God. God was not necessitated to create. Creation is not an emanation of God's being. Between God and creation stands the will of God. God's eternal will and counsel are the only reason of existence in the whole universe. And his will is unlimited, and beside, is a will of perfect wisdom. There was nothing that limited the will of God in creation. When man makes something, he is limited and determined on every side by the material out of which the proposed article must be fashioned. When an architect draws plans and specifications of an edifice that is to be constructed, he is subject to and must figure with all kinds of existing laws. He is limited by the means at hand.

Not so with God. Creation means that the universe is solely the product of his omnipotent will. And this will is limited by absolutely nothing. God is above all laws, and himself is the sovereign creator even of them. He proposes the end, and he creates the means. He conceives of the idea, and he calls into being the material of the world. The world is exactly as God willed it to be. Creation is an act of absolute freedom and sovereignty.

Hence, we may be assured that creation as God made it in the beginning is the revelation of perfect wisdom, and the highest possible revelation of the glory of God. When I say this, I am not simply referring merely to the world as it was formed in the beginning, but ultimately to the world as it is in the counsel of God. We may be sure, indeed, that this is the best possible world, and for that very reason the only world that God could create. In the abstract it may be granted, perhaps, that God could have created an indefinite number of worlds. This is often maintained and asserted, and considered a statement of great piety and reverence. But this world is the revelation of the highest purpose of God, adapted to the reflection of his greatest glory. This is the only world God, who can only make that which is characterized by highest perfection, could conceive of, the greatest and fullest revelation of his own excellent virtues.

Besides, we must not forget that God originally created the world as the God and Father of our Lord Jesus Christ. The end of creation is Christ crucified and raised. God ordained that in Christ all things in heaven and on earth should be reconciled and united, so that in him all the fullness should dwell. And the world in the beginning was adapted to the end with perfect wisdom. It was so created that through the deep way of sin and death it could be raised to the highest possible glory by the power of grace in Christ. God knows the end from the beginning, and the latter is adapted to the former.

When he created the world, he had that end in view, the highest realization and revelation of his tabernacle with men in Christ Jesus our Lord. When God in the beginning saw that all things were good, the meaning is not simply that they were perfect and flawless, without defect, as they had come forth from the hands of the Creator, but also that they were perfectly adapted to the end he had in view. And that end is the kingdom of heaven, the heavenly tabernacle of God with men in Christ. It is because of this that the things as they were made in the beginning are an image of the things to come, and that things are done, or take place, in parables. We cannot see this of ourselves in creation, but only through God's revelation in Christ, as we have it in the Scriptures.

The earthly creation reflects the things of the kingdom of heaven, is an image of things to come. Adam is an image of him that was to come, and Christ is the last Adam. The first paradise is an earthly picture of the paradise of God in the new creation, and the original tree of life is to be fully realized in its heavenly beauty when all things are made new. The seed that falls in the earth and dies and is quickened again is a parable of the resurrection, both in its scriptural and physical sense. The sun that dispels the darkness of the night is an image of the Sun of Righteousness. And the moon that floods the night with its mellow light and assures us that the sun is still there, though we do not see her, is a silent preacher of the promise of God that the Sun will rise again in all his glory in the day of the Lord. And so all creation, the lion and the lamb, the soaring eagle and the strong ox, the tall cedar and the sturdy oak, the mighty mountain and the barren desert, the flashing lightning and the rolling thunder, storm and zephyr, earthquake and eruption, color and number, as well as man in all the relationships of man and wife, of brother and sister, of father and son, of king and subject, all speak the language of redemption to us, if our ear is only attuned and made receptive by the word of God in Christ Jesus our Lord.

And so, all the works of God are one, even as he is one. They were one in the beginning, for God did not create a mere number of creatures, but a cosmos, rising by its creative power from the darkness of the chaos in a succession of creatures, higher and higher, until they reach their pinnacle in man, in whose heart the whole cosmos was united to the heart of God. A kingdom it is, in which all creatures must serve man, that man might serve his God. But they are also one in that the beginning is connected with and adapted to the end, the new creation that will forever be united with God in the heart of Immanuel, God with us.

A glorious confession this is, indeed: "I believe in God the Father, Almighty, Maker of heaven and earth." It means that God as the Father of our Lord Jesus Christ, who is the firstborn of every creature, created the world in the beginning. It means too that he speaks to us as the Almighty God, who is perfectly able to realize all his good counsel. It means too that as the Father of our Lord Jesus Christ, he is my God and my Father for his sake. It implies that on that omnipotent God, the creator of heaven and earth, the omnipotent Father, who loves me for Jesus Christ our Lord's sake, I may indeed rely in all circumstances of life. I may trust that he will provide with all things necessary for soul and body, for time and eternity. I may know that in the midst of this evil world he will cause all things to work together for my good, that I may obtain the eternal, incorruptible, and undefilable inheritance that never fades away.

For God is Father. He is Father of the Son within the economy of the Trinity. He is Father of our Lord Jesus Christ, the firstborn of every creature, the head of his church, who was crucified and raised again on the third day and exalted in the highest heavens. And he is Father of his own, the elect, whom he chose in Jesus Christ from before the foundation of the world.

It is true, indeed, that he is the Father of all in the sense that they were all created by him in the beginning. But in the true spiritual sense he is the Father only of his own, whom he gave to Christ in his eternal counsel. For through sin men became the children of their father the devil, and do his will. They neither have the right nor the power in themselves to be children of God. We must therefore not follow modernism in its boast of a universal fatherhood of God.

But in Christ and for his sake we obtain the right to be called the children of God. And by his grace we are also conformed according to the image of his Son. And all this is realized according to God's eternal purpose, that same purpose and good pleasure according to which he created all things and governs all things. That is the confession of the believer. Knowing that he is my Father for Christ's sake, I know that in his eternal wisdom he so arranged all things from the very beginning that all things must cooperate unto the final revelation of Christ and the salvation of all that are in him. Knowing that he is almighty, I may be assured that he will surely accomplish all his good pleasure, so that nothing can betide me, but by his will. Knowing that he loves me, and that too with an eternal and immutable love, manifested in the death of his Son, I trust that he will surely cause all things to work together unto my salvation. And so the believer in Christ relies on him entirely, confident that all things always work together for good to them that love him. And the eternal Father of our Lord Jesus Christ, the Creator omnipotent, the only Potentate of potentates, the God of our salvation, is my God and Father.

Chapter 3

THE LORD OF ALL

The first article of our apostolic confession does not mention what is called the providence of God, but nevertheless presupposes it. The creator of all, the Almighty God, is and must be the Lord of the universe. Of him all things are, but by him all things subsist and continue to exist. From moment to moment God is the Lord, and remains strictly and absolutely sovereign with relation to the world he created, not only because he created all things, but also because they are literally in his hand, and they exist only by his will. This is to be understood in the most unlimited sense of the word. The sun and moon and stars, the sea and the dry land, the mountains and the hills, forest and plain, trees and flowers, corn and wheat, rain and sunshine, gold and silver, the bread that we eat and the water we drink, the air we breathe, the light and the eye, the sound and the ear, our power of mind and will, the strength to labor and toil, all things exist and continue to exist, each in its own sphere and according to its own nature, only by the will and word of God, in whom we live, and move, and have our being (Acts 17:28). God is the Lord. Without him nothing could have had being at all, and without his will nothing would continue to exist even for one moment.

This implies, in the first place, that God alone is the absolute possessor of, the proprietor of all the universe. All things are his, things in heaven and things on earth and things under the earth: "The earth is the LORD's, and the fulness thereof; the world, and they that dwell therein" (Ps. 24:1). This is true, of course, of the brute creation and all it contains. His alone are the heavenly luminaries, the sun and the moon, the stars and the planets, that move in the firmament. His alone are all the gold and the silver and all the precious stones of the earth. His alone are the sea and the dry land, the mountains and the hills, the rivers and the sea, the forest and the plains, and all the forces and powers of the universe. For he says: "Every beast of the forest is mine, and the cattle upon a thousand hills" (Ps. 50:10).

But this absolute proprietorship is not limited to the brute creature. It includes no less the intelligent, the moral and rational creation. The angels that surround his throne in the highest heavens, as well as the devils that are chained with shackles of darkness, are his. And we ourselves, all men, whether great or small, righteous or unrighteous, are his possession. Our body and our soul, our mind and our will, belong to him. We are nothing and we have nothing that does not in the strictest sense belong to God. The eyes with which we see and the ears with which we hear, the mouth with which we speak, the mind we use to think and plan, the strength we use to labor and toil, the means we employ, our clothes, our homes, our money and our possessions, all belong to him.

They are his, not ours: not because we give them to him or dedicate them to him in his service, but they are his whether we devote them to him or spend them in the service of the flesh and corruption. His they are, because he is the sovereign creator of all things. He alone is Lord, who called the things that are not as if they were. And they still continue to be by the word of his power alone. Without him they never could have been at all. Without him nothing could continue to exist. He is therefore the only and sole Lord, proprietor of all there is and ever shall be. God is the Lord!

It is well for us to remember this. For it is the very nature of sin to deny this. The sinner really lives in the wicked and deceitful imagination that he is lord, lord of himself and lord of the universe. And this evil characteristic of sin becomes manifest, not only in the brute and open refusal to glorify God as the Lord and be thankful, but even in the more abominable form of false religiousness, of self-righteousness. We bring our tithes and offerings, and piously feel that the Lord thereby is obligated to us. Or we speak of doing something for him, and feel that we can claim our reward.

But over against this the church must insist that God alone is the Lord and proprietor of all things. He possesses all the universe. This means, first of all, that with all things he has the divine prerogative to do whatever he pleases. And no one has the right to open his mouth against him, to call him to account, and to ask, "What doest thou?" (Dan. 4:35). And his alone is this right. This implies, in the second place, that true religion can never consist in this, that we give something to God or that we can do anything in his behalf. Always we are obligated to him. Never does he become obliged to us. And even when, by his grace, we may understand this truth and glorify him as Lord of all, we may thank him for the blessing that we may do so. God is the Lord!

That God is the Lord implies, secondly, that he is the absolute ruler of the universe, and implies that he governs all things according to his decree and his eternal purpose. It is by his power that all things are preserved as they were originally created, but also that they move and function from moment to moment only through him. There are those called deists that deny this aspect of God's lordship. God is high above the world, they say, but he is not in the world. He created the world, but now the universe runs by itself. But this is not according to Scripture. God is not only transcendent above the world, but he is also immanent in the world. It is he who, in the world which he created, maintains and executes his own ordinances and strictly and sovereignly controls and directs the movement of every creature.

We must remember that the universe is not a dead, inactive thing or combination of motionless beings. It is a living, organic whole. It is the creation of the living Word of God. And so everything lives and moves in all the rich and wonderful creation of God. The planets move around the sun in the firmament, even as they rotate around their own axis; and so the sun rises every morning, to drive away the night, and sets every evening at its appointed time. The moon glides through the silent night, flooding it with its mellow, silvery light; and the planets, comets, and stars roam with incredible speed through the immensity of space, each keeping to its own appointed course.

Everything moves and lives. Light moves with a rapidity of 186,000 miles a second, and, though with far less speed, sound also travels. The reverberation of thunder, the howling of the wind, the whisper of the zephyr, the song of the lark, the cry of the young raven, the roar of the lion, the spoken word, the prayer that leaves your lips—all these, and thousands upon thousands of other sounds that constantly fill the universe, have wings and fly into space. The color of the lily and of the rose, as well as their fragrance, the lingering glow of the setting sun in the western sky, the silvery path struck by the moon across the lake, the reflection of your face in the mirror, the beautiful span of the rainbow in the heavens—they all live and move according to their own nature and laws. The clouds gather; the flash of lightning zigzags through the darkness; the rain descends; rivers and brooks restlessly meander to their destination; tides rise and fall; the seed falls into the earth and dies, to rise again; the seasons follow one another in regular succession; your heart beats, and the blood courses through your veins—everything is constantly in motion.

Besides, there is the movement of the living creature, of animals and men, of holy angels and wicked demons. The worm crawls along in its path; the sparrow takes off on its wings; the wild beast roams through the forest. Man thinks and plans, desires and chooses, speaks and acts. The angels sing and attend to the word of the Lord, and the devils believe and tremble. In all the wide creation there is nothing motionless or dead.

And all this living creation is controlled and governed and ruled from moment to moment by God, the Creator Almighty. This is the language of Scripture. Always the Bible attributes all the activities of all the creatures to God the Lord. It is he that sends "the springs into the valleys," to "give drink to all the beasts of the field" (Ps. 104:10–11). He waters "the hills from his chambers" (v. 13). He causes "the grass to grow for the cattle, and herb for the service of man" (v. 14). He makes "darkness, and it is night" (v. 20). And all creatures wait upon him, that he may "give them their meat in due season" (v. 27). He takes "away their breath, and they die" (v. 29). He covers the heavens with clouds, and prepares rain for the earth (147:8). He sends forth his word "upon the earth," and it runs "very swiftly." (v. 15). He gives "snow like wool," and scatters "the hoar-frost like ashes" (v. 16). He casts "forth his ice like morsels," sending out his word to melt them; he causes "his wind to blow, and the waters to flow" (vv. 17–18).

But this sovereign dominion of the Lord is not restricted to the irrational creature. It includes also the thoughts and intents, the desires and aspirations of the heart of man. Again, there are those who would deny this. Here, at least, they say, in the heart of man is a sphere that excludes even the sovereignty of God. Man is free. He is sovereign in his own domain. He thinks what he wills, and wills what he thinks, and freely, that is, sovereignly, follows the inclinations of his own heart. But it must be clearly understood that this free-will philosophy is not in harmony with the word of God. God is the Lord. He is Lord also over man, over angels and devils, over the righteous and the unrighteous alike. For "the king's heart is in the hand of the Lord, as the rivers of water: he turneth it whithersoever he will" (Prov. 21:1).

Assyria is the rod of the Lord's anger, to chastise his people Israel (Isa. 10:5). The haughty ruler of the world-power knows nothing of the Lord's purpose. On the contrary, he boasts of his own strength and glory. When the Lord uses him to "cut off nations not a few" (v. 7), he sets himself to destroy Jerusalem and the people of God. Yet, he is only the axe that boasts against the hand that hews therewith, and the saw that magnifies itself against the hand that draws it (v. 15).

The Lord Jesus was taken and crucified "by wicked hands," but only through "the determinate counsel of God" (Acts 2:23). And when Peter and John are released by the rulers of the Jews and returned to their own company, the church glorifies the Lord of all with one accord in these words:

24. Lord, thou art God, which hast made heaven, and earth, and the sea, and all that in them is:
25. Who by the mouth of thy servant David hast said, Why did the heathen rage, and the people imagine vain things?
26. The kings of the earth stood up, and the rulers were gathered together against the Lord, and against his Christ.
27. For of a truth against thy holy child Jesus, whom thou hast anointed, both Herod, and Pontius Pilate, with the Gentiles, and the people of Israel, were gathered together,
28. For to do whatsoever thy hand and thy counsel determined before to be done. (Acts 4:24–28)

All things therefore, small and great, rational and irrational creation, prosperity and adversity, health and sickness, peace and war, life and death, good and evil, are alike controlled absolutely by the absolute lordship of God, who is God. God is the Lord!

But even so, all is not said concerning that sovereign rule of the Lord. The world is not stationary: it develops. It passes through the ages of time. It is headed for some end. And the end of time, the omega toward which all things in time must tend, is the purpose of God. For God has his counsel. And this counsel is his eternal purpose, according to which he works all things. And the end of this eternal purpose is the glory of his own name, through the highest possible realization of his covenant with his people in Christ Jesus our Lord. For he has "made known unto us the mystery of his will, according to his good pleasure which he has purposed in himself, that in the dispensation of the fullness of times he might gather together in one all things in Christ, both which are in heaven, and which are on earth" (Eph. 1:9–10).

Things were not finished when God had created all things. He had provided some better thing for us. And they are not finished now. The final rest has not been attained. And they will not be finished until the first heaven and the first earth shall have passed away, the new Jerusalem shall have come down out of heaven upon earth, and the great voice out of heaven shall be heard: "Behold, the tabernacle of God is with men, and he will dwell with them, and they shall be his people, and God himself shall be with them, and be their God" (Rev. 21:3).

All things must tend unto that glorious day of the Lord. To this end he causes all things to be subservient. In a straight line and with unwavering progress he advances, through the course of centuries, from the beginning of the world to its end, toward his own eternal purpose. Through the dark depths of sin and death, he leads, by the wonder of his grace in Christ Jesus our Lord, all things to their consummation in the day of Christ, and through that day to the heavenly heights of his perfected kingdom. And to the attainment of this end all things serve him, willingly or unwillingly, in heaven or on earth or in the abyss. God is the Lord!

God, however, is the Lord also in the sense that his is all authority. He alone is the Lawgiver. By this we refer, of course, to his relation to his moral creatures that are created with a mind and will of their own and act consciously, as free agents: men and angels. And this relation is one of authority. God is the Lord, and his alone is the prerogative to declare his will for them, and to demand unconditional obedience. He alone determines what is good and what is evil, what is right and what is wrong, what we must do and what we must be. His word is law. And he alone is our judge, and has the power to execute his judgments.

His law and his judgments are righteousness and truth and justice, not because we judge them to be right, nor because they are in conformity with any standard of righteousness outside of God, but because they are in harmony with himself. God is his own norm. He is the sole Lord. From his tribunal there is no appeal. His authority covers the whole of our life. And it is our obligation to love the Lord our God with all our heart and mind and soul and strength. God is the Lord!

To submit in love to that authority of the Lord our God is something that we can do only through the grace of our Lord Jesus Christ, through whom we have been called out of darkness into his marvelous light, so that again we confess his lordship in all spheres and every department of life. By this grace of Christ Jesus, it is our earnest desire and endeavor to walk according to the confession: God is the Lord.

And, according as we live in the faith, in the conscious faith, that God is the Lord, we shall be without fear and terror in the world, because we shall live in the tranquil assurance that all things must work together for good to them that love God, to them that are the called according to his purpose. The God and Father of our Lord Jesus Christ is the one who manifested his love toward us in the death of his Son, and who surely will give us all things with him, that is the Lord of all. He holds the reins. And whatever betide, he will surely save his church.

As the church makes her voyage across the seas of the centuries, tempest may rage furiously and the waves may rise mountain-high. We know that our God is the Lord of the tempest, and that the waves must do his bidding. In the world we may have to suffer tribulation. But he is the Lord of the tribulation. And we may glory even in them. The sufferings of this present time are not worthy to be compared with the glory that shall be revealed in us. And therefore we will not be afraid, and

Though hills amidst the seas be cast,
Though foaming waters roar,
Yea, though the mighty billows shake
The mountains on the shore,[1]

though the nations rage furiously, and we hear of wars and rumors of war, yea though all hell break loose and all the powers of darkness set themselves against us, we shall not fear, but be of good cheer. For we know that we have a covenant with the only Potentate of potentates, and that we are of the party of the living God, who only doeth wondrous things. The Lord of Hosts is his name. And he is the Lord of all.

---

1   No. 126:1, in *The Psalter*.

Article 2

And in Jesus Christ,
his only begotten Son, our Lord

Chapter 4

THE NAME JESUS

The second article of the apostolic confession reads: "And in Jesus Christ, his only begotten Son, our Lord." In the present lecture we take only the first three words of this article, and speak to you on the name *Jesus*.

The name *Jesus* is of significance for us, first of all, because it is not of human, but of divine origin. Christ received the name *Jesus* because that name was ordained for him by God. This is very evident from Holy Writ. The name of Christ might not be left to the choice and determination of Joseph and Mary. God had ordained his name from all eternity. And by the name that God had ordained, he must be known to men. And so, just before the birth of Christ, when Joseph, naturally misinterpreting the condition of his espoused wife, contemplated putting her away privily:

20. The angel of the Lord appeared unto him in a dream, saying, Joseph, thou son of David, fear not to take unto thee Mary thy wife: for that which is conceived in her is of the Holy Ghost.
21. And she shall bring forth a son, and thou shalt call his name JESUS: for he shall save his people from their sins. (Matt.1:20–21)

And so Joseph "did as the angel of the Lord had bidden him, and took unto him his wife: and knew her not till she had brought forth her firstborn son: and he called his name JESUS" (vv. 24–25).

Also the gospel according to Luke refers to this revelation of the name: "And when eight days were accomplished for the circumcising of the child, his name was called JESUS, which was so named of the angel before he was conceived in the womb" (Luke 2:21). For not only to Joseph, but also to Mary, who preferred to keep things, pondering "them in her heart" (v. 19), it was revealed by the angel Gabriel that the name of the son whom she should bring forth must be called Jesus (1:31). And so the apostles can preach that "neither is there salvation in any other: for there is none other name under heaven given among men, whereby we must be saved" (Acts 4:12). The name Jesus, therefore, is of divine origin, and is the revelation of the eternal purpose and act of God. He is called Jesus because he is Jesus, the God of our salvation, reaching down to us in our misery, to redeem us and to deliver us from death.

And because the name is ordained by God himself, it stands to reason that it is of profound significance. As we know, the name Jesus is the Greek rendering of the Hebrew name Joshua, or Jehoshua, which means "Jehovah salvation" or "Jehovah saves." It signifies that Jesus is the revelation of the God of our salvation. He is Jehovah salvation. In him we behold Jehovah, the eternal, self-existent, immutable God, who is eternal and unchangeable in himself, and eternal and immutable also in relation to his people and his covenant, as he came down to us in our misery and death, reaching down with his mighty arm to save us.

The revelation of God in Jesus is more wonderful than his revelation in creation. Creation is the revelation of the Almighty, who calls the things that are not as if they were. But Jesus, that is, the Christ of the Scriptures, is the Son of God come into the flesh, bearing our iniquities, crucified and slain, raised on the third day, gone into the heavens, and exalted at the right hand of the Most High. And this Jesus is the revelation of Jehovah our salvation, who calls light out of darkness, righteousness out of sin, life out of death, heavenly glory out of the desolation and corruption of hell.

Mark you well, the name means that Jesus saves. He does not create a possibility of salvation, but he himself accomplishes all that is implied in the salvation of his people. Many in our day, while they loudly and emphatically proclaim that "Jesus saves," yet deprive him of all power to save unless the sinner gives his consent. This is indeed a great evil, and a very general and prevalent one in our day, all the more dangerous because those that thus preach Jesus ostensibly emphasize strongly exactly that which they nevertheless deny, that Jesus saves.

The name of Jesus is on the lips of many a preacher today who nevertheless proclaims a Jesus that is impotent to save. His arm is really too short to reach us.

The words "Jesus Saves" may be read on billboards and auto licenses, as well as above entrances to church buildings. But if you should inquire of those that are responsible for these advertisements just what they meant by that winged slogan, you would discover that they attach a meaning to it quite different from what the words actually express. For according to them, they do not mean that Jesus actually saves, but that he is willing to save, provided the sinner gives his consent, will let himself be saved by Jesus. If not, their Jesus is powerless to save. In other words, they do not find in their Jesus absolutely all things necessary to save the sinner, and that too, not a willing, but an unwilling sinner, that is dead through trespasses and sins.

But when the name Jesus was given to the child, as announced by the angel to Joseph, he did not say that his name should be called Jesus because we were willing, but because he shall save his people from their sins. He shall not throw out a lifeline, which you may perhaps grasp, that he may pull you to safety, or which you may, at your pleasure and folly, sneer at and refuse to grasp, so that you perish in the raging sea. But he *shall* save. He shall not beg you to allow him to save you, to come to him, to accept him, to let him in, so that you may make it possible for him to realize his name Jesus. But his name is Jesus because he shall surely save his people from their sins.

What is salvation? It is that marvelous work of God whereby he lifts me from our present misery into the glory of his heavenly kingdom and covenant.

What is the misery from which we must be saved? What is our natural state and condition, from which Jesus lifts us into eternal glory? Is it to be compared to the condition of a drowning seaman, struggling with the waves, whom you may save by calling to him to take hold of the lifeline? On the contrary, you must present him as a man that is already drowned. Not *drowning*, but *drowned* is the word that describes his condition. He is not dying, but he is dead. Salvation is no rescuing of the dying, but a raising from the dead.

Still more, that death is spiritual death. And spiritual death means that our nature is become so corrupt, that we are enemies of God and cannot be of ourselves anything else than enemies of the fountain of life. We will not, we cannot, and we cannot will anything but sin. We are in darkness. We are perverse of mind and heart. We are corrupt in all our thoughts and desires and ways. We are blind, deaf, dead. We are alive unto iniquity and dead unto righteousness. We love darkness rather than the light. We are hateful and hating one another. And in that condition we are enslaved as willing slaves. Our will is not free, except to do evil. We are shackled by sin and death, and we could not even will to let anyone break those shackles.

Yet more. We are in this condition because we are still under the guilt of sin. Sin makes guilty. For God is just, and he is angry with the sinner every day. We are born in sin, and we increase our guilt daily. Hence, we have no other right than to be damned. We have no right to life. We lie under the sentence of death. Such is our state and condition by nature. This is the testimony of all Scripture.

Now salvation is that work of God whereby he translates us from this natural condition of slavery into the glorious liberty of the children of God. Our state of guilt must be transmitted into that of righteousness before God. And our condition of darkness and corruption must be changed into one of light and holiness. We must be delivered from the power of death, both spiritual and physical, into the state of final heavenly glory.

Now God sent his Son into the world and called his name Jesus, because through him this entire marvelous work of salvation, from beginning to end, must be and is actually accomplished.

When we say, "I believe in Jesus," we mean that in him we are free from the guilt of sin and perfectly righteous before God. By his atoning self-sacrifice he fully satisfied for all our sins. Hence, the guilt of our sin is taken away. All our sins are completely and forever blotted out. This is simply a historic fact. More than nineteen hundred years ago,[1] on the cross of Calvary, God forever blotted out the sins

---

1   The reader should keep in mind that Hoeksema delivered this sermon on November 4, 1951.

of all his people, so that there is no condemnation for them that are in Christ Jesus.

The cross and the resurrection are the actual justification of all for whom he died and rose again. The cross and resurrection of Christ establish an actual fact, not a possible righteousness. Although we become partakers of this through faith, yet faith is not the cause of our righteousness. Objectively, before God, his people are righteous on the basis of the atoning blood that was shed vicariously for them by the gracious will of God over them by Jesus, Jehovah salvation. The actual blotting out of our sin does in no way depend on our faith. It is in no sense contingent upon the choice of our will. Jesus is savior because he fully satisfied for all our sins. He "was delivered for our offences, and was raised again for our justification" (Rom. 4:25); "For the love of Christ constraineth us; because we thus judge, that if one died for all, then were all dead; and that he died for all, that they which live should not henceforth live unto themselves, but unto him which died for them, and rose again" (2 Cor. 5:14–15).

"Christ has redeemed us," not will redeem us, or can redeem us if we will, but actually redeemed us "from the curse of the law, being made a curse for us" (Gal. 3:13). And he has "obtained eternal redemption for us" (Heb. 9: 12). "By one offering" has he "perfected forever them that are sanctified" (10:14). "Jesus saves," therefore, means that he actually redeems us from all our sin and guilt, and makes us righteous before God.

But there is more. Jesus not only redeems us from the guilt of sin, but also delivers us actually from the power and dominion of sin and death. How do we become partakers of the righteousness and of all the riches of salvation which Christ merited for us? Does Jesus simply offer it to whomsoever desires it and is willing to accept it? Does he merely throw out the lifeline of his atoning sacrifice, leaving it to the will of man to take hold of it? God forbid. If this were true, he would not be Jesus. This presentation of the matter would make of Jesus a possible savior, who merited a possible righteousness, and in whose death and resurrection there is the possibility of redemption, but who is dependent upon the choice of the sinner and his will for the realization of the mighty possibilities he created by his death. And such a possible savior is after all quite an impossible savior: for we are dead in trespasses and sins, enemies of God and of his Christ, only willing to reject the offer and to cast the lifeline far from us. And we cannot come to him unless the Father draw us (John 6:44).

But Jesus saves! And he shall save his people from their sins. And this salvation "is not of him that willeth, nor of him that runneth, but of God that showeth mercy" (Rom. 9:16). Not only the objective realization of our righteousness, but also the subjective application of it is solely the work of God, of the God of our salvation, which he accomplishes through Jesus Christ, our Lord. For God raised Jesus from the dead, and wrought "the exceeding greatness of his power" in him. And he "set him at his right hand in the heavenly places" (Eph. 1:19–20). And Jesus, exalted at "the right hand of God," received the Spirit and poured out that Spirit into his church (Acts 2:33). And through the Spirit of our Lord Jesus Christ we are made one plant with him, members of his body, and he applies himself, all the work of his salvation to us. He is Jesus because he also delivers us from the power of sin and death and the devil, and this, not upon the condition of the choice of our will, but without our will, as we are by nature, and entirely contrary to it.

Jesus saves! The Jesus of the Scriptures is not a Jesus who will save you, if you will, but who saves you although you do not will. Or rather, he makes you willing before you ever can will to come to him. He does not merely offer salvation, but powerfully, efficaciously, irresistibly he works it within you. He raises you from death, and regenerates you. He calls you with an almighty calling from darkness into light. He strikes you down in true repentance, and makes you cry out for him. He implants into your hearts the saving faith, and makes you one with him. He imparts himself to you, and pours forth all the blessings of his salvation into your hearts. He justifies you, and gives you peace with God. He sanctifies you, and gives you a new delight in his precepts. He dwells in you, and bears fruit in you and through you. He makes you persevere even unto the end, and glorifies you. And he ultimately raises your body from the dead, and with all the saints gives you a place in the eternal tabernacle of our covenantal God that will be with men. His name is Jesus, because he shall surely save his people from their sins.

Thus the name Jesus is a marvelous comfort for all that believe on him. He saves his people. And his people are those whom the Father has given him from before the foundation of the world. Indeed, he does not save all men. A universal Jesus is an impotent savior. And a mighty and effectual Jesus must needs be a particular savior. Either you offer a Jesus that is willing to save all men, but cannot; or you preach a Jesus that effectually saves, and saves his people only. And the name Jesus means exactly this. It signifies that he is an effectual savior of his people, not that he is a possible savior of all men.

And thus, and thus only, you may be sure of your salvation. Do you believe in Jesus? Then you know and are confident that he died for you on the accursed tree. Then you know and are confident that he brought the atoning sacrifice for you, which is the blotting out of all your iniquities and your righteousness before God.

Do you believe in Jesus, the Jesus of the Scriptures, that saves his people from their sins? Then you know that by his almighty grace, through his Holy Spirit, he has touched your heart, and has implanted into you the gift and the power of a saving faith. Then you know and are confident that he has and shall deliver you from all the power of sin and death, preserve you unto the very end, and lead you into the glorious liberty of the children of God. He is called Jesus, Jehovah salvation, because he is a perfect and infallible savior, who will certainly save all his people from their sin.

Chapter 5

JESUS THE CHRIST

"I believe in Jesus Christ, his only begotten Son, our Lord." Such is the second article of our apostolic confession. Previously we devoted our meditation only to the very first words of that article, and discussed the name Jesus. Proceeding with the discussion of the same article, we will contemplate the meaning of the name *Christ*.

Jesus is the Christ. And the importance of this confession is very strongly emphasized in Holy Writ. In 1 John 5:1 we read: "Whosoever believeth that Jesus is the Christ is born of God." The faith that the historical Jesus, who was born in Bethlehem, walked among us, suffered, and died on Calvary, is the Christ is here presented as a sure proof that one is born of God.

Without being reborn, it is impossible to believe that Jesus is the Christ. The disciples by the mouth of Peter confess that Jesus is "the Christ, the Son of the living God" (Matt. 16:16). And the Lord replies that "flesh and blood" did not reveal this unto Peter, but his "Father who is in heaven;" and "upon this rock," upon the rock of this truth, Christ will build his church (vv. 17–18). When the bread-seeking multitude in Capernaum have become offended in Jesus, and he turns to his twelve disciples with the question, "Will ye also go away?" they answer once more through Simon Peter: "Lord, to whom shall we go? thou hast the words of eternal life. And we believe and are sure that thou art that Christ, the Son of the living God" (John 6:67–69). The Samaritan woman reports to the men of Sychar that she has met the Christ. And after Jesus had taught two days in that city, the men of Sychar themselves believed "that this is indeed the Christ, the Saviour of the world" (4:42).

Gradually during Jesus' public ministry, as he taught the people and performed his marvelous works, it became the urgent and pressing question whether he were indeed the Christ. And there were many that believed that he was. On the other hand, the more it became evident that Jesus of Nazareth claimed to be the Christ, the more the carnal Jews and their leaders hated, opposed, and persecuted him. And it was no doubt because the Jews refused to acknowledge him as such that they finally conspired to kill him. They looked for a Christ, but for an altogether different Christ from this Jesus of Nazareth. And it was ultimately because of his confession under oath that he was the Christ, the Son of the living God, that the Sanhedrin declared him worthy of death. And when the apostles have been endowed with the power of the Spirit, they preach: "Therefore let all the house of Israel know assuredly, that God hath made that same Jesus, whom ye have crucified, both Lord and Christ" (Acts 2:36).

We may note also in passing that the significance of this name Christ is accentuated by the fact that in the new dispensation the powers of iniquity, the powers of the world, are called antichristian, and that the culmination of the manifestation of those powers is called the antichrist. We do not read of an anti-Jesus, but definitely of antichrist, a name which implies all the power and manifestation of the man of sin. The name Christ is therefore very important, and it is well that we carefully attend to its meaning.

Just as Jesus is the New Testament form of the name Jehoshua, so the name Christ is the same as the Old Testament name Messiah. The name signifies the Anointed. Jesus the Christ means Jesus the Anointed. The name is therefore a title, rather than a personal name. It is indicative of Christ's official dignity, rather than of his person and nature.

What is the meaning of the symbolic act of anointing? In the old dispensation there were many anointed ones, types and shadows of him that was to come. Those that were called to hold office in the kingdom of God as it existed in the old dispensation among Israel were anointed. Holy anointing oil, specially prepared for that purpose, was poured out over the head of the one that was called by God to function officially in the kingdom of God as prophet, priest, or king.

When we study Scripture, we discover that oil, also the anointing oil, was a symbol of the Holy Spirit. This is very evident, for instance, from Isaiah 61:1, where the gift of the Spirit is directly connected with the idea of anointing: "The Spirit of the Lord GOD is upon me; because the LORD hath anointed me to preach good tidings unto the meek; he hath sent me to bind up the brokenhearted, to proclaim liberty to the captives, and the opening of the prison to them that are bound." And because the anointing oil was a symbol of the Holy Spirit, there were especially two ideas expressed by this symbolic act, the ideas, namely, of ordination or appointment unto a certain office, and of qualification for that office.

That Jesus is the Christ signifies, therefore, that he is God's officebearer, ordained and qualified by God himself to function in behalf of God's covenant and kingdom in the world. As the officebearers of the old dispensation were but types and shadows of him that was to come, and all officebearers of the old dispensation are but reflections of him and function through him, so Christ is the Anointed One *par excellence*. He is the Prophet of all prophets. He is the High Priest over the whole house of God. He is the Lord of lords, the King of kings.

What is meant by an office? In general we may say that by office is meant the position of a servant-king in relation to God. An officebearer is the official representation of the invisible God in the invisible world. An office is a position in which man is authorized and qualified to function in the name of God and in his behalf in God's covenant and kingdom, to serve him and to rule under him. And the name Christ means that he is ordained and qualified from all eternity to occupy that position. But that one office may be distinguished from a threefold aspect, namely, that of prophet, priest, and king. Christ is therefore *the* Prophet, *the* Priest, and *the* King. And to each of these aspects we must call your attention briefly.

What is a prophet? In the popular mind a prophet is one that is capable of foretelling future events. The idea of predicting the future is regarded as essential to the prophetic office. However, this is hardly correct. It is true that it belongs to the work of the prophet to speak of things to come with relation to the kingdom of God. But this is quite different from saying that foretelling the future is the main and one calling and task of a prophet. In general a prophet is one that has the knowledge of God, that speaks in his name, and thus declares his praises and glorifies him.

In that general sense we may indeed say that Adam in the state of rectitude was a prophet of God. He was called to receive the knowledge of God in his heart and mind and to stand in the midst of the created world with the praises of God on his lips. But the fall of Adam caused a radical change in this relationship. The knowledge of God was not only lost, but was subverted into its very opposite. Instead of light there was darkness. Instead of the truth there was the lie. And man by nature became the false prophet, a prophet in the service of the devil.

However, all this does not destroy or frustrate the counsel of the Most High, but must serve its realization. It is true: by willful disobedience man violated God's covenant and fell away from his high estate of rectitude, so that he, and not God, is the author of sin. But this must not tempt us to deny that God is the Most High, and that he does whatsoever he pleases, even when the first Adam falls, violates the covenant, and becomes a servant of Satan. For even though it was no doubt the purpose of the devil to silence forever the voice of true prophecy, to change the truth into the lie, and the praise of God from man's lips into blasphemy, yet God's promise was the revelation of his greater glory, and his counsel must stand.

He had anointed his own prophet from before the foundation of the world. That prophet is Christ. And as our chief prophet, he accomplishes three things. First of all, he represents, as prophet, the whole church before the face of God, to glorify him.

In the second place, as our chief prophet he reveals unto us the Father and the whole counsel of God unto salvation. As such he functions throughout the old dispensation through the prophets and shadows. As our prophet he spoke to us face to face in the days of his flesh, and in his public ministry he revealed the Father through his person, his word, and his work. But even so his prophetic office does not terminate with his death and resurrection. He is our eternal prophet. For he died and was raised from the dead. He was exalted at the right hand of God and received the promise of the Holy Spirit. And in that Spirit he returned to us on the day of Pentecost, to dwell in the church and to abide with her forever. And he is with us as our chief prophet, our teacher, who instructs us by his Spirit and word.

There is no instruction, there is no preaching of the word, there is no exhortation or consolation, there is no gathering of the church, except by him, our only and chief prophet.

And even unto all ages of ages it will be of him and through him, as our prophet, that we shall receive and rejoice in the perfect knowledge of the God of our salvation. For, in the third place, Christ through his Spirit and word also makes us again true prophets of God, so that we too know the Father and declare the praises of him who called us out of darkness into his marvelous light.

Secondly, to the office of Christ belongs his priesthood. What is a priest? Usually we connect the priesthood with the offering up of bloody sacrifices for sin. But this is only one phase of the priesthood, a phase that became necessary because of sin. The central idea of the priestly office is that of consecration of one's self and all things to the living God. A priest is a servant of God. He consecrates himself to the Holy One, and loves him. He serves in God's tabernacle, in his home.

In this sense Adam was surely priest of the Most High in the state of rectitude in the midst of the earthly creation. But he fell away from his maker, became corrupt and unholy, and subjected himself to be a priest of the devil. But also in this respect the fall of Adam must serve the counsel of God and the coming of Christ as the high priest over all the house of God. He is priest according to the order of Melchisedec, according to Scripture, a royal priest forever and ever. As such, it stands to reason that at the head of his sinful and guilty people he must offer up the sacrifice of himself for the satisfaction of sin. This our high priest did on the cross of Golgotha, where he shed his life-blood as a sacrifice of atonement.

But with this phase of his priesthood his office as priest did not terminate. He is priest forever after the order of Melchisedec. He was raised from the dead and exalted into highest glory. And in the heavenly tabernacle he offers continual intercession for his people. And upon his prayer to the Father, he as the head of his people and mediator of redemption and salvation receives all the blessings of grace, to bestow them upon them whom the Father has given him from all eternity. As priest, therefore, he sacrificed himself, intercedes for us, and blesses us with all heavenly, spiritual blessings.

And again, by his grace he also makes us priests of the Most High, delivering us from the dominion of sin and death, filling us with a new life and holiness, so that we too consecrate ourselves to the Holy One of Israel, fight the good fight of faith in the midst of the world, until at last we shall enter into the heavenly glory in the tabernacle of God, where we shall serve him in the new creation and dwell with him forever in heavenly perfection, consecrating all things unto him through Jesus Christ, our high priest.

Thirdly, to the office of Christ also belongs his kingship. He is king forever. Also of this royal office of Christ there was a reflection in Adam in the state of rectitude. For the first man too was king under God, expressly ordained by God to that position in the earthly creation. For God gave him dominion over all things, that is, over all things in the earthly creation. This first servant-king of the Lord, however, rebelled against his sovereign Lord, rejected his word, preferred the lie of the devil, and became the latter's servant. And with his dominion he is made subject to God's curse and to the power of death.

All this, however, again stands strictly in the service of God and of his eternal good pleasure. For he had provided some better thing for us, and before the foundation of the world he had ordained his servant to be king over all the works of God's hand. For the purpose of God was not to perfect all things in the first man, Adam, but to unite them all under the kingship of the last Adam, the Lord from heaven.

Hence, Christ is king, king over all, Lord of lords and King of kings. By grace he reigns over his church. He rules over his church by his word and Spirit, and therefore by grace. He writes his law into their inmost hearts, so that it becomes their delight to do his will. And by his Spirit he remains in them and abides with them forever. The result of that spiritual reign of Christ over his people is that they repent of sin and, hearing his word, follow him wherever he leads. And they fight the good fight, even unto death, that no one take their crown.

But as king over his church he also defends and preserves his own in the redemption and salvation he obtained for us. For the present, the church, though redeemed and victorious in her Lord, is in the midst of a hostile world, and is surrounded by enemies that always aim at her destruction. Besides, believers are not yet delivered from the body of this death, and the motions of sin are still in their flesh. And in the midst of, and over against all these powers of darkness, the church as a whole and believers individually must be preserved and defended; and through them all they must be led on to eternal glory and victory. This also belongs to the work of Christ as the king of his church. He is able to defend them, for by his power he rules mightily over all things, and causes all things in this present world to work together for their salvation. For he is king not only by grace over his church, but also by his mighty power over all things, even over principalities and powers, over the rulers of this world, over all the forces of darkness. And all things are subjected under his feet even now. And again, as our everlasting King, he also makes us kings over all things under God.

Thus, when all things shall have been accomplished, the last of the elect shall have been called, the measure of iniquity shall have been filled, he will come again in great power and glory, and establish his eternal kingdom in the new creation, that he may reign everlastingly over his church, and with all his people as the royal priesthood over all the works of God's hands. For Christ is an eternal king. His dominion is an everlasting dominion. And although it is true that he, as the perfect Servant of the Lord, will also himself subject himself to the Father, this does not mean that he will ever abdicate and cease to be king. On the contrary, he is king forever, even as he is an eternal priest after the order of Melchisedec. And in the eternal kingdom of glory all things shall serve Christ and his people that they may serve their God, and he may be all and in all forevermore.

Chapter 6

THE ONLY
BEGOTTEN SON

Thus far we discussed the first part of the second article of the apostolic creed. That article reads: "I believe in Jesus Christ, his only begotten Son, our Lord." This time we call attention only to the phrase, "his only begotten Son."

We must remember that the subject here is Jesus Christ. It is not the second person of the Trinity as such that is the subject of our discussion, but Jesus Christ. That the Son of Man, the historical Jesus, who was born in Bethlehem in the fullness of time, who grew up in the home of Joseph and Mary in Nazareth as an ordinary child, who sojourned among us, who taught the people, and who performed his mighty works during the three years of his public ministry, and who finally was crucified and slain by his enemies, nailed to the accursed tree, but who according to the Scriptures was raised on the third day and exalted on the right hand of the Majesty in the heavens, that this Jesus is very God, not born, but begotten, "God of God" and "Light of Light,"[1] is the subject of the second article of the apostolic creed.

That Jesus is the Christ, and that he is "the only begotten Son of God, begotten of the Father before all the worlds, God of God... very God of very God,"[2] is the confession of the church of the New Testament of all ages. Besides, this is the clear testimony of Scripture. Before the church made this confession, even during Christ's sojourn in the flesh of his humiliation, the apostles confessed that he is the Son of God.

---

1   Nicene Creed, in Philip Schaff, ed., *The Creeds of Christendom with a History and Critical Notes*, 6th ed., 3 vols. (New York: Harper and Row, 1931; repr., Grand Rapids, MI: Baker Books, 2007), 2:58.

2   Nicene Creed, in Schaff, *Creeds of Christendom*, 2:58.

Thus Nathanael, the Israelite in whom there was no guile, exclaimed at the very beginning of Jesus' public ministry: "Rabbi, thou art the Son of God; thou art the King of Israel" (John 1:49). When Jesus was with his disciples in the coasts of Caesarea Philippi, after having inquired of them as to men's opinion about him, he placed them before the personal question: "But whom say ye that I am?" (Matt. 16:15). And Peter replied in the well-known confession: "Thou art the Christ, the Son of the living God" (v. 16). And the Savior sealed this confession both as to its truth and with respect to its fundamental importance, when he said: "Blessed art thou, Simon Bar-jona: for flesh and blood hath not revealed it unto thee, but my Father which is in heaven. And I say also unto thee, That thou art Peter, and upon this rock I will build my church; and the gates of hell shall not prevail against it" (vv. 17–18). And Thomas, who would not believe unless he put his finger in the print of the nails, overcome by the glory of the risen Lord, cried out in adoration: "My Lord and my God" (John 20:28).

And this indeed is the teaching of Scripture throughout. For,

1. In the beginning was the Word, and the Word was with God, and the Word was God.
2. The same was in the beginning with God.
3. All things were made by him; and without him was not any thing made that was made.

14. And the Word was made flesh, and dwelt among us, (and we beheld his glory, the glory as of the only begotten of the Father,) full of grace and truth.

18. No man hath seen God at any time; the only begotten Son, which is in the bosom of the Father, he hath declared him. (John 1:1–3, 14, 18)

"And without controversy great is the mystery of godliness: God was manifest in the flesh, justified in the Spirit, seen of angels, preached unto the Gentiles, believed on in the world, received up into glory" (1 Tim. 3:16). "Who is he that overcometh the world, but he that believeth that Jesus is the Son of God?" (1 John 5:5). And again: "We know that the Son of God is come, and hath given us an understanding, that we may know him that is true, and we are in him that is true, even in his Son Jesus Christ. This is the true God, and eternal life" (v. 20). The apostle Paul writes: "Whose are the fathers, and of whom as concerning the flesh Christ came, who is over all, God blessed for ever" (Rom. 9:5).

Moreover, in all Scripture divine attributes are ascribed to Jesus, virtues such as eternity, omniscience, omnipotence. And he performs divine works: he creates, sustains all things, forgives men's sins, raises the dead; and himself declares that he and the Father are one, that means they are one in essence (John 10:30).

Very important and very necessary it is for the church to maintain this confession and to insist on that very language, "the only begotten Son." For the church confesses to believe in Jesus Christ. Now if in this confession she does not also clearly and definitely maintain that this Jesus Christ is very God, her faith is nothing but hero worship, faith in man, ultimately faith in self. Then Jesus is not the revelation of the Father, the God of our salvation, reaching out to us from the mysterious depths of eternity and infinity, but merely the noblest product of the human race, the revelation of the wonderful possibilities that lie in human nature.

If Christ is not very God, there is no Immanuel, no incarnation, no union of God and man, no tabernacle of God with men, no covenant of friendship, no revelation of God the Father. If he who died on Calvary was a mere man, was not the Son of God in the flesh, there was no perfect sacrifice for sin on that accursed tree, there is no atonement. Then God did not reconcile us unto himself in the blood of his Son. If Christ is not very God, his own resurrection is but a beautiful myth, and he cannot be the resurrection and the life for us.

In one word, if Christ is not essentially and eternally God, our faith is vain, we are still in our sins, we are without God in the world. Then Jesus is not the revelation of the righteousness and wisdom and sanctification and redemption of God, but of the righteousness and wisdom and holiness and redemption of man. Then the beautiful philosophy of the Man of Galilee must take the place of the Christ of the Scriptures.

But the faith and hope of the church cannot rest in man. When the church says "I believe," the object of that faith is always God, the only God, the one that dwells in the light that no man can approach unto, the eternal, the infinite, who is not comprehended by time or space, but who himself spans the chasm that separates him from us by his revelation. He is the one whom no one knows, save the Son, and those to whom the Son will reveal him. Deny that this Jesus is very God, and the article of our faith by which we confess that we believe in Jesus Christ means: I believe in man. But confess with the church of all ages that Jesus Christ is the only begotten Son of God, and that too in an altogether unique sense of the word, and your faith and hope are still in the only true God.

Oh, it seems so easy to look upon Jesus as a mere man. For in Jesus Christ and his incarnation, God came so dangerously near unto us, that he, as it were, challenged us, challenged sinful men, to deny that he is very God. In creation God reveals his eternal power and Godhead, and sinful men refuse to glorify him and to give him thanks. The heavens declare the glory of God, and the firmament shows his handiwork. On Sinai he is hid in smoke and darkness, the mountain quakes and trembles at the approach of the Most High. And from its summit roars the voice of the Almighty as the voice of thunder, striking terror into the hearts of men.

But in Jesus the chasm between the infinite Majesty and mere sinful men, between the Creator and the creature, the eternal and time, the infinite God and finite dust, the only Lord and his servants, appears to be completely abridged, eliminated, hid. In the revelation of Jesus Christ God seems totally concealed. In the manger he is a babe, helpless and dependent. In Nazareth he grows up as a child, as any other child. He increases in wisdom and stature. He dwells among us, eats and drinks, speaks and works, is tired and sleeps, is troubled and weeps. Men can see him, hear him, understand him, touch him, even contradict him, oppose him, mock him, take hold of him and bind him, judge him and condemn him, kill him and bury him, God in the flesh, in the likeness of sinful flesh.

Oh, how easy it is, therefore, to deny that he is God at all. And this is exactly what men always did, and still do. They denied it when, in the days of his flesh, he walked and tabernacled among us. And they even killed him because he confessed that he was the Son of the living God. And they denied it from Arius to the present time. They admitted that he was a wonderful man, a good man, a man that was more deeply God-conscious than any other man before him, a man that was entitled perhaps to the name of the Son of God, a man that was appointed to be Son of God. But they denied that he is God. They denied that he is the only begotten of the Father. And they still deny it.

But the church must maintain this confession. For it is the rock upon which it is built.

It must maintain this confession, moreover, in all its distinctiveness. We must maintain it in distinction from the sonship of angels, who are also called the sons of God. We must maintain it in distinction from the sonship of Adam, who was created as the son of God. We must distinguish it also from the sonship of believers, who certainly are also called the sons of God, but by no means in the same sense as the Bible speaks of the only begotten Son. Believers are children of God by grace, for the sake of Christ Jesus their Lord. They are children by adoption and by regeneration.

But the sonship of Christ is altogether unique. Christ is not born, but begotten. He is the only begotten Son. Another son of God that is begotten there is not. Other sons of God, as we already stated, are created, or they may be children by reason of a gracious act of adoption. They may even be born of God. But they are never begotten.

Christ is begotten of God. He is not created, that is, he is not the Son of God through an act of God's omnipotent will, in virtue of which he calls the things that are not as if they were. Christ is not an adopted son, that is, the right and privilege of being called Son of God are not bestowed upon him by grace. Nor is Christ born of God, that is, he is not made a being outside of God, endowed with a creaturely reflection of God's virtues. No, Christ is "the only-begotten Son of God...God of God, Light of Light, very God of very God."[3]

True, he was also born. He is "the firstborn among many brethren" (Rom. 8:29), "the firstborn of every creature" (Col. 1:15), "the firstborn [of] the dead" (v. 18). But all this is true only of the Son of

---

3   Nicene Creed, in Schaff, *Creeds of Christendom*, 2:58

God in human nature. In his divine nature he is not born, but begotten. He does not have his origin in the divine conception, in the divine will, in the divine counsel. On the contrary, with the Father and with the Holy Ghost he is the subject of that counsel. He is begotten by an act of the Father within the divine essence. Christ is God.

Christ, therefore, is the eternal Son of God. And this means, to be sure, that as Son of God he has no beginning and no end. There is no distinction of time between the Father and the only begotten Son, as if the Father were first in time and thereupon gave being to the Son of God. The Father was never without the Son; the Son was never without the Father. And the Father and the Son were never without the Holy Spirit. But that Christ is the eternal Son of God also implies that the divine act within the divine being, whereby the Father begets the Son, takes place in eternity, not in time at all. There is a chasm between eternity and time that can never be abridged, even as there is such a chasm between God and the world, between the Creator and the creature, between the divine and the human.

That Christ is the eternal Son of God means that he is Son in virtue of an unchangeable act of God the Father within the divine essence, in which the Father is active with all the infinite fullness of his Godhead. Eternally, with infinite perfection of activity of the whole divine being, the Father gives life to the Son. This unfathomably deep mystery the church tried to express by the term *eternal generation*. And therefore, Jesus Christ, the only begotten Son of God, is himself God, possessing in and of himself all the divine perfections. He is almighty, all-wise, omniscient, omnipresent, eternal, independent, self-existent, incomprehensible, the implication of all infinite perfections, and the overflowing fountain of all good. Christ is the Son of God.

And mark you well, Jesus is that only begotten, that eternal Son of God. He, the eternal Son, when he became flesh, did not change into man. He did not shed his Godhead. For the Godhead is unchangeable. His incarnation, his coming into the flesh, did not mean that he left the bosom of the Father in order to become mere man. No, this Jesus, this Christ, this babe in the manger, this child of Nazareth, this man of Galilee, this sufferer on the cross, is very God. If God himself in the flesh of Jesus Christ was not shedding his lifeblood on the accursed tree, the cross is vain. And therefore, the church confesses in the words of Isaiah 9:6, "For unto us a child is born, unto us a son is given: and the government shall be upon his shoulder: and his name shall be called Wonderful, Counsellor, The mighty God, The everlasting Father, The Prince of Peace." Jesus is very God.

"I believe in Jesus Christ, his only begotten Son." Such is the confession upon which the church of Christ of all ages is built. And being built upon that foundation, the gates of hell shall never overwhelm it. Only when we believe that Jesus is the only begotten Son of God can we maintain that he is our Savior. Only then can we confess that by grace we too are children of God. For in him and through him God adopted us, who were no children, and bestowed upon us the glorious privilege of being called the sons of God. For that adoption was realized through the cross of the only begotten Son of God in the flesh.

In ourselves we have no right to be called the children of God. But the only begotten Son of God assumed the flesh and blood of the children; took the whole burden of their guilt and sin upon his mighty shoulders; and with that burden of sin upon him, took the place of God's judgment and wrath in their stead, and in their behalf offered the perfect sacrifice for sin and obtained for his own perfect and everlasting righteousness, the right to be called the sons of God. Only because we confess that Jesus is the only begotten Son of God can we also confess that we are God's sons for his name's sake.

Moreover, only because Christ is very God in human flesh can he possibly have the power to make us sons of God in reality. For he makes us partakers of the adoption unto children by the faith he works in our hearts through the gospel, by which we embrace Christ and all his benefits, are confident that we are justified, and that for the sake of Christ we are the sons of God, with all the rights of children. Besides, by his Spirit he witnesses with our spirit that we are the sons of God indeed. And the same Spirit also realizes the adoption by causing us to be born of God, by restoring within us the image of God and making us like the image of the Son as the firstborn from the dead. Christ will keep us by his glorious power as the Son of God in the flesh, preserve his church even unto the end, and lead us on to glory, into the glorious liberty of the children of God forever.

Chapter 7

CHRIST OUR LORD

"And in Jesus Christ, his only begotten Son, our Lord." Thus reads the second article of the apostolic creed. Thus far we have discussed the significance of the name Jesus as the revelation of the God of our salvation; the meaning of the name Christ, the Anointed of the Father, our prophet, priest, and king; and the last time we pointed to the great significance of the confession that the historical Jesus is the only begotten Son of God. This time we wish to discuss the last two words of that article, and therefore speak to you on the significant fact that this Jesus the Christ, the only begotten Son of God, is our Lord.

We must never separate the lordship of Jesus Christ mentioned in the second article of the apostolic confession from his unique sonship. It is the only begotten Son of God that is our Lord. It's true that in the way of sin and grace this lordship of Jesus receives a new and deeper meaning. For the only begotten Son of God was also conceived by the Holy Ghost and born of the virgin Mary. He suffered under Pontius Pilate; was crucified, dead, and buried; and descended into hell. He was the one that was raised on the third day and is exalted in the highest heaven at the right hand of God. And in this way he became our Lord in a new and deeper and richer sense than could ever have been revealed in his lordship as the creator of all things. Yet, even so it dare never be forgotten that this Jesus, crucified and raised, exalted at the right hand of God, is the only begotten Son of God, and that as such, even while he is our mediator in human nature, we call him our Lord. And he is Lord indeed!

This must be maintained, because only thus can we maintain that the lordship of Jesus is unique and can never be mentioned in one breath with any other lordship. The saints of the early church were placed before the choice of saying, "Jesus is lord, but Caesar is also lord," or being burned at the stake, cast before the wild beasts, or into a cauldron of boiling oil. And they preferred the latter. They confessed that Jesus is Lord alone, and that there is no lord next to him or beside him.

And, if we do not maintain that Christ is the only and eternal Son of God, very God of very God, the confession that he is our Lord is emptied completely of all its real significance. For then he is Lord as mere man, a lord among other lords—more powerful, perhaps, than all, yet strictly limited in his authority and might, both with regard to its scope and with respect to its power. In that case his lordship becomes a matter of relative significance. Then he is Lord really because we call him so, just as other religious groups in the world might call their leaders "lord." Then we may, perhaps, claim that comparatively he is worthy to become Lord of all the world because the religion he founded is much purer and nobler than any other religion; or we call him Lord because he has done so much for us, and therefore we are willing to serve him. But nevertheless, we deny his real and essential and unique lordship.

And therefore we must emphatically maintain that when we call Jesus Christ our Lord, we do not place him in a class, in a category of lords, such as we know many in the world, but that we acknowledge him as the sole Lord over us and over all. The expression "our Lord" in the confession of the church does not refer to a limited, but to an unlimited lordship. It does not tolerate other, perhaps inferior, lordship next to, or even under, the lordship of Jesus Christ, but is strictly exclusive of them and wholly intolerant.

His lordship is not contingent or dependent upon anything we may do. He is not and does not become our Lord because we acknowledge him as such, and we are willing to serve him. But on the contrary, our acknowledgment of him as our Lord is strictly dependent on the sovereign exercise of his lordship over us. Even the marvelous fact that we are able to say, "I believe in Jesus Christ our Lord," is only a manifestation of his mighty and sovereign lordship. No man can say that Jesus is Lord, except by the Holy Ghost.

But to maintain this unique lordship of Jesus Christ, we dare not separate that lordship from his unique sonship. The only begotten Son is our Lord. It is true, we are dealing now with the lordship of the only begotten Son of God not as he created us, but as he redeemed us, body and soul, from all our sins, not with gold and silver, but with his precious blood, and delivered us from all the power of the devil, and thus made us his own property. The only begotten Son is surely our Lord also by virtue of creation. He is our creator, and therefore also our Lord. But in this connection we speak of him as our Lord, not as the creator, but as our redeemer and deliverer.

With Thomas the church confesses: "My Lord and my God" (John 20:28). It is he of whom the apostle Paul writes: "For the same Lord over all is rich unto all that call upon him. For whosoever shall call upon the name of the Lord shall be saved" (Rom. 10:12–13). "The only-begotten Son of God, God of God, and Light of light,"[1] who was manifested in the flesh, who died and was raised, and who was exalted at the right hand of God, but who is still very God himself—him we call our Lord. And him we call our Lord, and that in a far deeper sense than ever before, him whom in our natural state we refused to acknowledge as Lord, the God of our salvation.

For God, do not forget, is our Lord also by virtue of our creation. Also in that sense the only begotten Son is our Lord. But against this Lord we rebelled. We refused to acknowledge him as our Lord. We turned away from him, rejected his word, and gave heed to the word of the devil in preference to his precepts. And thus we became slaves of the devil, and were held in the bondage of sin and corruption.

Not, you understand, as if this affected the lordship of our God, or as if we really succeeded to dethrone the Lord of heaven and earth: he is, and forever remains, the sole and sovereign Lord of all. Even the fact that by our rebellion we became slaves of Satan, lost in sin, guilty and damnable, so that we were incapable of doing any good and inclined to all evil, dead through trespasses and sins, unspeakably miserable, is but a manifestation of his lordship, the execution of his sentence upon us. But although he is and ever remains Lord, we nevertheless preferred the lordship of the devil as our rightful lord. And we refused to acknowledge God as Lord, whom to know and to serve in love is life. Him we hated in unspeakable folly.

God, however, will never give his glory to another. Before the

---

1   Nicene Creed, in Schaff, *Creeds of Christendom*, 2:58.

foundation of the world he had determined to reveal his lordship and to be known and acknowledged as the sole Lord, and to be served and glorified as Lord in a far higher and deeper and far more intimate and glorious sense than could ever have been possible in creation. Accordingly he had ordained his only begotten Son, the image of the invisible God, to be the firstborn of every creature, and that too as the firstborn from the dead and as the firstborn among many brethren, at the head of the elect, the head of the church.

And according to this eternal good pleasure of God, the only begotten Son of God, the eternal Word, in the fullness of time was manifested in the flesh. Our Lord, whom we had rejected, and against whom we had rebelled, came very near to us, spoke to us face to face and mouth to mouth, united himself with us in an inseparable union. What's more, he reached down into our misery, into our darkness of sin and death, where in our folly and by divine sentence of this same Lord we were held in the slavery of sin and Satan. And he redeemed us. He purchased us, purchased us free from the bondage of Satan, not as if he paid the price of redemption to the devil—for he had no other right over us than that which was implied in the divine sentence of death.

But Christ, the Son of God in the flesh, our Lord, paid the price of our redemption to the Father, whose revelation he is, and therefore—O wonder of wonders—to himself. And he did not pay a mere external price. He did not dig into the treasure of his own creation: for all the gold and silver in the world would not have been sufficient unto our redemption. But he redeemed us with his own precious blood, the price of an eternal love. And thus he obtained for himself, that is, at the bar of divine justice, the right to make us his property. Not, you understand, as a mere possession with which he may do as he pleases, but as a precious property of love. He obtained for himself the right of that lordship according to which we may once more, and now in a far deeper sense than ever before, love him, trust in him, and serve him as our Lord.

Thus Christ Jesus, the only begotten Son of God, our Lord by virtue of our creation, now also became our Lord in unfathomable love.

But even so, all is not said.

The question arises: how do we ever find him and acknowledge him as our Lord?

Is it thus, that perhaps this Jesus, this only begotten Son of God, this Lord of all, now sends the message of his love to us, offers us his lordship instead of the lordship of the devil, so that we are persuaded by the sight of that beautiful love to forsake the service of sin and Satan and to enter his service?

God forbid! On the contrary, Christ himself realizes his lordship also in us. He delivers us from the dominion of sin and from all the power of the devil. His lordship is always *his* lordship, whether in creation or in redemption. We never make him our Lord. And no man can say that Jesus is Lord, except by his own Spirit. And if anyone has "not the Spirit of Christ, he is none of his" (Rom. 8:9).

He exercises his lordship over us. He, the only begotten Son of God, the eternal Word, our rightful Lord, against whom we had rebelled, and whose enemies we are by nature, and who became flesh, was crucified and raised and exalted at the right hand of God, and is become the quickening Spirit—he himself, having destroyed him that had the power of death, that is, the devil, now comes to visit us in our prison of sin and death, and delivers us. He dethrones the devil and sin from our hearts. He breaks the shackles of corruption and death in which we are held. He removes the enmity against our rightful Lord from our inmost mind. He dispels the darkness of our folly. He enlightens us, sheds abroad in us the love of God, and then he calls us by his own mighty and sovereign word through the gospel.

And thus, and thus alone, we come. Thus, and thus alone, we see the folly of our sin, the unspeakable foolishness of ever having wanted to rebel against his blessed lordship, the unspeakable wretchedness of the slavery of the devil. Thus, and thus alone, we begin to love him, our Creator-Lord, now as our Lord-Redeemer, and to long for him, to cry out to him from the depths of our hearts. Then, and then alone, we trust in him, surrender ourselves to him, and fall down before him in adoration with the words of glad worship on our lips: "My Lord and my God!"

That Jesus is our Lord implies that he is our possessor, our proprietor. He alone is our Lord, and we are his property. We are his with body and soul, with heart and mind and will, with wife and children, with brothers and sisters, with all our life and possessions. He owns us completely. Our heart and all the issues of our heart are his. Our thoughts and desires, our intentions and our motives are his. The sight of our eyes, the hearing of our ears, the speech of our mouth, the actions of our members belong to him. They are his alone. They belong to no one else. And when we say, "Jesus is Lord," we imply that with all our heart and mind and soul and strength we forsake the world, crucify our old nature, and walk before him in the way of his precepts.

That Jesus is our Lord also implies that he is responsible for us and for all that we are, with body and soul, in life and death, for time and all the ages of eternity, to keep us, to love us, to defend us, and to lead us on to the final victory, to the glory of God's everlasting tabernacle. It means that he alone can bear that responsibility, that no one else can possibly share it with him. And the confession that he is our Lord implies that we completely trust in him, and surrender ourselves to his responsibility, that we trust in no other lordship, neither are fearful or terrorized by any other. Under his lordship there is complete freedom from fear.

Finally, that Jesus is our Lord means that he rules over us not by force and compulsion, but by grace and by the impelling power of his love. It signifies that his mind is our mind, that his will is our will, that his word is our law, and that his law is our delight. And he alone it is that determines not only what we shall do, but also what we shall think and feel and desire and by what motives we shall be governed. It means that he has dominion over the life of our body and the life of our soul and over all our relationships in the midst of this present world, in the home and in the shop, in labor and industry, in the school and on the street, in the church and in the state, in peace and in war, in prosperity and in adversity. And the confession that he is our Lord implies that we gladly and willingly acknowledge his lordship, and that it is our earnest desire and endeavor to know his will and to obey no other word than his in any department of our life in the world, no matter what may be the cost, yea, though we should lose our very life in his service.

For do not forget, we are still in the world. And the world hates his lordship and hates those that consistently confess it. Hence, if you represent the cause of the Son of God, our Lord, in the world, you must expect tribulation. Only by compromising this strictly intolerant lordship of Jesus Christ can you escape this. We must suffer with him. But even so we may be and are of good cheer. For we know that he is responsible for us, and that he has overcome the world. And if we suffer with him, we shall surely also be glorified together. The victory is our Lord's!

Article 3

*Who was conceived by the Holy Ghost,
born of the Virgin Mary*

Chapter 8

BORN OF A VIRGIN

The third article of our Apostles' Creed reads as follows: "Who was conceived by the Holy Ghost, born of the Virgin Mary."

In these simple words of our confession the most astounding wonder is expressed, the wonder of wonders, the mystery of godliness: *God* is come into the flesh. He himself, God, who is God indeed, came into our human nature. The Unchangeable was born, and presently became a growing child, who could suffer and die. The Eternal One came within the limits of time. In Bethlehem the Infinite is wrapped in swaddling clothes. The Sovereign Lord of all came under the law. The Holy One of Israel appears in the likeness of sinful flesh. The Potentate of potentates became a servant.

Such is the mystery of godliness, the reality of the incarnation. Jesus the Christ is the Son of God come into the flesh. And as we approach the Christmas season, it is but fitting that we pay special attention to these words of the apostolic confession: "Who was conceived by the Holy Ghost, born of the Virgin Mary." And in the present sermon we expect to call attention particularly to that virgin birth.

The two parts of this confession, that Christ as to his human nature was conceived by the Holy Ghost and that he was born of the virgin Mary, are intimately related, and constitute one whole. They are aspects of one and the same truth: that God alone is the Father of our Lord Jesus Christ, even according to his human nature, although he was not created, but had a human mother and was born of us. It is the truth that the birth of the Son of God is a human impossibility, a revelation of the God of our salvation. Christ was born without the will of man.

That the Scriptures plainly teach that Christ was born of a virgin, and therefore without the will of man, there can be no doubt. Even in the old dispensation the sign of the virgin that would conceive and bear a son was given: "Therefore the Lord himself shall give you a sign; Behold, a virgin shall conceive, and bear a son, and shall call his name Immanuel" (Isa. 7:14).

Those that would deny the virgin birth of Christ argue that the Hebrew word used in this text for *virgin* may also refer to a young woman recently married. Fact is, however, first of all that the word signifies the age of puberty, a person of marriageable age, but not yet married. And secondly, we must not overlook the fact that the text speaks of a sign. And the sign is that a virgin shall conceive and bear a son. Now a sign is a phenomenon that draws attention of men by its extraordinary character, its being radically different from the facts of experience, a wonder of grace. But there certainly would be nothing extraordinary in the fact that a young married woman would conceive and bear a son. We maintain, therefore, that the prophecy in Isaiah 7:14 ultimately looks forward to the wonder of the birth of our Lord from the virgin Mary.

This is moreover corroborated by the passage in Matthew 1:18–25. We remember that Joseph, having noticed Mary's condition, had been minded to leave his espoused wife secretly. But the Lord had revealed to him in a dream that she was quite innocent of the sin he had suspected her to have committed: "For that which is conceived in her is of the Holy Ghost" (v. 20). And then we read in verses 22 and 23: "Now all this was done, that it might be fulfilled which was spoken of the Lord by the prophet, saying, Behold, a virgin shall be with child, and shall bring forth a son, and they shall call his name Emmanuel, which being interpreted is, God with us." The word "of the Lord by the prophet" is evidently a reference to Isaiah 7:14. The passage in Matthew, therefore, is not only in itself a clear proof for the virgin birth of the Savior, but also corroborates the view that in Isaiah 7:14 this amazing wonder was already foretold.

But there is more. Also the gospel according to Luke, in chapter 1:26–38, plainly teaches that Christ was born of a virgin, without the will of man. In this passage we read about the annunciation of the birth of Christ by the angel Gabriel to the virgin Mary, who at that time was living in the village of Nazareth. The angel saluted Mary with the words: "Hail, thou that art highly favoured, the Lord is with thee:

blessed art thou among women" (v. 28). And when Mary evidently was troubled at this strange salutation, the angel continued:

30. Fear not, Mary: for thou hast found favour with God.
31. And, behold, thou shalt conceive in thy womb, and bring forth a son, and shalt call his name JESUS.
32. He shall be great, and shall be called the Son of the Highest: and the Lord God shall give unto him the throne of his father David:
33. And he shall reign over the house of Jacob for ever; and of his kingdom there shall be no end. (vv. 30–33)

And thereupon Mary asks the question of astonishment: "How shall this be, seeing I know not a man?" (v. 34).

Did you ever consider the significance of this question of Mary? What induced her to ask such a question? Might not the words of the angel have been interpreted to mean that she would become a mother in the natural way? To be sure, she was not yet married when the angel Gabriel addressed her. But we read that she was espoused to a man named Joseph, and that therefore she was about to be married. How then could she be so absolutely certain that she would know not a man? Certainly there was nothing in the words of the angel that would suggest this, far less raise it beyond a doubt that she would become pregnant without the normal intercourse to cause such a condition. Could she not interpret the words of the angel as meaning that she would get married to Joseph as soon as possible, and that then in the normal way she would become with child? Would not that have been the most natural conclusion for her to draw from the announcement of the angel, rather than at once think of the astounding possibility that she would conceive without knowing a man? Yet, as is evident from the question, of this she at once is absolutely sure: she will not know a man.

How must this certainty on the part of Mary be explained?

The only answer, to my mind, is that there was no man for her to know, that is, there was no man left in the royal line of the promise that could beget the promised Messiah. That Davidic generation of royal seed, which according to the promise was expected to bring forth the Christ, had ended in a virgin. The realization of the promise had become a human impossibility. There was no male descendant in the line of the generations of the promise. Only a virgin was left. And therefore the prophecy of Isaiah 53:2 was realized, that Christ should come forth as "a root out of a dry ground." And Mary, realizing this fact, asked the question: "How shall this be, seeing I know not a man?"

Only in this light can we really understand the question of Mary. And this explanation is based also on the conviction that in Matthew 1:1–17 the evangelist gives us not the genealogy of Joseph, as is usually supposed, but that of Mary. In the first place, in this genealogy we have what is called "the book of the generation of Jesus Christ" (v. 1). This therefore refers not simply to the legal, but to the organic line of the generations of Christ. This book of generations in Matthew is designed to show that Christ according to the flesh was in the loins of Abraham. But this certainly could not be the case if what we have here is the genealogy of Joseph, for Joseph certainly was not the father of Jesus.

It is true that verse 16 of the same chapter seems to offer a difficulty. For there we read: "And Jacob begat Joseph the husband of Mary, of whom was born Jesus, who is called Christ." But this difficulty can easily be solved when we remember that the Jacob mentioned in that verse had no male children, that Mary therefore was the only heir, and that when Joseph married Mary he was received and inscribed legally in the registers of generations that ran from David over Jacob to the mother of Jesus. In this legal sense Joseph was of the house and lineage of David.

And although it is quite impossible completely to harmonize the two genealogies of Jesus, that in Matthew and that in Luke, also in the latter we do not have the genealogy of Joseph, but that of Mary. For in Luke 3:23 we read: "And Jesus himself began to be about thirty years of age, being (as was supposed) the son of Joseph." In reality he was not the son of Joseph, but of Mary. But Joseph was supposed to be the father of Jesus because he took the place of Mary in her genealogies. And therefore Joseph was not of that line of generations, that continued line of Davidic kings that would culminate in the Messiah. Mary alone was left. It is not impossible that she often pondered this in her heart (Luke 2:19) before the angel came to visit her with this amazing message, and that the question that had frequently troubled her soul arose to her mind at once as she listened to the angel's words: "But how shall this be?" How shall the promise be fulfilled, seeing there is not a man, and I am the only one left of the royal line of the generations of David!

Is it important that we maintain the truth of the virgin birth of Christ? It certainly is. In the first place, the denial of the virgin birth of Jesus usually implies or leads to the denial of the incarnation of the Son of God, that Jesus Christ came into the flesh. It is true, there are those who would maintain the truth of the incarnation and of the real divinity of Christ, but who nevertheless deny that he was born of a virgin and claim that Christ's assuming our human nature did not necessarily require his birth of a virgin. The Son of God, according to them, could just as well unite himself with our nature as it is normally conceived and born from a human mother and by the will of man.

Now, that this is possible is, to say the least, a proposition that is difficult to prove, if not impossible. We know very little about the mystery of the conception and birth of a normal child, much less about the birth of the Son of God in the flesh. Even though we may not be able to demonstrate the truth of this proposition on the basis of Scripture, we much rather assume that the virgin birth of Christ was strictly necessary, that is, that the Son of God could assume the human nature only by way of elimination of the will of man. Besides, we must not forget that God purposely creates the sign of the virgin birth to make known unto us that Jesus Christ's coming into the flesh is his act exclusively, and that Christ is born not by the will of man, but by the conception of the Holy Spirit.

God reveals himself where all human possibilities have come to an end. The incarnation does not take place until the generations from which he was to be born according to the promise have ended in a virgin, that is, until an impossible situation has been created, in order that he may be revealed as the Lord, who not only calls the things that are not as if they were, but who also quickens the dead. Only when we are forced to ask the question, "How shall this be?", does God give us the answer: What is impossible with men is possible with God (Luke 18:27).

The confession that Christ is born of the virgin Mary is therefore intimately and inseparably connected with the other confession, that he is conceived by the Holy Ghost. And this truth is also directly taught in Holy Writ. For in answer to her question of astonishment the angel replied: "The Holy Ghost shall come upon thee, and the power of the Highest shall overshadow thee: therefore also that holy thing which shall be born of thee shall be called the Son of God" (Luke 1:35). In this answer to the question of Mary it is very plain that in the birth of Christ the will of man is entirely eliminated. Mary asked the question, "How is it possible that a virgin shall conceive and bear a child?" And the answer of the angel is, very plainly: through the conception by the Holy Ghost.

We must refrain, of course, from any attempt to explain this profound mystery. All we can say about it is that it signifies that the Son of God himself, by his Spirit, that proceeds from the Father and of the Son, so operated upon the flesh and blood of the virgin Mary that she conceived in her womb and brought forth her firstborn son. The incarnation is the wonder-work of the Trinity, of God the Father, God the Son, and God the Holy Ghost. Eliminating the will of man, the person of the Son of God, sent by the Father into the flesh, prepared his own human nature, and that too from the flesh and blood of the virgin Mary, by the power of the Holy Ghost.

Thus we can understand by faith that Christ is very God and very man. The incarnation implies, on the one hand, that Jesus is flesh of our flesh and blood of our blood. But it also implies, on the other hand, that as to his person he came from without, from above, out of eternity to unite himself with us forever. As to his divine nature he is God of God and Light of Light. But as to his human nature, he is of our flesh and blood. He does not stand outside of us. He is not especially created. But he is conceived and born.

With God nothing shall be impossible. With these words the angel concludes his message to the virgin Mary. Just as it is humanly impossible that a camel shall go through the eye of a needle, so it is humanly impossible that Christ be born of a virgin. But do not forget that on this human impossibility rests the whole of the divine possibility of our salvation.

The vicarious atonement of Christ on the cross of Calvary is also a human impossibility, but possible with God. The resurrection of Jesus Christ from the dead is also a human impossibility, but possible with God, for whom all things are possible. The exaltation of Christ into the highest heavens, through which he is Lord over all, the outpouring of the Holy Spirit, by whom all the blessings of salvation are applied to the heart of the sinner, the justification of the ungodly through the blood of Christ, his deliverance from the power of sin and death, and his ultimate resurrection and glorification in the day of Christ—all these are absolutely impossible from a human point of view. But what is impossible with man is possible with God. And by faith, as an evidence of things unseen, we cling to Jesus Christ as the God of our salvation, who was conceived by the Holy Ghost and born of the virgin Mary.[1]

---

1   See Appendix 1 for an additional message on the same subject.

Chapter 9

CHRIST IN OUR NATURE

Once more we call your attention to the third article of the apostolic confession: "Who was conceived by the Holy Ghost, born of the Virgin Mary." And this time we would like to consider the question: what kind of human nature did Christ assume?

In answer to this question we maintain, first of all, on the basis of Scripture, that he assumed a real human nature, in every respect like ours, sin excepted. Christ was very really born. He was not created, but born of the virgin Mary. Even though he was conceived without the will of man and born of a virgin, his was not a strange or a specially created human nature, but he took upon him the flesh and blood of the children. He was very really organically connected with us. As to his human nature he did not come from without, but was brought forth by us. He did not stand next to men, but among them. He partook of the flesh and blood of the children. He was flesh of our flesh, blood of our blood, bone of our bone.

This is the very plain teaching of Scripture. According to the message of the angel to Mary, she would conceive in her womb, and bring forth a son (Luke 1:31). That which was conceived in her developed in the womb of Mary like the seed of any other human being, and its growth required the same length of time. For while Joseph and Mary were in Bethlehem, "the days were accomplished that she should be delivered. And she brought forth her firstborn son" (2:6–7). When Mary visited her cousin Elizabeth, before the birth of Jesus, the mother of John the Baptist, filled with the Holy Ghost, greeted her in the following words: "Blessed art thou among women, and blessed is the fruit of thy womb. And whence is this to me, that the mother of my Lord should come to me?" (1:42–43). Besides, Scripture teaches us that "when the fulness of the time was come, God sent forth his Son, made of a woman, made under the law, to redeem them that were under the law, that we might receive the adoption of sons" (Gal. 4:4–5).

This truth, that Christ was not especially created, that his human nature was not outside of ours, but that he was of us, organically connected with our race, must be maintained lest we lose the faith of our redemption and deliverance from sin and death through him. Christ must redeem us. And in order to redeem us, he must bear our sin, and bear it away forever. He must make satisfaction for our sins, and suffer death in our stead, vicariously. But if this were to be done, he must suffer death as the punishment for our sins in our nature. For the same human nature that sinned must bear the wrath of God to the end.

Now if Jesus had not been of us, if his human nature had been especially created, he would have been a stranger to us. He might have been like us, but he nevertheless would have stood outside of us. In that case his death would not have been our death. He would have suffered death, suppose this even were possible, entirely apart from us. In that case God would really have left the human race in Adam in their sin and condemnation, and created something entirely new. In that case we did not die with Christ, neither were we raised with him, and our life cannot possibly be hid with Christ in God. The truth therefore that Christ really assumed the flesh and blood of the children is essential to the gospel of redemption.

Secondly, the truth that Christ assumed the real human nature also implies that this nature is complete, consisting of body and soul. We must not conceive of the incarnation of the Son of God in such a way that by this wonder of grace the divine nature came to inhabit a human body, took the place of the human soul, or even that the person of the Son of God took upon him a human body and a human soul, but that the divine nature took the place of the human mind or spirit. On the contrary, the whole human nature he assumed in his incarnation. He was completely human, even as he is truly divine.

That this is true is evident from all we read of the revelation of Jesus Christ in the days of his flesh. That Christ assumed a real human body is evident from all that we read in the Scriptures of his dwelling among us in the days of his flesh. But also that he possessed a real human soul is emphatically declared in Holy Writ. Shortly before his death the Savior himself declares: "Now is my soul troubled" (John 12:27). And as he entered into the garden of Gethsemane, he complained: "My soul is exceeding sorrowful, even unto death" (Matt. 26:38). The person of the Son of God, therefore, in the incarnation assumed a complete human nature, body and soul.

Nor must we ever say that the human nature of Jesus was a sort of general human nature. On the contrary, we must maintain that Jesus the Christ, in the days of his flesh, was an individual, that he possessed a very concrete human nature, in every respect like ours, sin excepted. To say that it was a general human nature is tantamount to saying that it did not historically exist, that it had no tangible reality. But this is indeed absurd. It is evident that our Lord, according to the flesh, had a very concrete form of the human nature. It is even not erroneous to assume that he looked like his mother Mary, perhaps more than any other child ever resembled his mother.

In the days of his flesh he certainly could have been photographed, although it may indeed be considered fortunate that we do not have a photograph or even a painting of Christ, lest we commit the folly of idolatry. Christ had a very concrete body. He was of a certain measurable height, weighed a certain number of pounds, had a certain color of eyes, had a certain color of skin, and possessed certain definite features by which he was recognized in distinction from his fellow men.

And what is true of Jesus' body is equally applicable to his soul. Even though the gospel narratives are not at all interested in a life of Jesus, and although it is certainly true that one looks in vain in them for a description of his character, the conclusion is not warranted that Jesus had no character, that he had a general human soul. That the gospel narratives are not interested in a description of a life of Jesus is due to the fact that they mean to be only the revelation of Jesus Christ the incarnated Son of God, who died for me and rose again and is seated at the right hand of God. But it certainly must be maintained that both according to soul and body the Lord possessed a real, concrete, definite form of the human nature, both body and soul. He was of the seed of David, the son of Mary, and took upon himself the flesh and blood of the children.

We would rather say that the Son of God took hold of the very center of our human nature from the virgin Mary. This too is in harmony with the Scriptures. He assumed his nature not from the Romans or from the Greeks, not from the sons of Ham or from the sons of Japheth, but from the seed of the promise. The Son of God took hold of the human nature in the holy line, the line of the covenant. He is the seed of the woman, the son of Adam. But in the generation of Adam he is the seed of Seth, not of Cain. He is of Noah, but in the generations of Noah he is the seed of Shem, not of Japheth or Ham. And again, in the generations of Shem he is in the line that culminates in Abraham, in the generations of Abraham he is of the seed of Isaac. And in the latter generations he is not of Esau, but of Jacob.

Gradually, in the generation of Jesus Christ the line becomes narrower and more defined. The line runs through Israel, but in Israel it is the tribe of Judah that bears the Christ in its loins. And within the tribe of Judah the house of David is pointed out as the everlasting royal line that must culminate in the Christ. And this royal line of David culminates finally in the virgin Mary. Thus the generations of Jesus Christ are like a pyramid, with its base in the seed of the woman and its apex in the virgin Mary. And in the fullness of time the Son of God took hold of the very heart of the seed of the promise, and thus assumed the flesh and blood of the children. A very definite and concrete, but at the same time a central human nature Christ took upon himself in assuming our flesh and blood.

Moreover, it must be said that Christ assumed a weakened human nature from the virgin Mary. His was not the original human nature, as Adam possessed it in paradise, in the state of rectitude. Adam, although mortal in the sense that it was possible for him to fall and to die, was nevertheless not subject to death. But with Christ this was different. He assumed the flesh and blood of the children. He could hunger and thirst. His soul could be troubled and sorrowful. He can sympathize with all our infirmities, because he was subject to them himself. He was subject to suffering and death. The only exception to this was his sinlessness. For he came "in the likeness of sinful flesh"; not in sinful flesh, but in its likeness (Rom. 8:3). And "it behoved him in all things to be made like unto his brethren" (Heb. 2:17). And "we have not an high priest which cannot be touched with the feeling of our infirmities," but one who "was in all points tempted like as we are, yet without sin" (4:15).

The only exception to this was, as has already been said, that Christ was absolutely sinless. In a corrupt human nature the Son of God could not have dwelt. He was the holy child Jesus. He was separate from sinners: "For such an high priest became us, who is holy, harmless, undefiled, separate from sinners, and made higher than the heavens" (Heb. 7:26).

The sinlessness of Christ implies especially three elements. It means, first of all, that he was without original guilt. We are born in original guilt and condemnation. The sin of Adam is imputed to us, we being reckoned in Adam forensically. But Christ does not fall under this imputation because, although he assumed a human nature, he is not a human person, but the person of the Son of God. And therefore the guilt of Adam could not be imputed to him. Personally he did not lie under the wrath of God and under the condemnation of the human race. He was separate from sinners.

Secondly, the sinlessness of Christ implies that he was not depraved, that his nature was without corruption, that he assumed a holy human nature. Being without original guilt, he was entitled to a sinless human nature, for he was personally not subject to the sentence of death. And this sinless human nature he assumed not from a holy virgin, who herself was immaculately conceived, but because the Son of God formed his own human nature through the conception of the Holy Spirit in the womb of the virgin Mary.

And, lastly, this implies that Christ never had an actual sin, that his whole existence, from the manger to the cross, was without spot or blemish. He was tempted in all things, even as we are, yet without sin (Heb. 4:15).

It is sometimes maintained that although Christ did not actually sin, he was nevertheless capable of sinning. But this is an error. There was not the slightest possibility that Christ should fall into sin. The first Adam was lapsible; the second Adam was not. And this impossibility was due not to the holiness of his human nature alone, for Adam was also righteous and holy, yet he fell. But in the first place, objectively this is due to God's decree that in him all things should be made perfect; and subjectively, to the union of the human nature to the divine in the person of the Son of God.

To maintain that also for Christ there was a possibility of falling into sin is to deny God's immutable decree that he should be made perfect as the captain of our salvation, and is also tantamount to the statement that the person of the Son could become disobedient to the Father in human flesh. And this is absurd. Hence, it must be maintained that Christ could not sin. This does not render the reality of his temptations less real. He was tempted in all things, even as we are, yet without sin. The trial or test of anything does not become less real because it is certain from the outset that it will not and cannot break. The strain put upon the obedience of Christ in his suffering and death is nonetheless real and heavy because it was *a priori*[1] established that he could never be crushed under the strain of the temptations. Also in this respect Christ was separate from sinners. He could never fall. In him the realization of God's everlasting covenant is assured from the beginning, because he is the Word become flesh.

Thus, and thus only, can he be our mediator, who is able to bring the perfect sacrifice for our sins and to deliver us from all the dominion of sin and death. He is the Lamb of God that could take away the sin of the world. For he is the Lamb without spot and blemish, that therefore can deliver up a perfect and acceptable sacrifice to God.

Thus, and thus only, Jesus Christ is our savior. He is able to deliver us from the power of sin and death. He only is able to translate our guilt into his righteousness before God. He alone is able to change our pollution and our corruption into holiness. He alone is able to translate our death into life everlasting. He redeems us from the guilt of sin by his perfect righteousness, and he clothes us with eternal righteousness that makes us worthy of eternal glory. He makes us lovers of God and lovers of one another. He finds us slaves of the devil; and he makes us servants of the Most High. He cut the shackles of sin and sets us into the perfect liberty of God's eternal covenant. He comes into our death and brings us with him into the glorious life of the resurrection. He finds us in hell and lifts us up into the highest glory of God's heavenly tabernacle. But remember, all this is possible only because Jesus Christ is come into the flesh, and therefore is based on the confession of the Apostles' Creed: "Conceived by the Holy Ghost, born of the Virgin Mary."

---

1   Beforehand, in advance.

Chapter 10

GOD AND MAN

"I believe in Jesus Christ…Who was conceived by the Holy Ghost, born of the Virgin Mary." This we were discussing in our last two sermons, and will conclude in the present sermon.

Jesus Christ is the only begotten Son of God, very God of very God. But he is also man, born and conceived through an amazing wonder of grace, but nevertheless conceived and born, and therefore very man of very man. This, of course, is the mystery of the incarnation. We will never be able to comprehend it, and we can receive it by faith only on the basis of God's own revelation. That the Infinite assumed the finite; that the Eternal came into time; that the Unchangeable became clad in garments of the changeable; that the Creator appeared in the form of the creature; that God assumed the form of a man; and that in it all he did not cease to be God, nor did man cease to be a creature—this is indeed the truth of the incarnation of the Son of God, but is at the same time the mystery of mysteries, the most astounding wonder of revelation.

But although the truth of the incarnation of the Son of God is a profound mystery, yet, on the basis of Scripture it can nevertheless be expressed and defined and formulated. And this the early church has done in a most beautiful confession that has since remained unchanged.

> We, then, following the holy Fathers, all with one consent, teach men to confess one and the same Son, our Lord Jesus Christ, the same perfect in Godhead and also perfect in manhood; truly God and truly man, of a reasonable [rational] soul and body; consubstantial [coessential] with the Father according to the Godhead, and consubstantial with us according to the Manhood; in all things like unto us, without sin; begotten before all ages of the Father according to the Godhead, and in these latter days, for us

and for our salvation, born of the Virgin Mary, the Mother of God, according to the Manhood; one and the same Christ, Son, Lord, Only-begotten, to be acknowledged in two natures, inconfusedly, unchangeably, indivisibly, inseparably; the distinction of natures being by no means taken away by the union, but rather the property of each nature being preserved, and concurring in one Person and one Subsistence, not parted or divided into two persons, but one and the same Son, and only begotten, God the Word, the Lord Jesus Christ, as the prophets from the beginning [have declared] concerning him, and the Lord Jesus Christ himself has taught us, and the Creed of the holy Fathers has handed down to us.[1]

In this beautiful and amazingly correct and precise formulation the church expressed the truth that the divine and the human natures of Christ subsist in unity of divine person, without fusion or mixture, without change, without division, and without separation. And in this confession, therefore we have a more concise expression and formulation of what was expressed in the Apostles' Creed, namely, that Jesus Christ is the only begotten Son of God, conceived by the Holy Ghost, born of the virgin Mary.

It is very important that we maintain the truth that Jesus Christ is one person. He has two natures, a human nature and a divine nature; but he is only one person, and that one person is not human, but divine. Christ is the person of the Son of God.

I do not know whether it is possible for me to explain somewhat what is meant by a person. But nevertheless I must say something about it. Let me say, then, in the first place, that a person is always a being with a rational and moral nature, a being that can think and will. You would never call a tree a person; nor would you call a cow or a horse or a dog a person. That any being is a person is expressed and manifest in his face. You really cannot properly speak of a face of a dog, or of the face of a cow, or of a face of a horse. We speak of a face of a man, because his intelligence, his intellect and will, his rational and moral nature, shine forth in his face.

---

1   The Symbol of Chalcedon, in Schaff, *Creeds of Christendom*, 2:62–63.

Further, let me say that my person is that which I call my ego, my *I*. It is the subject of all my actions. I do not say that my legs walk, but I walk. My hands do not work, but I work. My eyes do not see, but I see. My ears do not hear, but I hear. My mouth does not taste, but I taste. My mind does not think, but I think. I act, I see and hear, I speak and run, I think and will, all through my human nature. And the marvel of it is that my person remains the same from the cradle to the grave. My nature undergoes many changes, but I know that I am still the same person nevertheless, the same person that was nursed at my mother's breast. And even through death my person remains the same, retains its identity. It is I that die, and I through the grace of Christ that will be raised at the last day.

Now this I, this person, in Christ is not human, but divine. It is the person of the Son of God, the second person of the Trinity. He is the subject of all the divine acts in the divine nature. And he is the subject of all the human acts in the human nature. But it is the same subject throughout. It is he that is born in Bethlehem as to his human nature, but that was never born but eternally begotten as to the divine nature. But it is the same person. It is he that grows up in the home of Joseph and Mary in Nazareth in the human nature, but that is from eternity to eternity the same in the divine nature. But it is the same person of the Son of God. It is the person of the Son of God that converses with the doctors of the law in the temple when he is twelve years old, that is baptized and enters upon his public ministry when he was about thirty years of age—all, of course, in his human nature.

The person of the Son of God, who is in the bosom of the Father as to his divine nature, appeared in the form of a servant in the human nature, tabernacled among us, spoke to us, performed his mighty works among us. The person of the Son of God as to his human nature is captured in Gethsemane, condemned by the Sanhedrin, delivered over unto death by the human governor. The Son of God suffers death, is raised from the dead, exalted at the right hand of God, and receives a name that is above every name—all in his [human][2] nature.

---

2   This word in square brackets is not in the original transcript, but the context indicates that it is to the human nature of Christ that the author is referring.

Always he is the same person, not parted or divided into two persons, but one and the same Son and only begotten Word, the Lord Jesus Christ. If he were two persons, he would not be Immanuel; the union of God with us would not be established in him. If he were two persons, his death would have no other significance than any human death; atonement would not have been made through him. And he could not be the object of our adoration and worship. We could not address him as "my Lord and my God" (John 20:28).

The two natures of Christ, the human and the divine, are united therefore in the one person of the Son of God.

Of these two natures the church confesses that they are never mixed or fused. The two natures remain distinct in all their attributes. According to his divine nature Christ is eternal; according to his human nature Christ exists in time. According to his divine nature Christ is infinite. He is infinite in power, in knowledge, in wisdom, and he is the implication of all infinite perfections. According to his human nature, however, Christ is limited, limited in power and knowledge and wisdom, limited in time and space. It is true that even while he was on earth his divine power often flashed through his human nature, as, for instance, in his mighty works. It is also true that his divine knowledge often was revealed through his human nature. But this was true only because of his union of the divine and human natures in the one person of the Son of God. In itself, however, the human nature was limited, as our human nature. He was very God, but also very man.

And therefore it is very important that we maintain the confession of the early church that the two natures subsist in the person of the Son of God without fusion or mixture. The Son of God, who is coequal with the Father, and the Holy Ghost, God of God and Light of Light, assumed the real and complete, that is, the finite human nature, body and soul, but so, that the two natures remain forever distinct. God and man are most intimately united in him, yet so that the two are never fused into one nature.

But there is more.

The two natures of Jesus Christ also subsist without change. Neither the divine nor the human nature was essentially changed when the Word became flesh. We must never say that the Son left the glory which he had with the Father as Son of God. He was in the bosom of the Father eternally. In the bosom of the Father he is, according to the divine nature, at the same time that according to the human nature he lies in the manger of Bethlehem. According to his divine nature he is in the bosom of the Father at the same time that in his human nature he grows up as a child in Nazareth, walks among us in the form of a servant. In the bosom of the Father he is, when he dies on the accursed tree, and when in the human nature he cries out: "My God, my God, why hast thou forsaken me?" (Matt. 27:46). In the divine nature he is in the bosom of the Father, when he is interred in the grave of Joseph of Arimathea, as well when he is raised from the dead and is exalted at the right hand of God. For of course, the divine nature is unchangeable.

Nor must we say that the Son of God put aside the divine virtues, although it is certainly true that they were hid in human flesh. The Infinite was not changed into the finite, but he assumed the finite. The Eternal did not empty himself in time, but he assumed the temporal. The Lord of all did not cease to be Lord, but he assumed the form of a servant. Nor did the human nature in any sense change into the divine, or assume divine attributes. In our human nature he lived our life, thought human thoughts, had human desires, and spoke human language.

Yea, as we have said before, he even assumed the weakened human nature from the virgin Mary, body and soul. For he came "in the likeness of sinful flesh," though without sin itself (Rom. 8:3). He was made like unto us as to his human nature in all things, sin excepted. And therefore, in the divine nature he is eternally God, perfectly equal with the Father and the Holy Ghost. But in his human nature he became truly man, with all the limitation and weaknesses of the human nature. And therefore, with the confession of the early church we must also maintain that the two natures of Christ subsist in the person of the Son of God without change.

Still more we must say about the human and divine natures of Christ.

We must also insist that the two natures of Christ, the human and the divine, subsist in the person of the Son of God without division. That is, Christ was not part God and part man, but he was wholly and completely God and wholly and completely man. When the early church, in its formulation concerning the natures of Christ, expressed this limitation, they had reference to a very definite error that had already been introduced into the church concerning the natures of Christ.

Some had indeed taught the heresy that the natures of Christ were divided into parts, and that parts of these natures were joined in the incarnation. Christ had assumed, according to this heresy, a partial human nature, not the entire human nature. He was not completely human. In the incarnation, according to them, the Son of God assumed a human body and a human soul, but he did not take upon himself spirit or a human mind. A vacuum was left in the human nature, and this vacuum was occupied by the person of the Son of God and by the divine spirit. Christ, therefore, was human, but he was not completely human.

It is my experience that many believers entertain some such notion of the incarnation of the Son of God. On questioning them, it seems that some have the notion that the divine nature inhabited a human body, and that in that human body the Son of God took the place of the human soul. Also in that case we lose the reality of the human nature of Christ. And therefore it must be constantly made clear and emphasized that the whole infinite divine nature was joined indivisibly to the whole human nature, body and soul. Christ is very God and completely man.

One more thing must be said about the two natures of Christ subsisting in the one person of the Son of God.

It is this, that the two natures, although never mixed or fused, although each retains its own attributes and virtues, although they are both complete and do not supplement each other, yet they are never separated. On the contrary, they are intimately united in the person of the Son of God. Although in the manger of Bethlehem we certainly cannot see God in that little babe, although God in Christ in that manger seems to be completely hid, in him we have Immanuel, the union of God and man. Although on the cross he cries out, "My God, my God, why hast thou forsaken me?", yet even there the divine nature was never separated from the human, as our own confession has it: "In the mean time the divine nature always remained united with the human, even when he lay in the grave; and the Godhead did not cease to be in him, any more than it did when he was an infant, though it did not so clearly manifest itself for a while."[3]

Although the human nature in Christ never partook of the divine, through the intimate union of the two natures in the person of the Son of God there was a constant inner connection between the human nature and the divine, between his human mind and human spirit and the Spirit of God, between his human power and the power of the Almighty, instructing him from within and making him obedient unto death, sanctifying him and sustaining him, even in his deepest affliction. He is therefore the perfect revelation of the Father in human nature. And because of this intimate union he could endure the terrible moment of the pouring out of all the vials of God's wrath without being crushed.

Thus, and thus only, can we maintain that the death of the cross is the death of the Son of God. And thus, and thus only, can we maintain that in and through that death perfect satisfaction is made for our sins. If Christ was a mere man, if it was not the Son of God that died on the cross, the cross is made vain. No mere man, even if he were righteous, could ever bear the full punishment for sin and finish it. Still less could a mere man make satisfaction for others, and that too for countless millions of sinners.

Only the Son of God could taste the depth of death. Only he could bear the full burden of the wrath of God and sustain it to the end. Only he could make his death an act of obedience, and voluntarily lay down the life he had voluntarily assumed. Only he could finish death in dying. And only he had the right and the power to take the place of the elect, and satisfy the justice of God in respect to their sins. Only his death, the death of the Son of God himself in human nature, could be so deep, so precious in the sight of God, that by his obedience many could be made righteous. Only when the death of the cross is the death of the Son of God can we have the assurance that our sins are blotted out forever and that in Christ we have the righteousness of God by faith. And therefore we must maintain that Christ is the only begotten Son of God, conceived by the Holy Ghost, born of the virgin Mary.

---

3   Belgic Confession 19, in Schaff, *Creeds of Christendom*, 3:405.

Article 4

Suffered under Pontius Pilate;
was crucified, dead, and buried;
he descended into hell

Chapter 11

CHRIST BEARING
THE WRATH OF GOD

T he fourth article of the Apostles' Creed is indeed very significant. It reads: "Suffered under Pontius Pilate; was crucified, dead, and buried; he descended into hell."

This article therefore speaks of the vicarious suffering of Jesus Christ our Lord, the only begotten Son of God. And I am sure you will not take it ill of me if I elaborate a little on this article of the Apostles' Creed. That Jesus suffered and died for us is from a certain viewpoint the heart of our faith and the ground of our salvation. Never the people of God grow weary, therefore, of hearing of the suffering of Jesus Christ our Lord. And therefore we will elaborate upon this article of the confession, and explain the vicarious suffering of Jesus step by step.

How simple and how utterly common, we would say, is the account of Jesus' life as it is presented in the Apostles' Creed. He was born, he suffered, he was crucified, dead, and buried. What human being ever lived of whom this same review might not be written? There certainly would seem nothing in this confession that could serve as a basis for a biography of Jesus. The modernist, who likes to emphasize the goodness of the Man of Galilee and to glorify Jesus as an example for us to follow, must certainly be disappointed and very much dissatisfied with the account of Jesus' life and ministry as presented by the apostolic confession: born, suffered, crucified, dead, and buried. There certainly seems to be nothing special or distinctive in all this.

Yet, it is exactly in these words that one must find the revelation of Jesus Christ as far as his earthly life and ministry are concerned. Oh, it is true, many other works may be attributed to him, and could be mentioned here—so many, in fact, that if all were written, the whole world could not contain the books. He taught and revealed the Father. He performed many wonderful works. He stands out in the midst of all men as the One no one could ever convict of sin. But all this would have no significance for us if he had not suffered and died. And if the revelation of Jesus Christ is to be expressed in a brief confession, the words of the Apostolicum must surely have the preference to any "life of Jesus" or character description of the Man of Galilee: born, suffered, crucified, dead, and buried.

These words of the confession are not to be divorced from the preceding declarations concerning Jesus Christ, nor from what is stated subsequently in the same confession. It is only in their proper connection that their special significance can be understood. Taken by themselves, they describe only what is common to all men. All men are born, all men suffer, all men die. And although all men are not crucified, there is nothing unique even in this. Thousands of men were crucified about the time of Jesus' life; and untold thousands more have suffered even greater agonies, were tortured, sawn asunder, torn apart limb by limb on the cruel rack, burnt alive at the stake, or left to rot slowly in dark dungeons.

Yet, the suffering of Jesus Christ is not to be compared for one moment with this suffering of all men. The special significance of the suffering of Christ must be found in the subject of this suffering. It was he, Jesus Christ, the only begotten Son of God, our Lord, that was born, that suffered, that was crucified and buried. God himself came in the flesh and was born. God himself suffered in the flesh. God himself was crucified in the flesh. God himself died in the flesh. God himself was buried in the flesh of Jesus Christ our Lord. Therein, and therein alone, lies the altogether unique and tremendous power and significance of the words of the confession.

And only when we first confess that it is Jesus Christ, the only begotten Son of God, our Lord, that was born, suffered, was crucified, and died, is it possible to continue this confession concerning the revelation of Jesus Christ. When a mere man dies, you cannot continue. It is, as far as we are concerned, the end. You can indeed write the real biography of every man, no matter how illustrious a name he may have made for himself among men, in these words: born, suffered, died. Such indeed is the reality of all human existence. In these words the most important facts concerning man's existence are related. All is vanity. Death is in all man's life and activity. And there is no way out. But for that very reason you cannot continue the description of a man's life after you have said: "He died."

But the revelation of Jesus Christ is not finished with death and burial. Exactly because it is the only begotten Son of God that suffered and died, the confession of the church can continue: "On the third day he was raised again from the dead, ascended into heaven, and sitteth at the right hand of God the Father, Almighty. From thence he shall come to judge the quick and the dead." That, and that only, is emphatically the revelation of Jesus Christ.

Now the essential difference between the suffering of Christ and the suffering of any other man in the world consists, according to Scripture, in this, that he bore the wrath of God against the sin of all his people. This is the teaching of Scripture. In that marvelous chapter, Isaiah 53, which might have been written in the shadow of the cross, we read: "Surely he hath borne our griefs, and carried our sorrows: yet we did esteem him stricken, smitten of God, and afflicted. But he was wounded for our transgressions, he was bruised for our iniquities: the chastisement of our peace was upon him; and with his stripes we arc healed" (vv. 4–5). And in verse 12 of the same chapter: "He hath poured out his soul unto death: and he was numbered with the transgressors; and he bare the sin of many, and made intercession for the transgressors." And in 1 Peter 2:24, "Who his own self bare our sins in his own body on the tree, that we, being dead to sins, should live unto righteousness: by whose stripes ye were healed."

Now the question is: in what sense did Christ bear our sins and the wrath of God against them? And how is it possible that one bear the sin of others?

For a proper understanding of this mystery of salvation it may be well first of all to recall the distinction that is frequently and very properly made between state and condition. This distinction is important with a view to the question as to how Christ could bear and sustain the wrath of God. In popular speech the two words, *state* and *condition,* are often promiscuously[1] used. Yet they should be carefully distinguished. By *state* is meant one's legal position as determined by the sentence of the judge or magistrate; while *condition* denotes the mode of being, the sum total of the properties of any being at a given time. When someone enters this country as an immigrant, his state is that of a foreigner. Under the American law he has no right of citizenship. When a few years later he receives his naturalization papers, his state is changed. However, his condition remains practically unchanged. He still has foreign blood in his veins, and his outward appearance reveals that he is foreign born.

Now a man is a sinner both as to his state and as to his condition. As to his state, that is, his legal position according to the judgment of God, he is guilty. As to his condition, he is totally depraved. In this state of guilt he is worthy of death, object of the just wrath of God. As to his condition, he is incapable of doing any good and inclined to all evil.

Applied to Christ, this means that he entered into the state of sinners, but not into their ethical corrupt condition. In God's eternal decree he was ordained to be the head of his sinful people, so that he represented them before the law of God and before the bar of the Judge of heaven and earth. He therefore assumed their guilt. And in the fullness of time he willingly entered into that state of guilt decreed for him in God's eternal good pleasure. He, who is himself the eternal Lord, became a servant, entered into the state of a servant, so that he was obliged to fulfill the law. He, who was above the law, placed himself under the law. Moreover, seeing that he placed himself under the law, and that, too, according to God's decree as the representative head of his sinful people, he entered the state of guilt. And in that state he was obliged to bear the wrath of God to the end to fulfill all the demands of the justice of God against the sin of his own.

Through all this his personal state remained that of perfect righteousness before God. He was born without guilt. For he was the person of the Son of God, and while under the law and even under the wrath of God he remained perfectly righteous. And as to his ethical condition, he was and remained holy and blameless. While he entered

---

1   Without distinction, indiscriminately.

into the state of sinner, he remained separate from sinners as to his condition, except in so far as he must bear the wrath of God and therefore be subjected to suffering and death. He, the Son of God, who is Lord above all, came under the law, and entered into the state of a servant. The holy child Jesus, who was personally righteous, both as to his state and as to his condition, entered into the state of sinners, not into the condition of sinners. And yet, he entered into their condition in as far as their suffering and death are concerned.

In this sense, then, Christ bore the wrath of God against the sin of his people. But once more: what does that mean? Was God ever angry with Christ personally? The answer to this question is negative. First of all, in his person our Lord is the only begotten Son of God, who is in the bosom of the Father eternally. And certainly it would be blasphemy to assert that the Father is ever angry with his Son.

But was he perhaps angry with the man Jesus? Was his anger directed against Christ as the Servant of Jehovah personally? Again, the answer is negative. This is equally impossible. And besides, it is contrary to all that we ever read of the Savior as man in relation to God. If he suffered the wrath of God all his life, this certainly cannot mean that God was angry with his holy child Jesus during his entire lifetime, and that our Savior was conscious of this anger of God against him. All his life is one testimony of the fact that he lived in perfect fellowship with the Father and was conscious of his approval and favor. What was announced from heaven at his baptism, and again at his transfiguration, on the mount, covers his relationship to the Father during his whole life: "This is my beloved Son, in whom I am well pleased" (Matt. 3:17).

God is angry with the wicked, certainly not with the righteous. And Jesus was the righteous, the obedient Servant of God in his whole life. Always God was well pleased with him, even as a man. Yea, we may say that there was never a moment in which God was so perfectly pleased with him and in which Christ was so perfectly obedient and in harmony with the will of God as that very moment in which he cried out: "My God, my God, why hast thou forsaken me?" (Matt. 27:46). The wrath of God, therefore, was not personally upon the obedient Servant of Jehovah.

But what does it mean that our Savior bore the wrath of God?

It signifies, first of all, that he suffered the expression, the concrete effect of the wrath of God against sin, against the sin of others. What is the wrath of God? It is the reaction of his holiness against all the workers of iniquity. God is holy. He is the Holy One. For he is the only good. He is the implication of all perfections. Hence he is always consecrated to himself. He seeks himself, knows himself, loves himself, glorifies himself; he seeks his own glory also in the creature.

For man this holiness of God means that it is his everlasting obligation to be consecrated not to self but to God. He must love God with all his mind, and with all his strength. If he does this, God embraces him in his blessed lovingkindness and favor, and he is unspeakably happy. But if he fails to do just that, if he turns against the Holy One, rejects him, rebels against him, ignores him, tramples his glory underfoot, God reacts against that rebellious sinner in his anger, pursues him constantly with fear and terror, makes him inexpressibly miserable, casts him down into everlasting darkness of desolation. This is his attitude toward the sin of all mankind. And the expression of this wrath, that is, the pain and agony, the suffering and misery, the sorrow and anguish of soul, the desolation and darkness, the fear and terror, the death and hell that becomes the experience of him against whom God directs his wrath, Christ experienced. And it is in this sense that our Lord and Savior Jesus Christ bore the wrath of God against the sin of his people.

We shall, of course, never be able to fathom this astounding mystery. We can explain and rejoice in the paradox of the cross, but we can never fathom it. At the moment of the cross, which is at the same time the moment of his perfect obedience, Christ endured the agonies of the damned. At the moment when God is most highly pleased with him as the obedient Servant, he experienced all the terror of being forsaken of God.

It is exactly because of this that when Christ at the cross descended into hell and suffered all the agonies of hell, hell was nevertheless still a question for him, an outcry of God for an answer. This paradox of the cross is the reason why even from the darkness of hell and in the condition of utter desolation the obedient Servant can still cry out:

"My God, my God, why hast thou forsaken me?" He that knew no sin was made sin for us.

And too, this is the reason why this question, pressed from his utterly forsaken and agonized soul, has an answer. In the hell of mere sinners there is no question. Hell is the answer, the final answer, the answer of everlasting wrath. But the suffering Servant of Jehovah, exactly because he is obedient and yet forsaken, has a question: "Why me? Why hast thou forsaken me?" And that question presently receives an answer, an answer from God in heaven, an answer to which the Servant of Jehovah responds even at the cross: "It is finished" (John 19:30).

And therefore, looking at the cross, and believing that Christ suffered for us, by his death defeated and broke the power of death forever, by his hellish agony forever took the fear of hell away from his people, we respond to that victorious outcry of the Servant of Jehovah on the cross: "It is finished." Finished is our sin, and we are righteous in Christ. Finished is the power of sin and death within us, and we are forever delivered. Finished is the power of death, and we have everlasting life. Finished forever is the fear of hell, and we look for the city that has foundations, whose builder and maker is God. Christ bore the wrath of God. He was forsaken of God, that we might never be forsaken of him, but forever live in his glorious tabernacle with men in the heavenly Jerusalem.

Chapter 12

ACTIVE SUFFERING
ALL HIS LIFE

The distinction, we said, between the suffering of Christ and all other suffering is that he bore the wrath of God against the sin of his people. In all his suffering he tasted the wrath of God. This time we want to emphasize the truth that Christ not only suffered, but that his suffering was an act of obedience, of the obedience of love. Only because his suffering was an act which he performed in perfect obedience of love to the Father, only because he not only suffered the wrath of God, but sustained it, could his suffering be the satisfaction of justice and an atonement for sin.

Atonement is the perfect satisfaction of the justice of God with respect to sin. And this satisfaction must be an act. In a certain sense we can say that the damned in hell also bear the wrath of God. But they can never sustain that wrath, and therefore in hell there is no atonement and no satisfaction for sin. But Christ's bearing of the wrath of God was an act of perfect obedience in the love of God.

Sin is an act. Atonement for sin must also be an act. Sin is an act of rebellion and of disobedience. Atonement must be an act of perfect self-subjection and obedience in love. Sin is an act of enmity against God. Atonement must be an act of the perfect love of God. Only thus can the law of God be satisfied, and therefore his justice.

For we must remember that the fundamental demand of the law of God upon man is expressed in the one commandment: "Thou shalt love the Lord thy God" (Deut. 6:5). This demand is unchangeable. God never relinquishes it, not even when he subjects fallen man to his wrath, to the suffering of the curse. Man must love his God, even when he suffers the wrath of God. For the wrath of God is righteous and holy. It is an expression and revelation of his goodness and perfection in respect to sin. Hence, the guilt of sin can be removed only by an act of love under the wrath of God. He that would atone for sin must willingly, motivated by the pure love of God, seek to fulfill all the justice and righteousness of God against sin. He must will to suffer all the agonies of the expression of that wrath in death and in hell and that too for God's sake alone. Only such an act is a sacrifice, and only such a willing sacrifice of love is satisfaction of God's justice, and therefore atonement.

And therefore, we must say that Christ not only bore the wrath of God passively, as the damned in hell bear it, but that he *sustained* that wrath. He not only suffered the wrath of God, but in suffering he performed an act of perfect obedience. The distinction that is often made between the active and passive obedience of Christ may be accepted, provided it is rightly understood. By the former, then, must be understood that Christ without fail was obedient to the law of God in all his walk and conversation. He never failed to love the Lord his God with all his heart, with all his mind, with all his soul, and with all his strength. He was always the perfectly obedient Servant. But by the latter, that is, by passive obedience must be understood that Christ was obedient also in his suffering. Never was Christ purely passive. Always he was active. He was active in his suffering, and he actively died on the accursed tree. He willed to suffer, and he willed to die. He willed to fulfill all righteousness. He was determined to satisfy the justice of God against sin. Voluntarily he assumed the obligation to suffer the wrath of God. And actively, in the love of God, he bore that wrath even unto the end. And thus his suffering was the perfect *yes* of obedience and love over against our rebellious *no* of sin.

And this act of obedient and willing suffering Christ performed during his entire sojourn on earth, and not only on the cross. It is true, the cross was the climax of his sufferings. In the cross he finally tasted death as the final and perfect expression of the wrath of God. Nevertheless, he sustained the wrath of God against sin all the time that he lived on earth.

Nor is it difficult to see that Christ's suffering extended over his entire life. Oh, this does not imply that he was subject to special diseases or even to the common sicknesses of mankind. If we consider the life of Jesus in as far as we become acquainted with it from the gospel narratives, we can find no special suffering of pain or sorrow that distinguishes him in any respect from other men. Although it is true that according to the gospel he took all our sickness upon himself, not once does the gospel mention that he was sick. It is not even improbable that he never was sick in that special sense of the word. But we must remember that he sustained the wrath of God. He, the Son of God in the flesh, the Sinless One, assumed the likeness of sinful flesh. And this means that he took upon himself the corruptible human nature, in which life is nothing but a continual death. And this continual death he tasted as the heavy hand of the wrath of God against sin.

Moreover, in the likeness of sinful flesh he came into a world that was sinful, and under the curse of God. The creature itself was made subject to vanity and was subjected to the bondage of corruption. And the person of the Son of God, in the sinless human nature, tasted and suffered in and through that human nature in the midst of this present world all the just wrath of God.

Add to this that he suffered from men, who hated him, and that also in this hatred he very keenly tasted the wrath of God against sin. He suffered the contradiction of sinners against himself. He dwelled among men that loved the darkness rather than the light. Daily he came into contact with men who hated God and who hated one another. Daily he came into contact with men in the corruption of whose nature he apprehended the wrath of God revealed from heaven. And we need not try to discover some special suffering, sicknesses, or calamities in the life of Jesus on earth, in order to understand that in the corruptible and mortal flesh which he voluntarily assumed and in the midst of the world filled with enmity against God and of a creation that bore the curse of God, Christ's life was nothing but a continual death, and that in this death he experienced as the holy and righteous Servant of God his wrath during his entire sojourn in the world.

Not only so, but we should never forget that all his life Christ lived in the shadow of the cross. The cross was always before him as the end of his way. With ever increasing consciousness he moved deliberately in the direction of that cross. He had come under the law, not only under the moral law, but under the entire Mosaic institution of ordinances and shadows. And that meant that he came under the curse, and that it was his task to remove that curse. Always he was conscious of the program of his suffering, as is evident from the repeated and rather detailed announcement of his suffering to his disciples.

When he was in the way from Caesarea Philippi, after he had asked the disciples, "Who do you say that I am?", and Peter had answered, "Thou art the Christ, the Son of the living God" (Matt. 16:16), he immediately informed his disciples about his coming suffering and death, and that too in minute detail. For we read in Matthew 16:21, "From that time forth began Jesus to show unto his disciples, how that he must go unto Jerusalem, and suffer many things of the elders and chief priests and scribes, and be killed, and be raised again the third day." And again, after Jesus had had a taste of his future glory on the mount of transfiguration, and had come down from the mount with his three disciples, he said unto his disciples: "Let these sayings sink down into your ears: for the Son of man shall be delivered into the hands of men" (Luke 9:44). And in the same connection, in the same chapter, we read: "And it came to pass, when the time was come that he should be received up, he stedfastly set his face to go to Jerusalem" (v. 51).

In John 10:11 we read: "I am the good shepherd: the good shepherd giveth his life for the sheep." And again: "I am the good shepherd, and know my sheep, and am known of mine. As the Father knoweth me, even so know I the Father: and I lay down my life for the sheep" (vv. 14–15). And once more, in verses 17–18: "Therefore doth my Father love me, because I lay down my life, that I might take it again. No man taketh it from me, but I lay it down of myself. I have power to lay it down, and I have power to take it again. This commandment have I received of my Father."

From all these passages, and from many others, it is very evident that Jesus during his entire lifetime on earth was conscious of the cross. In a sense, therefore, all his life was a Gethsemane, an anticipation of the hour of the righteous judgment of God, when all the vials of God's wrath would be poured out over his head. And therefore we may certainly say that Christ bore the wrath of God against the sin of his people during his entire sojourn in the world. He was the Man of Sorrows, the Suffering Servant of Jehovah.

Nevertheless, it was especially at the end of his life that he suffered and sustained the full concentration of God's holy wrath against sin, and finished it. Of this final suffering on the cross of Calvary we must speak later. But even now we must remember especially two elements in this connection. First of all, we must remember the truth that in all that final suffering inflicted upon him through the wrath and fury of evil men, his passion in the garden, his suffering before the Sanhedrin, his humiliation before Pilate and Herod, his agony on Calvary, in all his being forsaken and denied, despised and rejected of men, beaten and buffeted and scourged and spit upon, in his condemnation and death, he tasted and suffered the wrath of God against the sin of his people, of those whom the Father had given him.

And secondly, it is important to remember that he bore the wrath of God voluntarily, in the obedience of love, even unto the end. Always his suffering was an act of perfect obedience. And thus, and thus only, his passion was the sacrifice of reconciliation, by which he obtained for us redemption from everlasting damnation not only, but also that everlasting righteousness that makes us worthy of that higher and heavenly glory which the Scriptures denote by the term "eternal life." So infinitely precious was the death of the Son of God that by it he merited the right to lift us out of the depths of hell and desolation into the glorious tabernacle of God with men.

Yes indeed, the suffering and death of Christ was infinitely precious. It is sometimes said that this death of Christ was so infinite in value that even if through his death he had saved all men without distinction, yea, even if he had saved other worlds besides our own, he would not have had to suffer more than he did suffer. But this must be taken with a grain of salt. In the first place, this must never be applied in such a way as if Christ suffered and died and brought the sacrifice of atonement for every man individually, nor even that it was his intention to do so. He did not lay down his life for all men, but only for his sheep, that is, for those whom the Father gave him out the world.

Nor may the expression that the sacrifice of Christ is of infinite worth and value be understood in the sense of general atonement.

Once more, Christ did not die for all men. For if he had died for all men, he would certainly have represented them on the cross. And if he had thus represented all men, all men certainly would have been saved by his suffering and death. But according to the testimony of all Scripture, Christ died only for his own, for those whom the Father had given him, for the elect. Them, and them alone, he represented according to the counsel of God. For his own, for the sheep the Father had given him, he laid down his life. He did not suffer more than was necessary to redeem them; not one drop of blood that was shed by the Savior was shed in vain. Those for whom he suffered are surely redeemed and saved.

It is true that in Scripture we find expressions that would almost point to a general atonement. John the Baptist points him out as "The Lamb of God, which taketh away the sin of the world" (John 1:29). And the apostle John writes: "And he is the propitiation for our sins: and not for ours only, but also for the sins of the whole world" (1 John 2:2). But even these expressions, as well as similar terms, must be understood organically rather than individualistically. They refer indeed to the whole organism of the race, to the elect from every nation and tongue and tribe, but not to every individual man. After all, mankind, and not a few individuals, is saved. But it is saved in the elect. The world is redeemed, but it is the world of God's love, not every individual man. For those in whose stead and in whose behalf he bore the wrath of God are surely redeemed by his blood. Everlasting righteousness and eternal life he obtained for them. And what he obtained for them by his suffering he surely bestows upon them by his sovereign grace and through the application of this salvation by his Holy Spirit.

Chapter 13

SUFFERED
UNDER PONTIUS PILATE

It is not improbable that the phrase in the Apostles' Creed, "Suffered under Pontius Pilate," was designed to be a temporal modifier, indicating that at the time when Pontius Pilate was governor of Judea, Christ suffered and was crucified. Nevertheless, this temporal modifier has undoubtedly a deeper significance. It meant at least that he was publicly condemned by the worldly judge.

It is very evident from the history of the suffering of Jesus Christ in the gospel narratives that it was through God's very special direction that the Savior was brought before the Roman governor. It certainly was not the intention of the Jews to lead Jesus to his death in the way of a public and official trial. Their original intention was quite different from its final execution. For when shortly before the final passover the chief priests and the scribes and the elders of the people assembled in the palace of the high priest to conspire against Jesus, they "consulted that they might take Jesus by subtlety, and kill him. But they said, Not on the feast day, lest there be an uproar among the people" (Matt. 26:4–5).

This intended program of the Jews, however, was completely frustrated. And it was not they but God who determined according to his counsel both the time and the manner of Jesus' death. Things were taken out of the hands of the Jewish leaders. An important factor in the way in which this was done was the dismissal of Judas from the upper room in which Jesus celebrated the last passover with his disciples. This dismissal of Judas forced the issue. It is evident that Judas at the time did not intend to betray Jesus that very night. But by the dismissal of Judas it became very evident that all the secret plans of the Jews were known to the Lord, and that even their employment of the traitor could not serve them to realize their purpose of taking and killing the Lord by subtlety. And thus it came about that they hired a band of soldiers that night, that the capture of Jesus as well as his trial before the Sanhedrin that night could not remain a secret, that it had become impossible to kill him secretly, and that therefore they were virtually forced to bring the Lord to the Roman judge and seek confirmation of the death sentence they had already pronounced. All this, of course, was necessary, because the death of the Savior might not be secret, but must become a public spectacle. And besides, he must not be stoned, but he must die the death of the cross. He must shed his lifeblood for the sins of his own.

But there is more. He must also be publicly condemned by the temporal judge. And herein especially lies the deeper significance of the phrase in the apostolic confession: "suffered under Pontius Pilate."

Let us ask the question: why was it necessary that Christ be publicly judged by the Roman governor, by the worldly judge?

The answer to this question is undoubtedly partly that Christ must be publicly condemned, in order that his personal innocence and righteousness might be manifested, and that therefore it might become evident that his suffering and death were vicarious, that he suffered for his people, in order to obtain for them freedom from condemnation. God presides over all the judgments and verdicts expressed by the worldly judge. And he used the judgment of the Roman governor to establish the innocence and righteousness of Christ publicly and officially. And thus it became openly manifest that at the cross the innocent one was condemned to death, in order that he might bear the sins of his people. It also became very evident from this public trial and judgment of Pilate that the Lord did not rebel against this judgment in as far as it was a judgment of man, that he did not rebel against this unrighteous condemnation, but that he voluntarily bowed under it, in order that he might bear the wrath of God on the cross. For this reason it was necessary that Christ should not be put to death secretly, that he might not be killed in an uproar, but that he might publicly be tried and examined in order that his innocence might be brought to light and that it might be established that he who had first been declared innocent was now condemned, not because of his own guilt, but because of the sins of those whom the Father had given him before the foundation of the world, that he might take the place of them in the judgment of God. Hence, Christ must suffer under Pontius Pilate.

But there is undoubtedly more.

The condemnation of Jesus by the Roman governor was the judgment of the entire world. It was the answer to the question: what does the world think of Jesus the Christ? And because it was the public and official answer of the world to this question, the trial and condemnation of Jesus by the Roman governor was at the same time the condemnation of the world.

Thus the Lord himself had spoken a few days before he stood before the Roman governor, delivered by his people to be tried by that representative of worldly justice. We read in John 12:31, "Now is the judgment of this world: now shall the prince of this world be cast out." There can be no doubt about the fact that the Lord spoke these words with a view to his own condemnation and death. What was historically, as men view the events of this world, the trial and condemnation of Jesus by the world, was in reality, and according to the purpose of God, the trial and judgment of the world.

This must be understood in the most literal sense of the word. It is not a mere figure of speech. The world, the whole of sinful humanity as it reveals itself and develops in the present world, the world in its ethically evil sense, with its lust of the flesh and lust of the eyes and pride of life, was tried, weighed in the balance of God's justice, exposed as corrupt and found wanting, and condemned, when it passed judgment upon Jesus the Christ, the Son of God in the flesh. It is true, Scripture teaches us that there will come a final day of judgment, a day when the ever righteous judgment of God shall be revealed, and when all that is implied in the judgment of the cross shall be openly and clearly manifested. But that does not alter the fact that nineteen hundred years ago the world stood in judgment before God and was condemned in the cross and resurrection of Jesus Christ from the dead. The world, the corrupt and sinful world, therefore, is already judged and condemned.

In the hour of the cross, when the world judged the Christ, that world was well-represented. This was necessary, for in and through those that were present and took an active part in the trial and condemnation of Jesus the whole world, of all ages, from the beginning to the end of time, is judged and condemned by God. There may therefore be no room for complaint on the part of the world that it possibly was not legally and justly and fairly represented. Its representatives must belong to the very best which the world is able to produce. Not a tribe of ignorant savages or a band of criminals from the lowest strata of society, not men whom the world itself draws into its courts to judge and condemn them, may kill the Christ of God. Not on the outskirts of the world, far from the pale of civilization, may this judgment of the cross take place. Not in a period of darkness and ignorance, when human culture stands on a very low level, is the Christ of God to be tried and condemned by the world.

On the contrary, in the very center of the world, in the very heart of civilization, in the fullness of time, Christ is judged. And in that very judgment the world is condemned. That center of the world and of history was at that time, in the year 33 of our era, in Jerusalem. There indeed the whole world, in all its culture and civilization, was present. There were the representatives not only of culture and philosophy and human justice, but there also were the representatives of the world of religion as it had been enlightened by the law and the prophets. There were the leaders of the Jews, the theologians of that day, teachers of Moses sitting on Moses' seat, proud of their knowledge and keeping of the law. And, there also was the Roman court of justice, famous for its knowledge of what is right and true among men. And therefore the world was tried and exposed as evil through the trial and condemnation of the Christ of God.

By the trial of Jesus Christ the world was very really called before the bar of divine justice, examined and exposed in its corruption, its hypocrisy, its worthiness of damnation. It was forced to cast off its mask of goodness and nobility, of justice and love of the truth, in order to become manifest in its inner wickedness and rottenness, its love of darkness rather than the light, its constant suppression of the truth in unrighteousness, its enmity against the living God. For this purpose the world must judge the Christ, God's Son, the holy child Jesus. And in this judgment they must give an answer to the question:

what think ye of the Christ? They must give an answer to this question, not in the way of theological contemplation or as a result of philosophical thought, not in a disinterested, impersonal way, but as a revelation of their ethical worth, as a revelation of the thoughts and intents of the heart.

The question was a searching one. It was a question of life and death. It was intended to reveal whether they loved or hated the truth, whether they were in harmony with or opposed to the will of God, whether they were children of God or children of their father the devil. Christ, as it had become very evident to all, represented the light. It had become very evident in all his public ministry that there was no darkness in him at all. He had gone throughout the land doing good. And he had revealed the Father. And in that final hour he stood before the world without power and without defense. Freely, without fear of human might or revenge, the world could express its judgment, reveal its inmost heart, and in judging the Christ of God principally answer the question: "What will you do with God, his truth, his righteousness, his holiness, if he is represented by a weak and helpless man?" And the answer they gave with one accord was: "Then we will kill him."

Now to that world also belonged the power of the state, the sword power, as instituted by God for the punishment of evildoers and the praise of them that do well. And that power at this particular time was represented by the Roman governor, Pontius Pilate. Pilate ultimately was the representative of the highest worldly tribunal, without whose verdict Jesus could not possibly have been crucified. Christ suffered under Pontius Pilate—thus we read in the apostolic creed. And, these words are of tremendous significance when we consider that in the judgment of Pilate the whole world is finally tried and condemned.

One of the most remarkable and striking features of this trial, as reported by the gospel narratives, is that the judge repeatedly and most emphatically declares that Jesus is righteous, that he is innocent. He makes it very plain that he, the Roman judge, is perfectly convinced of the righteousness of Christ. Repeatedly he expresses that he finds no guilt in him. When he finally renders the verdict that is to send Jesus to the death of the cross, his sentence is by no means the result of a mistrial or a misunderstanding on the part of the Roman governor.

Nor is he then finally convinced that Jesus is guilty. On the contrary, to the very last he emphasizes that Jesus is innocent. He washes his hands of the whole affair. His original judgment is never changed: "I find no guilt in him at all."

Yet, even so, the way is open for the Roman judge to answer the question: what will you do, then, with the righteous Jesus? The light in darkness, the revelation of the Father? An answer he must give. He represented the sword power of the world. And he is very deeply conscious of the fact that he has power to release Jesus and power to send him to his death. But in this particular instance he does not like his position. He is not pleased with the power that is given him.

Under ordinary circumstances he would have revealed little or no hesitancy to send the innocent to his death. And even now it was not the love of truth and righteousness that caused him to hesitate and waver. But he was afraid. Caring little for truth and justice as such, he was anxious about his own position. On the other hand, he was afraid of Jesus. He had undoubtedly heard about him. And his calm and majestic appearance at the trial must have deeply impressed the Roman judge. Besides, his wife's report of a dream and her request that he would have nothing to do with this righteous man increased his anxiety and trouble not a little. On the other hand, however, he was afraid of the Jews; and above all, of course, he was afraid of Caesar. By all means he must remain Caesar's friend, for otherwise he would lose his position as Roman governor, and this must at all costs be avoided.

Hence, the judge was not motivated by a love of righteousness or justice or truth. But he was tossed to and fro by these various motives and circumstances, and therefore he repeatedly seeks a way out and tries to release Jesus. Desperately he attempts to avoid a definite answer to the question: what will you do with the perfectly righteous? He has to rid himself of the troublesome case by sending Jesus to Herod. He places the people before the choice of Barabbas or Jesus. He tries Jesus scourged, and brings him out to the people, perhaps to evoke their pity. But it is all of no avail. Pilate must answer God's question: what will you do with the righteous Christ? The perfectly righteous one, in whom according to your own judgment there is found no guilt at all? And the inevitable answer of Pilate, the answer of the heart, is finally:

"I have no regard for the righteous; I have no regard for righteousness and truth; let the blood of the righteous be shed."

This answer the Roman governor gives as the highest representative of the world. It was his condemnation, but at the same time the condemnation of the whole world. To be sure, Pilate was not the sole representative of the world that judged and condemned Christ and that itself was condemned. Judas had given answer to that same question. So had the church institute, represented by the Sanhedrin, Annas, Caiaphas, the leaders of the Jews. So did Herod, that fox, face and answer the question, when by way of intermission in the trial by the Roman governor the Lord was sent to him. So did the soldiers, the representatives of Roman might, give an answer to the same question, when they made him the object and victim of their ribald and cruel mockery. And so did the church as a congregation, when they voted in favor of a murderer, and demanded that the Christ of God be crucified. Yet when we read in the apostolic confession, "Suffered under Pontius Pilate," it means that the Roman judge stood as representative of the entire world, of his time and of all times, and that in the judgment which he passed the world was condemned. And its condemnation and blood-guiltiness can never be removed, unless its guilty stains are washed away by the very blood that was shed on Calvary.

But God be thanked that in and through that very blood that was shed by the world God reconciled the world unto himself. For God was in that Christ the only begotten Son of God, in the flesh was innocently condemned to death by the worldly judge, in order that as he voluntarily submits to this unrighteous judgment and willingly goes the way of the cross, we might have a strong assurance that he bore not his own, but our transgressions on the tree, and bore them away forever. For those, that is, for the sheep whom the Father had given him, for the elect, who are washed from their sins by the judgment of the cross, the condemnation of the world is removed by God's verdict in the resurrection of Jesus Christ from the dead. For he was delivered for our transgressions, and raised for our justification.

Chapter 14

THE DEATH OF
THE ACCURSED TREE

Jesus died. And his death was the death of the cross. This too is mentioned in the fourth article of the Apostles' Creed: "Suffered under Pontius Pilate; was crucified, dead, and buried." And the question must be asked and answered: Why was the death of the cross necessary for Christ to make the sacrifice of atonement? Why might he not simply die in the normal way? Why might he not be stoned to death? Why might he not even be secretly stabbed to death by the enemies? What was there in the death of the cross, according to Scripture, that was necessary for the Savior to bear our sins before the face of God?

The answer to this question is found in Deuteronomy 21:22–23, as interpreted in Galatians 3:13. In Deuteronomy we read:

22. And if a man have committed a sin worthy of death, and he be put to death, and thou hang him on a tree:
23. His body shall not remain all night upon the tree, but thou shalt in any wise bury him that day; (for he that is hanged is accursed of God;) that thy land be not defiled, which the Lord thy God giveth thee for an inheritance.

The reference in this text is not to capital punishment by hanging, but to the hanging and public exposure of the bodies of those that had been put to death by the sword or by stoning. Such a public hanging was considered an intensification of capital punishment. It was therefore the hanging itself, and not the death by hanging, that was an abomination and that caused the hanged one to be accursed of God.

And this passage of Deuteronomy is explained in Galatians as follows:

10. For as many as are of the works of the law are under the curse: for it is written, Cursed is every one that continueth not in all things which are written in the book of the law to do them.
11. But that no man is justified by the law in the sight of God, it is evident: for, The just shall live by faith.
12. And the law is not of faith: but, The man that doeth them shall live in them.
13. Christ hath redeemed us from the curse of the law, being made a curse for us: for it is written, Cursed is every one that hangeth on a tree. (Gal. 3:10–13)

Now the quotation in verse 10, "Cursed is every one that continueth not in all things which are written in the book of the law to do them," is from Deuteronomy 27:26. And the context of that passage is remarkable, in as much as it shows how really as many as are of the works of the law are under the curse. Do you not remember how Moses gave commandment to the people of Israel that when they should have crossed over Jordan into the land of Canaan, half of the tribes were to take their position on Mount Gerizim, the mount of blessing, and the other half on Mount Ebal, the mount of cursing? On that mount the children of Israel had solemnly covenanted to take this curse of the law upon them.

But Israel as such, by itself, could never bear that curse and live. It could never work its way through the curse, so to speak, unto the promise and unto the inheritance of eternal life. It would seem to have been nothing short of sheer recklessness on their part to assume responsibility for the curse at all. But in Christ they could assume that responsibility. Christ was in their loins. And that Christ was able and would bear the curse for them, in their behalf and in their stead. And he did so in the fullness of time.

Christ too came under the law. And with the people, his own, the heirs of the promise, he also came under the curse, though by a voluntary act of his own. He, so to speak, took up his position on Mount Ebal, the mount of cursing. And to him too the curse of the law was read, even as unto the children of Israel. And he too responded, even as Israel did in the old dispensation, by a solemn *Amen*. And he was able to assume that responsibility and to fulfill it. For he was the holy child Jesus, the Son of God in the flesh. He could bear that curse in such a way that the demands of the law were satisfied, so that it would no longer curse the children of the promise. He could work his way through the curse to the promise, through death into life, through hell into eternal glory. And this he did. Figuratively speaking, his cross was planted on Mount Ebal, and there he fulfilled once and forever the curse of the law. For Christ became a curse for us, as it is written: "Cursed is every one that hangeth on a tree" (Gal. 3:13).

It was principally Christ that covenanted with God on Mount Ebal to assume responsibility for the curse of the law. And it was Christ again, this time on the real Mount Ebal of Calvary, that fulfilled that responsibility, and becoming a curse removed the curse forever.

Such is the meaning of the cross.

No other death, therefore, than that by crucifixion, might the Lamb of God, that must take away the sin of the world, die. For him it would not have been proper had he died suddenly, of heart failure, or of some common disease, or of the weakness of old age. Nor might the enemy stone him to death, as they sometimes sought to do even before his hour had come; or cast him down from the precipice, as they meant to do at Nazareth; or with the help of the traitor sneak upon him unawares, and secretly put him out of the way, as must have been their intention when they covenanted with Judas for thirty pieces of silver. All these attempts were frustrated. The counsels of the enemy were brought to nothing. And by God's special direction the events of his hour were so arranged that the ultimate outcome was the death of the cross. For Christ had to bear God's curse against the sinner. And the path of the cross was accursed of God. Thus it was written: "Cursed is every one that hangeth on a tree."

However, this is not the only meaning of the cross. And it is not the only reason why our Lord must die the death of crucifixion.

Jesus' death must be a sacrifice for sin.

This implied, first of all, the shedding of his blood. In Christ the priest and the sacrificial victim were one. He was both. He must, therefore, shed his own blood, and himself carry it into the inner sanctuary, as did the high priest among Israel on the day of atonement. For,

11. Christ being come an high priest of good things to come, by a greater and more perfect tabernacle, not made with hands, that is to say, not of this building;

12. Neither by the blood of goats and calves, but by his own blood he entered in once into the holy place, having obtained eternal redemption for us.

13. For if the blood of bulls and of goats, and the ashes of an heifer sprinkling the unclean, sanctifieth to the purifying of the flesh:

14. How much more shall the blood of Christ, who through the eternal Spirit offered himself without spot to God, purge your conscience from dead works to serve the living God? (Heb. 9:11–14)

And again: "And almost all things are by the law purged with blood; and without shedding of blood is no remisson" (v. 22). If the death of Christ were to be an atoning sacrifice, his blood must be shed. And this was one of the reasons why he might not die some other death, but must suffer the death of the cross.

That the death of the cross must be a sacrifice for sin implied secondly that he must lay down his life voluntarily, in willing and loving obedience to the Father. His death must be an act of the High Priest. He must offer himself, as he did while he tabernacled among us:

11. I am the good shepherd: the good shepherd giveth his life for the sheep.

15. As the Father knoweth me, even so know I the Father: and I lay down my life for the sheep.

17. Therefore doth my Father love me, because I lay down my life, that I might take it again.

18. No man taketh it from me, but I lay it down of myself. I have power to lay it down, and I have power to take it again. This commandment have I received of my Father. (John 10:11, 15, 17–18)

But if he were to lay down his life, if he were to shed his own blood, the very form of his death must be such that it offered him an opportunity to do so. To this end the death of the cross was eminently adapted.

In the case of the Old Testament sacrifices the priest and the sacrificial victim were two different beings. All that was required, therefore, was that the priest should stab the victim as quickly as possible, and sprinkle the blood upon the horns of the altar and upon the mercy seat to realize that idea of a sacrificial offering. The victim did not have to be slowly tortured to death in order to make its death a voluntary offering. It was the priest, not the victim itself, that brought the sacrifice.

But with our Savior this was different. He was the priest, but also the offering. He had to shed his own blood. Hence, the very form of his death must be such that it gave him the opportunity to pour out his life in a voluntary sacrifice, to carry his own blood into the heavenly sanctuary, sprinkle it upon the horns of the altar and on the mercy seat by an act of conscious obedience. Had our Lord been stabbed to death, so that he died instantaneously, this act of voluntary and loving obedience could not have been performed. But now it was different. He died the death of the cross. And this meant not that the enemies killed him instantly, but that they merely opened his body, broke it, that he might shed his own blood.

For six long hours Christ poured out his life unto death. This was a completely voluntary act on his part. At any moment during those six hours he might have refused to remain suspended on the accursed tree, and have taken up the challenge of the enemy to come down from the cross. But he remained on the tree, and continued to pour out his life. In every drop of blood that slowly trickled from his hands and feet there was an expression of perfect obedience, of the love of God and the love of his own. Through the death of the cross he, the High Priest, poured out his own blood, sacrificed himself as the Lamb of God without spot, and carried the blood of atonement into the sanctuary of God.

Finally, through the death of the cross our Lord could taste death, could experience the fullness of horror there is in the reality of death, as a punishment for sin. This too was necessary in order to make his death a sacrifice for sin. He must not merely die as quickly as possible, but he must pass through the full experience of the agony of death. Every bitter drop of death in all its misery he must taste, as he drinks his cup. And the death of the cross was eminently adapted to this purpose.

Thus the death of the cross was the means through which Christ took upon himself and suffered the curse of God that is upon the sinner. God's curse is the expression of his holy wrath against the workers of iniquity. It is the opposite of his blessing. It is the word of his wrath and hot anger, expelling us from his house, causing us to experience him, God, as a consuming fire, casting us away from him, forsaking us in utter terror of darkness and desolation, making us unspeakably wretched. This curse of God was upon Christ as he was made sin for us, that we might be made the righteousness of God in him.

The question may be asked: What did the cross have to do with Christ's tasting the horror of the curse of God against the sinner? Was it merely a symbol, expressive of the curse? Or did it serve as a means through which the bitter experience of God's wrath in the curse was conveyed to the consciousness of the sufferer on Calvary?

The answer must be that it was both. On the one hand, the cross of Christ is a symbol, a sign, expressive of the fact that he bore the curse of God that was upon us. For the victim of crucifixion was a castaway. There was no room for him in all God's wide creation. Suspended between heaven and earth, he was the embodiment of the judgment that there was no place for him on the earth among men, and no room for him in heaven with God. Men did not want him. God did not receive him. Such is the symbolism of the cross of Christ. And therefore, by the symbol of the cross, conceived not merely as man's, but as God's cross, we are assured that Christ bore the curse that was upon us.

But for Christ it was also a means through which he actually tasted the horror of God's curse upon the sinner. For let us not forget that the cross was a word of God. It was not man, but God himself that had spoken the word: "Cursed is every one that hangeth on a tree." On the cross, therefore, God himself by his own word placed Christ in the category of the accursed. The category, I say, for the word of God in Deuteronomy emphatically speaks of *every one* that hangs on a tree. There was no exception to this rule. In that category, therefore, also belonged the cross of Christ, and that too by the word of God. On Calvary through the means of the tree God spoke his own word of wrath to the crucified one: "Cursed is every one that hangeth on a tree. Cursed art thou, even as thou here standest in the place of sinners."

And Christ heard that word of God and trembled, and became unspeakably miserable. He felt the oppressing hand of God's wrath in an increasing measure, as the slow moments of his dying hours were measured by the equally slow trickle of his blood from hands and feet. More heavily laden with the wrath and the curse of God he became every succeeding moment. And to every moment of God's fierce anger the Savior responded, so to speak, by every drop of blood, sprinkled with fervent love and perfect obedience upon the mercy seat before the face of God. Accentuated was the word of the curse by the darkness that spread its horrible wings over the scene of that judgment of God on Calvary. And the Savior became completely occupied with the tremendous task of tasting the horror of God's cursing wrath and of responding to it in obedience of love through his dripping blood. Thus he descends into the depths of woe. And thus it is somewhat understandable that at the moment when God's cursing wrath is most oppressive, at the same time that his love and obedience are most perfect, the question of amazement should be wrung from his sorely vexed soul: "My God, my God, why hast thou forsaken me?"

Such is the meaning of Calvary. Looking by faith upon that bloody, that accursed tree, we know that our Savior, Jesus Christ, the only begotten Son of God, took upon himself, completely bore, and removed forever the curse that was upon us. Christ indeed has redeemed us from the curse of the law, having become a curse for us. And having redeemed us from the curse, he made us the objects of God's everlasting favor and grace, so that instead of facing the eternal desolation of hell, we now look forward in joy to the eternal inheritance, incorruptible, and undefiled, and that fades never away, reserved in heaven for us, who believe in Jesus Christ, the only begotten Son of God, who suffered under Pontius Pilate, was crucified, dead, and buried, in order that we might live forevermore.

Chapter 15

DEAD AND BURIED

In the Apostles' Creed it is evident that the words "dead and buried" belong together. They belong to the series: "Suffered under Pontius Pilate; was crucified, dead, and buried." From this it is evident that the Apostles' Creed mentions the various elements of the suffering of our Lord in the order of time, or in the historical order. And this means too that the word *dead* in the creed refers to the fact that Christ died, that is, to the moment when he gave up the ghost and laid down his earthly life.

We are, perhaps, inclined when we speak of the death of Christ to overlook that final moment when his spirit departed from the earthly house of his tabernacle. After all, thus we are liable to reason, the death of the body is not the real and certainly not the only penalty for sin. The essence of death is the wrath of God, the curse, separation of our whole being from the favor of God's presence, to be forsaken of him. And therefore, if we are to speak of the death of the Son of God as a satisfaction for sin, we must not so much call attention to the moment when Christ gave up the ghost. After all, then his suffering and death were finished. It is true that he was buried, and that his body remained until the third day in the place of corruption. But even then his soul was already in paradise, and the suffering of the wrath of God had all been borne to the end. If, therefore, we wish to refer to the deeper meaning of his death as the expression of the wrath of God, we must not call the attention to the moment when Christ gave up the ghost.

Yet it is evident that in this connection we must speak particularly of that aspect of Christ's death that consisted in the departure of his spirit from his body, and that was as far as the body was concerned finished in the burial. This is evidently the meaning of the word *dead* in the series: "suffered under Pontius Pilate, was crucified, dead, and buried." We must therefore ask the question: What is the meaning of physical death, of the death of the body? What does it mean for sinful man to die? And what is the meaning of the grave?

In answer to these questions, we must say, in the first place, that physical death is the complete dissolution of our earthly house, the end of our earthly existence. And the grave is corruption, our return to the dust whence we are taken.

Death, therefore, is an utter loss. In death the organism of the body collapses and is dissolved. And with it man's entire earthly existence is completely destroyed. As far as the present world is concerned, he is no more. For it is through the body that man is a living soul. Through his physical organism, with its senses of sight, hearing, touch, taste, and smell, he has contact with the outside world, the world of his present experience. When his body is dissolved, that entire world as the object of his experience dissolves with it. In death he sees and hears, he tastes and touches and smells, he eats and drinks, he thinks and speaks, he desires and pursues, he craves and delights in the things of this world no more. Everything is taken away from him.

It is true, he is not annihilated. He continues to be, though he cannot possibly conceive the mode of that existence on the other side of death and the grave. But in and through death he is left utterly naked. From the viewpoint of his present existence death means that he is deprived of all rights and privileges. And the grave seals it all, and signifies that there is no return. There is no way out as far as his own knowledge and power can conceive of and effect such an escape. In the grave, the corruption and dissolution of his body are finished. He becomes a mere heap of dust without form and meaning. Such is the meaning of physical death as far as we can even now interpret its mystery.

But in the light of the word of God we know far more about death. For Scripture reveals to us that death is not a normal process, but rather a violent intervention of the hand of God to take away our name. Death is punishment. It is the wages of sin. It is the expression of the wrath of God, the revelation of his justice against the sinner. We do not simply die as a matter of fact. But God kills us. And therefore, death is God's verdict over us. In death God declares that we are wholly unworthy to have a place and a name in this world, that we have forfeited the right to be, and that, on the other hand, we have made ourselves worthy of destruction: "The day that thou eatest thereof thou shalt surely die" (Gen. 2:17).

But there is more. Death, so Scripture informs us, is the end; but it is also the beginning. It is the end of all existence in the world. It is for the sinner the beginning of eternal desolation. Physical death for him is only the entrance of a dark and horrible pit, the pit of hell, of outer darkness, where there is nothing but the experience of the just wrath of a righteous and holy God. There shall be weeping and gnashing of teeth, and nothing else. That is really the principal reason why man is terribly afraid of death. And, always being in the midst of death, the fear of death holds him in bondage throughout all his present living.

And this fear of death for the sinner is certainly no act of cowardice. For the sinner apart from Christ it is mere folly, and also haughty rebellion, to pretend that we are able to face death without fear. How can mere man speak of courage over against an enemy which he cannot successfully hope to oppose, and which he cannot even begin to fight? We may cover our coffins with beautiful flowers, and decorate our graves; but through it all the grim specter of death mocks our vain attempts to deny him, and strikes terror into the heart of every man.

But Christ also died. And he died also the physical death. And, he too was buried. And his dying unto death was from beginning to end a voluntary act of his own. From the very beginning he, the Son of God, until he gave up the ghost at the cross, performed an act of dying. We lie in the midst of death. All our present existence is oppressed by death. Death surrounds us on every side. And the fear of death pursues us every moment.

And to his incarnation the Son of God entered into this death. He became like unto us in every respect, sin excepted. For he assumed the flesh and blood of the children. He took upon himself the likeness of sinful flesh. And in that likeness he was even as we are, in the midst of death. But he entered into this death voluntarily. For he is the Son of God. He came from without, though he is born of a woman. Into the prison of our death he entered by an act of his own, in obedience to the Father.

All his life he tasted death. He could taste death in all its horror because he was the Son of God in sinless human nature. He knew and experienced the reality of death, for he apprehended it as the expression of the wrath of God, as the execution of God's justice against the workers of iniquity. He felt that in death the hand of God was heavy upon him. And, he deeply experienced the fear of death. This fear was aggravated as his hour approached. Just hear him complain, as the shadow of the cross begins to creep over his soul: "Now is my soul troubled; and what shall I say? Father, save me from this hour: but for this cause came I unto this hour" (John 12:27). Or behold him on the eve of his deliverance into the hands of sinners, as he casts himself down in the dust of Gethsemane, a worm and no man, his soul exceeding sorrowful, even unto death, his agony so great and deep that his sweat became as it were great drops of blood, crying from the depths of fear to the Father that the cup may pass from him, if it were possible.

Yet, in all his fear and suffering he never became for one moment disobedient. Nor did he ever despair. His was the true courage, the only possible courage over against death, the courage that is based on the assurance that God was with him in all his dying, even unto the end. For, first of all, his dying was an act of perfect obedience in the love of God. Knowing death as the just judgment of God against sin, and standing in the place of his sinful people, he willingly assumes the suffering of death. In all his life he died, and in all his dying he was obedient. And being obedient in dying, he never lost the consciousness of God's favor upon him personally, even while he experienced God's wrath in dying. And in the consciousness of his perfect obedience and of the favor of his God, he trusted that God would not leave his soul in hell, nor suffer his holy one to see corruption.

And in the second place, in this consciousness he was constantly assured of the victory. He had power to lay down his life, and he had power to take it again. Trusting in God, he saw through death and looked forward to the resurrection. Hence, suffering the fear of death, he was not afraid.

It was certainly necessary that Christ too should die the death of the body. He might not simply suffer the agonies of death on the cross, in order then to be revived, or glorified, in the sight of the enemies. He must bear the wrath of God to the end. The sentence of God in physical death is that the sinner has absolutely forfeited every right to his existence in the world. This sentence must be executed upon Christ also. God takes away his entire earthly house, his very name perishes. His body too collapses. And he gives up the ghost. Also upon him the sentence is pronounced that he is unworthy to exist on the earth.

Only as the head of his people he agrees with the sentence of God with all his heart. He makes of death an act. His life he lays down, even as God takes it. His spirit he commends to God; his body he delivers over into the place of corruption. His name and position he freely offers up to the righteousness of God. And in delivering up his soul unto death he confesses: "Thou, Father, are just and righteous when thou judgest that the sinner has no right to be, should be utterly destroyed from the earth, and should sink into everlasting desolation. Take my life, my name, my all. Freely I offer it, all love to Thee. For even now it is my meat to do thy will, O God."

And so Christ was also buried. For he must die unto that very end. He too must enter into the place of corruption. He must deliver his body to the humiliation of the grave, to the place where the sinner returns unto the dust. In perfect obedience to the Father he enters into Hades, and commits his body to the grave. We say that he himself committed his body to the grave, for we must never forget that even his burial was an act of his own. Even as he entered into the womb of the virgin, and thereby into the likeness of sinful flesh; even as he voluntarily suffered the reality of death during his entire lifetime on earth; and even as he voluntarily entered into death finally, and gave up the ghost; so he obediently submitted to the sentence of God, "Dust thou art, and to dust thou shalt return" (Gen. 3:19), and entered into the grave. He could do so as an act of his own, because he was the Son of God, and the person of the Son of God was never separated from his human nature even in the grave. And so he accomplished all of death and fulfilled all righteousness.

Thus satisfaction was made for sins. Atonement and reconciliation could be made only by the death of the Son of God.

Is not this too bold an expression: "the death of the Son of God"?

Is not the Son of God very God himself? Does he not have life in himself? And is it not therefore, perhaps, blasphemy to speak of the death of the Son of God? Was it after all not simply the man Jesus that died on the accursed tree, while the Son of God lives eternally in everlasting glory? Nevertheless, it is very necessary that we maintain this expression. At the cross it was the Son of God that died.

It is quite true, of course, that the divine nature cannot suffer death. God is the Lord. He is the living God. He is life. In his divine being he cannot suffer. But we must remember that Christ is the person of the Son of God. As such he subsists eternally in the divine nature. And in that divine nature he is in the bosom of the Father, and lives the life of infinitely perfect divine friendship with the Father and the Holy Ghost in infinite bliss. But this same person of the Son of God also assumed the human nature. He is not two persons, a human and a divine. But he is and remains one person, the divine person of the Son of God, subsisting in two natures, the divine and the human. And it is this person of the Son of God that committed his spirit to God, and that was buried in the sepulcher of Joseph of Arimathea. Only, it must be remembered that he suffered all this not in the divine nature, for once more: the divine nature cannot suffer and cannot die. But he suffered in the human nature, in soul and body. And so it is perfectly proper to speak of the death of the Son of God.

And this expression must be retained because only by the death of the Son of God, and by no one else, could satisfaction be made for our sins, and could reconciliation of us to God be accomplished. If it was a mere man that died on the cross, the cross is made vain. No mere man, though he were righteous, could ever bear the full punishment for sin and finish it. Still less could a mere man make satisfaction for others, and that too for countless millions of sinners.

Only the Son of God could taste the depth of death. Only he could bear the full burden of the wrath of God and sustain it to the end. Only he could make of death an act of obedience, and voluntarily lay down his life for the sheep, the life which he had freely assumed. Only he could finish death in dying. And only he had the right and the power to take the place of the elect, and satisfy the justice of God in respect to their sins. Only his death, the death of the Son of God himself in human nature, could be so deep, so precious in the sight of God that by his obedience many could be made righteous. Only, therefore, when the death of the cross is the death of the Son of God can we have the assurance that our sins are blotted out forever, and that in Christ we have the righteousness of God by faith. Only in and through the death of the Son of God can we possibly have the right to everlasting life and to the place of everlasting glory in the tabernacle of God with men.

Chapter 16

OUR TEMPORAL
DEATH

In the present sermon I wish to digress a moment from the material of the Apostles' Creed, in order to ask and to answer a question that often arises in connection with the significance of the death of Christ. It is this: why must believers still suffer death? If physical death belongs to the punishment of sin and the death of Christ is really satisfaction for sin, it would appear to follow that believers were also delivered from the temporal or physical death. Yet, this is evidently not the case. And therefore the question arises: why must those that are in Christ nevertheless die the physical death?

Several answers may be offered to this question.

First of all, we may suggest that if the believers were to escape the suffering of physical death in all its implications, they would have to be completely glorified at the moment when they were regenerated. Nay more, their regeneration, and also their glorification, would have to take place at birth. For the reality of physical death is not limited to the moment when we give up the ghost and our spirit leaves the body, but involves our entire earthly existence. We are born in the midst of death, with a corruptible and mortal body. The power of death reveals itself in all our life, in all the diseases, suffering, and sorrow of the present time. If, therefore, the elect were to escape physical death, they must be regenerated and completely renewed at their birth, and at once taken into heaven. But this is absurd. This would be impossible, for in that case the church of the elect could never be brought forth. The generations of the elect must be born. And to them we can give birth only in our present earthly and corruptible bodies. And in these corruptible bodies we lie in the midst of death, and must needs pass through the grave into glory.

Secondly, I would suggest that it is no doubt the will of God that the glory of his grace shall eternally shine forth in the church of the redeemed even in their consciousness. They must know by experience from how great a depth of sin and misery and death the marvelous grace of God redeemed and delivered them. But unto this end they must have experience of the suffering and power of death. From the depths they must cry unto God, that they may forever extol the wonder of his grace whereby they are redeemed. And therefore, they must pass through the darkness of death, that they may taste the goodness and glorious grace, the mighty power and dominion of God their redeemer, who calls the things that are not as if they were, and who quicks the dead (Rom. 4:17).

Thirdly, it is only in the body of this death that believers are able to fulfill their calling in this world according to God's good pleasure over them. For a time they must represent the cause of the Son of God in antithesis to the world of sin. They must be to the glory of the grace of him that called them in all their walk and conversation (Eph. 1:6). They must "fight the good fight of faith" (1 Tim. 6:12) and that too "in the midst of a crooked and perverse nation" (Phil. 2:15). And in this cause they are called to suffer with Christ, and to fulfill the measure of his suffering. Hence, their regeneration and glorification cannot be simultaneous. It is only in their present body, in which they are by nature one with the world and have all things in common with natural men, that they can serve this high purpose of God and be faithful even unto death.

Fourthly, we must not forget that the economy of things to which the ultimate and complete redemption belongs is not yet come. The believers shall be glorified body and soul, and inherit the kingdom of God, the incorruptible and undefinable inheritance, that fades not away. But this kingdom of God is heavenly. And to inherit it, all of the body of believers must be made to bear the image of the heavenly. The heavenly kingdom and the redemption of their body belong together. The one must wait for the other. Hence, the body of believers cannot be glorified until the consummation of all things, the moment of the resurrection when God shall make all things new, and create "new heavens and a new earth," in which righteousness shall dwell (2 Peter 3:13), and the tabernacle of God shall be with men (Rev. 21:3). Until that moment, the body of believers must rest in the grave, and await the resurrection of the dead.

Further, we must not forget that the death of believers certainly is no satisfaction for their sin. Satisfaction it could never be. Only the death of the Son of God could blot out all the guilt of sin. If the just wrath of God must fall upon us, we can only perish everlastingly. Then we must suffer death forever. But this is not the case. The death of believers can no longer be considered a manifestation of the wrath of God, an execution of justice, a punishment for sin. It is changed into something else for them that are in Christ. And this must be understood in its full sense. It must be applied not only to the final moment of dying, but also to all that is implied in death, to all the suffering of this present time. For we lie in the midst of death in this world. Dying we die. All the suffering and agony, all the sorrow and grief of this present time, are very really the operation of death. When, therefore, we confess by faith that our death is not meant as satisfaction for sin, it also implies that all our present suffering of soul and body are no longer to be considered as a punishment for sin, and an expression of the righteous judgment of God. Christ died for all our sins. And he bore all the punishment of sin. The debt has been paid in full, and God in his justice will not exact payment twice.

This is indeed a great comfort. But it is also a comfort on which believers often fail to lay hold. In the midst of suffering they will often express themselves in a way that clearly reveals their failure to consider their misery and death in the light of the cross and the perfect satisfaction of Christ for all their sins. They feel that they have deserved it all, and that they suffer exactly because they are worthy of death. They declare that God is righteous in visiting their sins upon their head, and that they have made themselves worthy of his wrath. They often seek a connection between their specific suffering and certain sins in their past life, and feel that the former is the expression of God's just wrath upon the latter. They still must make satisfaction for their sins.

This is an error. And the error is not that believers apprehend in their suffering the displeasure of God against sin. God is indeed displeased with sin, also with the sins of his children. It is very well that we humble ourselves before the face of God in our suffering and misery and confess that if God should deal with us according to our transgressions, we would not be able to stand before him, but would have to perish in eternal desolation. But the error is that in our suffering and in our apprehension of the righteous judgment of God we do not lay hold upon Christ by faith, and thus lack the joyous assurance that all our sins are blotted out, so that our death is no longer to be considered a punishment for sin. As soon as, and in the measure that we do take our sins and sufferings to the cross, we do indeed confess: "Lord, if thou shouldst mark transgressions, in Thy presence who shall stand?" But we also triumphantly shout: "But with Thee there is forgiveness, that Thy name may fear command."[1]

God does indeed chastise his children, but he never punishes them. There is a great difference between punishment and chastisement. The former is the expression of God's just and condemning wrath. The latter is an operation of his paternal love: "For whom the Lord loveth he chasteneth, and scourgeth every son whom he receiveth" (Heb. 12:6). If we are punished for our sins, there is no hope: for punishment means just retribution and the just retribution for our sins is eternal death. But if we are chastised, we may rejoice in the chastisement, for it is meant for our good, and it tends unto life. Punishment for sin in the suffering of this present time is for the reprobate wicked. Chastisement is the same suffering for God's elect children. Punishment is that suffering as it is mixed with God's fierce and holy anger. Chastisement is the same suffering mixed with saving grace. Punishment ends in destruction. Chastisement is for our good, for our correction and sanctification.

For thus the Scriptures teach us: "Furthermore we have had fathers of our flesh which corrected us, and we gave them reverence: shall we not much rather be in subjection unto the Father of spirits, and live? For they verily for a few days chastened us after their own pleasure; but he for our profit, that we might be partakers of his holiness" (Heb. 12:9–10). Although, therefore, also believers lie still in the midst of death and taste death in all the suffering of this present time; yet for

---

1   No. 363:2, in *The Psalter*.

them it is no punishment, no satisfaction for sin. Christ died and rose again. He fully satisfied for all their iniquities. And the sufferings they endure must be their servant and unto their eternal good.

Besides, do not forget that physical death means for believers the end of all sin and imperfection, and opens for them the gate to everlasting life. Those that are in Christ die in faith. And even though, judging from outward appearances, their death appears the same as that of unbelievers, even though they pass through the same struggle and suffer the same agony in departing from this present world, their death is essentially different. For as in that hour of death they cling by faith to their crucified Lord, they know that it is not the retributive wrath of God that is upon them in all the agonies of death, but his elective love, delivering them from death into life, and beckoning them home to the house of many mansions. By faith they may truly die in peace.

For believers death is indeed an abolishing of sin. The death of believers in Christ is not simply a separation of soul and body. It is much more. It is the final deliverance of the inward man from the bondage of the outward man and from all that pertains to it. When the believer dies, his outward man perishes completely. To that outward man belong many things. The earthly house of this tabernacle it is called in Scripture. His body and all his earthly life, his earthly experiences, his joys and sorrows, his earthly relationships, his name and position in this world, all belong to the outward man. But to that outward man also belongs the old nature in which the motions of sin are still active, in which operates the law of sin that wars against the law of his mind and brings him into captivity to the law of sin that is in his members.

In death this outward man perishes. It is completely and finally destroyed. And even though it is true that death is suffering and that the believer as well as the unbeliever, as long as he is in this earthly house, does not want to be unclothed, but clothed upon, so that he too dreads and hates the dissolution of his earthly house from a merely earthly point of view, yet by faith he may rejoice in the very suffering of death. For all his life he had to fight against the motions of sin in his members. And frequently he seemed to suffer defeat. The sin that is within him was a cause of profound sorrow and misery to him. And now, as he finally lays down his weary head upon death's pillow, he may rejoice in the prospect of final deliverance from the body of this death and of the enjoyment of the perfect liberty of the children of God.

And so, the death of believers is a passage into eternal life. Though the outward man perishes, the inward man never does. It cannot perish. It is the new principle of life, of the life of Christ, in him. And that life can never die. It is resurrection life. Death has no power and no dominion over it. With regard to the believer from the viewpoint of that inward man, our Lord said to Martha: "I am the resurrection, and the life: he that believeth in me, though he were dead, yet shall he live: and whosoever liveth and believeth in me shall never die" (John 11:25–26). According to his inward man the believer is firmly rooted in Christ, the resurrection. He passes through death, but himself can never die.

And therefore, in the case of the believer death has radically changed through the power of the death of our Lord, the Son of God. It is no longer satisfaction for sin. For the death of the Son of God has fully accomplished that satisfaction. It is a means to deliver us from the power of sin forever. Death is no longer a terrorizing lord. On the contrary, he is become a servant, opening for us the gates into the glory of everlasting life. And the grave, that dreadful tyrant that swallowed us up into everlasting desolation, has become a passage into the glory of the resurrection. Death is swallowed up in victory. And triumphantly we shout: "O death, where is thy sting? O grave, where is thy victory? The sting of death is sin; and the strength of sin is the law. But thanks be to God, which giveth us the victory through our Lord Jesus Christ" (1 Cor. 15:55–57). We are conquerors, yea, "more than conquerors through him that loved us" (Rom. 8:37). Our very enemies, including death itself, have become subservient to our salvation. And "I am persuaded, that neither death, nor life, nor angels, nor principalities, nor powers, nor things present, nor things to come, nor height, nor depth, nor any other creature, shall be able to separate us from the love of God, which is in Christ Jesus our Lord" (vv. 38–39).

Chapter 17

RECONCILED TO GOD

Seeing that my series on the fourth article of the Apostles' Creed coincides, just about, with the Lent season, I intend to broaden out a bit on the article and devote a few sermons to the fruit of the death of Jesus.

One of the outstanding fruits of Jesus' death is, of course, that by the blood of the cross we are reconciled to God. This is frequently mentioned in Scripture, both directly and indirectly. Thus, for instance, we read in Romans 5:10, "For if, when we were enemies, we were reconciled to God by the death of his Son, much more, being reconciled, we shall be saved by his life." In the well-known passage of 2 Corinthians 5:18–20 we read:

18. And all things are of God, who hath reconciled us to himself by Jesus Christ, and hath given to us the ministry of reconciliation;
19. To wit, that God was in Christ, reconciling the world unto himself, not imputing their trespasses unto them; and hath committed unto us the word of reconciliation.
20. Now then we are ambassadors for Christ, as though God did beseech you by us: we pray you in Christ's stead, be ye reconciled to God.

And in Hebrews 2:17, "Wherefore in all things it behoved him to be made like unto his brethren, that he might be a merciful and faithful high priest in things pertaining to God, to make reconciliation for the sins of the people."

Now, what is meant by reconciliation?

I would define it as the work of God whereby we, that is, the elect, whom God has given to Christ from before the foundation of the world, were translated from a state of enmity and estrangement and wrath into a state of eternal and unchangeable favor and most intimate friendship, a change that is effected by the removal of the cause of the estrangement, namely, sin, and the establishment of an eternal righteousness.

I would like to call your attention to especially five different elements in this idea of reconciliation. First of all, it is purely an act of God, not an act of God and the sinner both. God alone is the reconciler. Secondly, it presupposes an eternal relation of love on the part of God to his people. If this were not the case, reconciliation would be forever impossible. Thirdly, the relation of love and friendship on the part of God to his people is disrupted on the part of man by sin. If this were not true, reconciliation would not be necessary. Fourthly, reconciliation implies that the cause of the estrangement, namely, sin, is removed. And finally, reconciliation means that this removal of sin can be accomplished only in the way of perfect satisfaction of the justice and righteousness of God.

Let us briefly explain these various elements in reconciliation.

First of all, then, I want to emphasize that reconciliation is purely an act of God, and of him alone. It is true, of course, that we enter into the state of reconciliation by a true faith. But it is not true that reconciliation is mutual, an act of God and an act of us. God reconciles us to himself, but we do not reconcile God to us. Nor is it true that Christ is the mediator between two parties at variance, and that now he reconciles us to God and God to us. God alone is the reconciler. And in the work of reconciliation we have no more part than we have in the work of creation.

And not only do we not have a part in this work of reconciliation, but on our part we did not even desire it or seek it. On our part, we would do all we could to frustrate God's work of redemption. For do not forget that we were reconciled when we were still enemies. And this enmity against God on our part revealed itself never in a more horrible form than at the very moment when God reconciled us to himself. For it was at that moment that we revealed our enmity against God by killing his Son.

God, therefore, is the reconciler. And not only this, but we must also emphasize that God reconciled us unto himself, not himself to us.

Reconciliation is not the restoration of harmony between two parties, but it is the reconciliation of men to God. This is everywhere emphasized in Holy Writ. Never do we read in Scripture that God reconciled himself to us, but always that he reconciled us to himself.

And finally, we must also emphasize that this reconciliation is an accomplished fact. It is not something that must still take place, or that is constantly being realized. On the contrary, nineteen hundred years ago God was in Christ reconciling the world unto himself, not imputing their trespasses unto them. The work of reconciliation is accomplished once and forever. We are reconciled to God.

Secondly, I stated that reconciliation presupposes the love-relation on the part of God to us. God loved us with an eternal love. Long before the cross of Christ was ever planted on Calvary, and long before Christ shed his lifeblood for the sins of his own, God loved us. If this were not true, reconciliation would have been forever impossible. Never must we present the matter thus, as if God were filled with enmity against us, and Christ now by his cross and shedding of his blood changed that enmity of God into love toward us. On the contrary, God's sending of his Son into the world in order to shed his lifeblood on the accursed tree for our sins is a manifestation of the everlasting love of God.

This is evident from many passages of Holy Writ, but I will quote just one. We read in 1 John 4:9–10, "In this was manifested the love of God toward us, because that God sent his only begotten Son into the world, that we might live through him. Herein is love, not that we loved God, but that he loved us, and sent his Son to be the propitiation for our sins." In that everlasting love God is the reconciler. And without that eternal love of God reconciliation would have been forever impossible. According to his eternal purpose of election, God has an everlasting covenant with his people. And just because that covenantal relation of friendship rests only in God, it can never be destroyed.

God therefore never ceases to love his people. No matter what they may do or what they may become, he still loves them. Though their sins be as scarlet, and though they be red as crimson, he loves them still and will restore them to his favor and fellowship. He may be angry with his people in righteous wrath for a moment; but even in his anger he loves them. Reconciliation, therefore, is an act of eternal and infinite love, of unlimited grace, and of abundant mercy. That is the reason why we can read in Scripture that God loved his people even when they were his enemies.

Thirdly, however, reconciliation also presupposes that fact of sin, through which that love-relation is disrupted on our part, though never on the part of God. The love-relation on the part of man was disrupted when he rebelled against his sovereign friend in paradise. Adam was the friend of God, the object of God's favor. He knew God and was known of him. He loved God and was loved by him. He walked and talked with God, and was blessed by him. But in and through Adam the whole human race, and with the human race God's own elect in Christ Jesus our Lord, violated the covenantal relationship. They became guilty, the objects of God's righteous wrath, foolish and corrupt and enemies of God. Hence, as they are in their sin and death, they cannot be and cannot function as God's covenantal friends. Because of sin they are alienated and have forfeited the right to God's favor and love. The covenantal relationship has been violated and disrupted on the part of man through his fall into sin. And God is terribly angry with his people in their sin, and they are in themselves worthy of death and damnation.

Now, the question is: how and on what basis can this covenantal relation of friendship be restored? And the answer is, and this is the fourth element to which we call your attention in connection with the idea of reconciliation: that the cause of disruption, that is, the sin of man, must be removed. When we speak of reconciliation between men, such as between a man and his wife or a friend with his friend or a king with his subject, such a removal of the cause is neither possible nor necessary. All that is necessary is in that case that the guilty party repents and confesses his sin and promises henceforth to be faithful to the relationship that was violated. Thus, for instance, a wife that committed adultery may return to her husband in heartfelt sorrow and be received by him; and if the woman gives proof of repentance and renewed faithfulness, the reconciliation is accomplished.

But with God this is different. He cannot deny himself. He cannot permit his holy law to be trampled underfoot with impunity. He cannot simply forgive and forget, as if nothing had ever taken place. If the sinner's relation to him is to be restored, the cause of the separation must actually be removed, so that it is no more. The sin of man, therefore, must not simply be repented of and forgiven, but it must be wholly blotted out.

And this brings us to the cross of Christ. God was in Christ, reconciling the world unto himself. He himself removed our sin and blotted it out in boundless grace.

But the question is: How is this possible? How can sin be removed? How can the guilt of sin ever be blotted out? How can the guilty ever become righteous, so that the sinner is restored to the favor of God?

The answer is: only in the way of the perfect satisfaction of God's justice and righteousness. Atonement must be made for the sin that has been committed. And atonement consists in perfectly satisfying the justice of God.

What is atonement? The answer to this question is: the sinner must freely, voluntarily, motivated by the love of God and true sorrow for his sin, bear the punishment of sin, eternal death. He must not merely bear the punishment and suffer eternal death. He must do so willingly, in the love of God. The damned in hell also suffer eternal death, yet they can nevermore atone. But he that would satisfy the justice of God against sin must sacrifice himself. He must be so mightily moved by the love of God that he seeks death, that he seeks eternal desolation in hell, in order that he may atone, and that he voluntarily lays himself on the altar of God's holy wrath. For God can never relinquish his demand of love upon man. And even though man has become the object of God's consuming wrath, he must still love him in his wrath.

This is the reason why reconciliation is, on the part of man, forever impossible. He can never atone for his sin! No good works, suppose that he could perform them, will ever atone for his sin. For he is obliged to do them in the first place, and no man can ever pay back a debt by paying his current bills. Besides, man does not want to pay his debt. He is dead in sin. He cannot do any good before God. He stands in enmity against God. And his nature is so corrupt that he loves the darkness rather than the light. He is not at all concerned about the righteousness of God. How then could he possibly bring the sacrifices that would atone for his sin? Even if he would, he could not possibly bear the punishment of eternal death and finish it, so that he would live. But he will not seek God. He does not care to be reconciled to God. Hence, the case is helpless as far as man is concerned. Reconciliation cannot be of man, but must be of God, and of him alone.

And this is exactly the wonder of reconciliation. God reconciled us unto himself "while we were yet sinners" (Rom. 5:8). God was in Christ reconciling the world unto himself. Never change this truth into something else. Never say that Christ reconciled God to us and us to God. That would make of Christ a third party between God and us. And although it is certainly true that Christ in his human nature is the mediator of God and man, this mediator is entirely of God. And therefore, it is God himself, the Son of God, begotten of the Father eternally, who is eternally in the Father's bosom, God of God in human flesh, that accomplished our reconciliation. In Christ the strong arm of God, of the God of our salvation, reached down into our death, in order to remove the cause of our estrangement from him, and to restore and raise to a higher, heavenly, eternal level the covenant of friendship between him and us.

Such is the meaning of the cross.

God reconciled us unto himself through the death of his Son. In the cross of Christ God himself through his own Son in the flesh satisfied his own justice. The Son of God brought the sacrifice that was required to blot out the guilt of sin and to clothe us with an everlasting righteousness. He could do so because he was the holy child Jesus, the Lamb of God, without blemish, and the zeal of God's house consumed him. He could and did willingly, from the motive of the love of God, descend into lowest hell, to suffer for us the punishment of our sin, to bear for us the wrath of God to the very end. He stood in the place of judgment. And on him all the vials of God's wrath against sin were poured out.

And when he cried out, "It is finished" (John 19:30), he had completed his sacrifice, removed sin, obtained righteousness, a fact which God sealed when he raised him from the dead. For he was delivered for our transgressions, and was raised again for our justification (Rom. 4:25). And he was able to bring the sacrifices as an atonement for the sin of his people. For God had appointed him to be the head of his church, representing them. For them he died. And because it is not mere man, but the Son of God, that died on the cross, his death is abundantly sufficient to blot out the guilt of all his own.

This, then, is the glad gospel of reconciliation. It proclaims reconciliation, not as a possibility, but as an accomplished fact. The elect are surely reconciled once and forever through the death of the Son of God. God reconciled us through Christ. And he too sends unto us the word of reconciliation through the preaching of the gospel. And through the word of the gospel he comes to us with the earnest prayer: Be ye reconciled to me. And what is more, it is by his own grace that his own prayer is heard, and that the sinner turns to God the reconciler. For he causes the word of reconciliation to become a mighty power within us, a fire in our bones, so that we repent of sin in dust and ashes, and seek reconciliation with God in the blood of Christ. It is all of God, none of us. To him alone be the glory and the thanksgiving and adoration forevermore!

Chapter 18

EVERLASTING RIGHTEOUSNESS

> How blest is he whose trespass
> Hath freely been forgiv'n,
> Whose sin is wholly covered
> Before the sight of heav'n.
> Blest he to whom Jehovah
> Imputeth not his sin,
> Who hath a guileless spirit,
> Whose heart is true within.[1]

Thus the psalmist sings in Psalm 32. And every child of God, conscious of his own sin and undoneness, and conscious too of God's forgiving grace and of the everlasting righteousness, sings it after him. Or again, he sings after the psalmist of Psalm 130:

> Lord, if Thou shouldst mark transgressions,
> In Thy presence who shall stand?
> But with Thee there is forgiveness,
> That Thy Name may fear command.[2]

Or is there for the Christian ever a greater boon than the knowledge that his sin is blotted out, and that he stands forever as righteous before the face of God?

And what a marvel of grace this gift of righteousness which we have in Christ Jesus our Lord as the fruit of his cross and perfect obedience really is! It implies that we stand before the judgment seat of

---

1   No. 83:1, in *The Psalter.*
2   No. 363:2, in *The Psalter.*

God, as we always do, without fear. It implies that as we stand before the tribunal of God, he judges us, as he always does, and finds no guilt in us; yea, that he declares us perfectly righteous. It implies that God applies the perfect standard of his holy will to us, to our being and nature, to our life and walk, and that his verdict is that we are perfect. It means that he expresses his verdict upon us, and that he declares us so perfectly righteous, as if we never had or committed any sin, as if we had always perfectly kept his every commandment.

Such is the meaning of the blessing of justification.

But it means still more. It also implies that he himself inscribes the verdict by which he declares us righteous in our very hearts, so that we are conscious of it, are assured of our righteousness before God. He does so by his Holy Spirit and through the proclamation of his holy gospel.

A great marvel and wonder of grace, I say, is this blessing of everlasting righteousness. It is beyond our boldest comprehension. For it means that the holy and righteous God declares the unrighteous and ungodly perfectly righteous. Do not fail to understand this. For this is exactly the greatest source of comfort to the believing Christian. God declares the ungodly righteous, and that too in the very moment that they are still ungodly and unrighteous.

The justified sinner is not one that formerly was ungodly, and therefore was the object of God's condemnation, but who has now reformed, converted himself, became godly, pious, religious, and who now appears in the judgment of God with his new piety and good works, and on the basis of them is declared righteous. He who would present the matter in this light would deprive the Christian exactly of all his comfort. But the contrary is true. The sinner at the very moment of his justification is very really a sinner in himself, and as such he appears as far as his own conscience is concerned before the tribunal of God. He is, and he knows that he is, an enemy of God. His nature is corrupt, and there is no good in him at all. He is wholly inclined to all evil. He has transgressed all the commandments of God, and kept none of them. Yea, what is worse, at the very moment when he stands before the judgment seat of God he sins and violates all God's precepts.

And he knows it. He carries the testimony in his own conscience that he is a sinner, that he is worthy of damnation, that he is inclined to all evil, that he is incapable of doing any good, that he trampled God's holy law underfoot, and that even now, as he stands before God's holy judgment seat, he continues to transgress. He is deeply conscious of the fact that if God will ever enter into judgment with him, and deal with him according to his nature and deserts, he cannot stand for one moment, but must expect that he will be sentenced to eternal damnation.

And the marvel of justification is that this sinner, who has nothing to bring before God but corruption and rebellion, is declared righteous before God, and hears the verdict that he has no sin, that all his sins are blotted out and completely forgiven; yea, what is more, that he is clothed with an everlasting righteousness, that makes him worthy of eternal life and glory. Marvelous is this gift of grace indeed! Nevertheless, it is exactly what the Scriptures declare. We are "justified freely by his grace through the redemption that is in Christ Jesus" (Rom. 3:24). "By the deeds of the law...shall no flesh be justified in his sight" (v. 20). For by the law is their knowledge of sin. "But...the righteousness of God without the law is manifested...the righteousness of God which is by faith of Jesus Christ unto all and upon all them that believe (vv. 21–22). All boasting is excluded, for a man is justified by faith without the deeds of the law (vv. 27–28). God is indeed revealed abundantly as a God that justifies the ungodly. And the sinner is justified without any works of righteousness on his part.

You ask how this is possible! Can a righteous and holy God pronounce a sentence upon him that is guilty and corrupt, by which he becomes perfectly righteous? Oh yes, he can. And not only is it possible for him, but he accomplished this marvel of justification through Jesus Christ our Lord. We are justified freely by his grace through the redemption that is in Christ Jesus. In Christ God revealed himself as the one that justifies the ungodly. And again, we refer you to the cross of the Son of God. He is our righteousness and he alone. In Christ there is a righteousness that is so great and mighty that it blots out all our sins, and clothes us with an everlasting righteousness that makes us worthy of eternal life.

In the judgment of God Christ took our place. He assumed full responsibility for us. All our sins he took upon himself, and he bore them away forever. For he is the Lamb of God that bears away the sin of the world. And he not merely suffered the punishment for the sins of his own, but in suffering the wrath of God he was perfectly obedient, even unto the death of the cross (Phil. 2:8). As I have emphasized repeatedly, the death of Christ was an act. He laid down his life voluntarily. He sacrificed himself willingly. Motivated by the love of God he went down into the lowest hell, that there he might bear the wrath of God against sin. And thus he satisfied the justice of God. And satisfying God's justice, he made a perfect atonement for our sins. He removed the guilt of sin, and merited eternal righteousness. And God justified him and pronounced the verdict of his perfect righteousness upon him when he raised him from the dead and gave him everlasting glory and immortality. For Christ was delivered for our transgressions, and was raised again for our justification (Rom. 4:25).

In the death and resurrection of Jesus Christ from the dead God revealed himself as the one that justifies the ungodly. And by faith we receive the sentence of God's justification in our hearts. For this righteousness of God in Jesus Christ is imputed to all those for whom Christ died and was raised, so that we are perfectly righteous before God, as if we ourselves had performed that act of obedience on the cross which Christ performed for us. And by faith we lay hold upon this verdict of justification, so that we know that even though all things testify against us, and though our own conscience condemns us, and though our sins rise up against us, we are nevertheless righteous before God, and heirs of eternal life, according to the promise.

Christ died in our stead. He became a curse for us, and thereby removed the curse forevermore. You ask how this is possible? How could the justice of God permit another to die for our sins? In a worldly court that would, of course, forever be impossible and never permissible. If there one is found guilty of murder and the judge would inflict capital punishment upon another instead of upon the guilty, it would be considered a double injustice. How is it possible, then, that Christ could die in our stead? Not only so, but how could it be just that one man die for the sins of countless millions?

The answer is, friends, that Christ is not another, but he is the Son of God come into the flesh. He took upon himself our flesh and blood voluntarily. He became man by an act of his own will. He had power to lay down his life for others if he so pleased. And before the world was, he had been appointed the head of all his own, so that he represented them and was responsible for them, by God's eternal decree of election. God's people are one body. Christ, therefore, can be summoned before the bar of God's judgment and appear there for all his own, assume responsibility for them, take all their guilt upon himself, and pay for their sins by an act of perfect obedience on his part. And again, because he is not a mere man, but the Son of God in the flesh, his death is of immeasurable value, infinitely precious, capable of blotting out the sins of all his own and of procuring for them eternal righteousness and everlasting life and glory.

This is the meaning of Calvary! This is the marvelous grace of God in justifying the ungodly. He himself came down to us. He himself assumed our human nature. And in that human nature he assumed responsibility for our sins and became obedient unto death, yea, unto the death of the cross. Thus God blotted out the handwriting of our sins that was against us (Col. 2:14). And thus Christ not only obtained for us forgiveness of sins, but an everlasting righteousness, a righteousness that was far greater and far more valuable than the righteousness of Adam in the state of rectitude, a righteousness that was worthy of eternal life. In Christ God justifies the ungodly. We are justified freely by his grace.

Of this righteousness of God in Christ God himself makes us partaker by a true and living faith. In a sense we may certainly say that faith makes us righteous before God. Only he that believes on him that justifies the ungodly is righteous, no one else. In order to be justified, we must certainly believe on God as he revealed himself in Jesus Christ crucified and raised from the dead. There is no other way than that of faith, to become righteous before God, and to receive the merits of Jesus Christ our Lord. We must not even try another way. All our good works count for nothing. They are but "filthy rags" (Isa. 64:6). All our own goodness, all our piety, all our religiousness, and the very best of our religious acts must be utterly discarded as a ground of righteousness before God. We must come before God as naked sinners, damnable in ourselves, but believing on God that justifies the ungodly. By faith we are justified.

But what is this faith out of which and through which we are justified before God? Is it, perhaps, merely another work which we must perform in order to become righteous before God, instead of the work of the law? May we say, perhaps, that faith is a work which God reckons as righteousness instead of our perfect obedience to the law of God? God forbid. Then salvation would still be of works, and not of grace.

May we say, perhaps, that faith is necessary for us to do good works, and that now by the works of faith we are made righteous before God? Again, even then we are not freely justified through grace by the redemption that is in Christ Jesus, but we are really justified on the basis of our own good works. Is faith, perhaps, a condition, a prerequisite, which we must perform before God will declare us righteous before him? Also this is not true, for the simple reason that all the elect are justified before God from eternity, and they are objectively justified in the cross and resurrection of Jesus Christ from the dead.

No, not our faith is the ground or the condition or the cause of our righteousness, but only the cross and resurrection of our Lord Jesus Christ. His righteousness is imputed to us. But faith is an instrument, a means, whereby we are united with Christ. And it is the spiritual power whereby we lay hold on this righteousness, so that we know and wholly rely on the God of our salvation that justifies the ungodly.

Thus, and thus alone, all boasting is excluded. For let us not forget that faith itself is a gift of God. No man can or will of himself accept Christ and believe on God who raised him from the dead. God through Christ, by his Holy Spirit, works within our hearts the justifying faith. And so it is all of grace. By grace God came down to us in our sin and death, and in the person of his only begotten Son assumed our flesh and blood. By grace Christ died for our sins on the accursed tree. By grace he was raised on the third day for our justification. By grace God gives us the power of faith, thus uniting us with Christ and causing us to believe on him who justifies the ungodly. "By grace are ye saved through faith; and that not of yourselves: it is the gift of God" (Eph. 2:8).

And do not say that this doctrine of free justification causes men to become careless and profane. Such is forever impossible. For let us remember that we are justified out of faith, and that by faith we are united with Christ and live out of him. The same faith whereby we are justified is also the principle of our sanctification. It is quite impossible that one who lives out of Christ should deliberately continue in sin. For he has died with Christ and is raised with him unto "newness of life" (Rom. 6:4). Hence, he condemns his own sin and hates it. By faith he repents and cries out: "God be merciful to me a sinner" (Luke 18:13). By faith he "hungers and thirsts after righteousness" (Matt. 5:6), and lays hold on the righteousness of Christ. And by that same faith he abhors the ways of sin, crucifies his old nature, and walks in a new and holy life, to the glory of his Redeemer, who delivered him from the dominion of sin and called him out of darkness into his marvelous light (1 Peter 2:9).

Chapter 19

CRUCIFIED
WITH CHRIST

O ne of the fruits of the death of the Son of God is that we are crucified with Christ, so that sin has no more dominion over us, and we live unto him that died for us and rose again. This is plainly the teaching of Scripture in many places. In Romans 6:3–6 we read:

3.   Know ye not, that so many of us as were baptized into Jesus Christ were baptized into his death?

4.   Therefore we are buried with him by baptism into death: that like as Christ was raised up from the dead by the glory of the Father, even so we also should walk in newness of life.

5.   For if we have been planted together in the likeness of his death, we shall be also in the likeness of his resurrection:

6.   Knowing this, that our old man is crucified with him, that the body of sin might be destroyed, that henceforth we should not serve sin.

And in 2 Corinthians 5:14–15, "For the love of Christ constraineth us; because we thus judge, that if one died for all, then were all dead: and that he died for all, that they which live should not henceforth live unto themselves, but unto him which died for them, and rose again." Besides, "the cross of our Lord Jesus Christ, by whom the world is crucified unto me, and I unto the world" (Gal. 6:14).

It is plain, therefore, from the word of God that the power of the death of the Son of God is such, that by it the crucifixion, death, and burial of our old man is accomplished. Centrally the death of Christ is the death of all the elect. When he died, they all died as to their old man. When he arose, they all arose in newness of life.

The question is, however, in what sense is this true? How may it be said that sin has no dominion over the Christian even in this world? Is he entirely without sin? Or is it even so that the Christian in this world is capable of living in perfection, as the perfectionist would have it?

In Romans 6:1 the apostle Paul asks the question: "What shall we say then? Shall we continue in sin, that grace may abound?" We must remember that in all ages, even already in the time of the apostle Paul, the doctrine of free grace and free justification always found opponents. They alleged that such a doctrine makes men careless and profane. If, they say, the death of Christ is the satisfaction for all our sins, and if by faith we receive all his benefits and lay upon this satisfaction, then we have, so to speak, a general indulgence, the forgiveness of all sin, the sin we ever committed, still commit, or shall commit in the future. Then, so they say, we are perfectly righteous no matter what we do. No amount of good works can possibly increase our righteousness or make us more perfectly righteous before God than we are by faith in Christ. And no sin on our part can possibly deprive us of the perfection of the righteousness we have in Christ. What then would be more logical than the conclusion that we had better continue in sin, seeing that there is no condemnation for them that are in Christ anyhow? Yea, more, to continue in sin would yield the benefit that thereby the power of Christ's satisfaction and grace of God would shine forth more gloriously: let us therefore "continue in sin, that grace may abound" (Rom. 6:1).

To this objection, however, the apostle Paul replies with an emphatic, "God forbid!" (Rom. 6:2). In other words, he means to say that it is forever impossible that those that are in Christ and are justified by faith should ever become careless and profane. And he explains this emphatic answer by continuing to write: "How shall we, that are dead to sin, live any longer therein?" (v. 2). And that the believer is dead to sin the apostle explains in the verses that follow, verses 3–9, in the same chapter. The old man of sin in believers is crucified, dead, and buried. And this crucifixion of the old man is the direct result of the death of Christ. Believers are ingrafted into Christ, and thus they are partakers of his death. They are crucified, dead, and buried with him, so that, as we already said, the death of Christ is also the death of believers. When the power of the death of Christ is applied unto the elect, the old man also dies in them.

What is meant by the old man that is crucified with Christ? It is man in his corrupt and sinful nature. In this nature man lives unto sin. He is not free from sin, but bound in and unto sin. Sin has dominion over him. Sin is the queen that is enthroned in his heart, that issues her precepts, to whom he is enslaved, willingly enslaved to be sure, but enslaved nevertheless, and whom he does obey, whose will he honors, whose direction he follows, whose wages he receives. For the human nature in Adam is wholly corrupt, the understanding is darkened, the will is perverted, the heart is obdurate, the desires and inclinations are impure. His whole nature is motivated by enmity against God.

This condition, you must remember, is spiritual death. And death is the punishment of sin. The "old man" has no right to life, no right to be delivered from the bondage of sin and death. He is legally, according to the very sentence of God over him, a slave of sin. He is under the law of sin and death. In this sense it may be said that sin is legally his lord, that it is the power that is legally enthroned in his heart, and that it cannot and may not be dethroned until the guilt of sin is blotted out. The old man is a legal slave of sin.

If we bear this in mind, we will be able to understand that and how the death of Christ is the crucifixion, death, and burial of "the old man" for all the elect. For the death of Christ is the satisfaction for sin, the complete and final blotting out of the guilt of sin for all that are in Christ, for the whole church of all ages, and the establishment of a basis of eternal righteousness. Hence, the very basis of sin's dominion in the human nature of the elect was removed by the death of Christ. Legally sin has no more dominion over them. On the basis of righteousness, of the righteousness of Christ, the throne of sin in the human nature cannot stand: it must fall. When Christ died, therefore, all the elect were freed from sin. As the apostle writes in Romans 6:7, "He that is dead is freed from sin."

This is the meaning of Scripture in Romans 8:3, "For what the law could not do, in that it was weak through the flesh, God sending his own Son in the likeness of sinful flesh, and for sin, condemned sin in the flesh." Notice that in this verse it is sin that is condemned, not the sinner. Sin is, as it were, personified and summoned before the bar of divine justice. Before that bar she claims to have a right to sit enthroned and to rule as the queen in the human nature. And the law cannot condemn her, because the law itself condemns man to spiritual death, and therefore to the slavery of sin.

But what the law could not do, that is, condemn sin in the flesh, God himself accomplished by sending his own Son in the likeness of sinful flesh, and that too for sin, that is, in order to deprive sin of its right to rule in human nature. In this respect sin was condemned. It was juridically deprived of its dominion in the flesh, deprived of its right to rule in human nature. And this was accomplished by the death of the Son of God, by the accursed death of the cross. When God, through the death of the cross, had blotted out the iniquity of his people, sin was condemned. It could no longer claim the right to rule in human nature. Thus, then, the "old man" of all God's own is crucified, dead, and buried forever through the death of the Son of God.

And, by Christ's own power, that is, by the power of his Spirit, this freedom from the dominion of sin through the sacrifice of the cross is applied to all the individual elect in this world. For Christ is raised, and death has no more dominion over him. He is exalted at the right hand of God, clothed with all power in heaven and on earth. And having received the promise of the Spirit, he poured out that Spirit in the church, and through him dwells in his people and makes them partakers of all his benefits.

He gives them the justifying faith, and by that faith they become partakers of his death and resurrection, they receive the forgiveness of sins and the everlasting and perfect righteousness he obtained for them by his perfect obedience even unto death. And in this righteousness they possess their legal liberation from the dominion of sin over them, and they are conscious of this freedom. And being legally freed from sin's dominion, they are also actually delivered from the power of corruption, raised with Christ, and inducted into the glorious liberty of the children of God through the power of grace and by the calling of the gospel. And thus it is by the power of the cross that our old man is crucified, and that sin can have no more dominion over us. Thus it is that instead of living unto sin, we henceforth live unto God in Christ Jesus our Lord.

It is very clear that the grace of justification can never make men careless and profane, so that they indulge in sin. For exactly in being justified the believer is freed from the dominion of sin, in order that he may live unto God. An indulgence granted by mere man, even though he be the pope, may induce the sinner to live wantonly in sin. The mighty power of the death of Christ has the very opposite effect. By it sin is condemned, dethroned, its power destroyed, and the believer is become dead to sin. The corrupt inclinations of the flesh can no more reign in him. He may now serve the living God and offer himself a living sacrifice unto God.

The question still arises: how does this freedom from the dominion of sin reveal itself in the present life of the believer in this world?

In answer to this question we must state, first of all, that to be dead to sin does not mean the same thing as to say that sin is dead in us. Bitter disappointment must needs be the result, if we imagine that when we are ingrafted into Christ, crucified and raised with him, the death of sin follows. For sin is not dead in the believer as long as he is in this life. It does not die until he dies. Till then sin is very much alive. The motions of sin are in our members. In fact, in opposition to the new beginning of life in the believer these motions of sin are often more active and assert themselves more emphatically and insistently as the believer grows in the knowledge and grace of the Lord Jesus Christ. He has but a small beginning of the new obedience. And a small beginning it remains even in the very holiest of the children of God. And the believer must understand this, that he may watch and pray, lest he fall into temptation. Paradoxical though it may sound, though the old man is dead and buried with Christ, yet throughout his whole life in this world, until the very moment of his death, he must constantly fight to put off the old man and to put on the new man in Christ Jesus.

Yet, though sin is not dead, the believer is nevertheless dead to sin. The old man is very really dead and buried. That old man was characterized by his being legally and ethically enslaved to sin. And the believer is a free man. Death has no dominion over him. The old man was known by his inner harmony with sin. Sin was his proper sphere. He lived in sin. He loved iniquity. He found his delight in the service of unrighteousness. He hated the light and loved the darkness. Though he often was filled with the sorrow of the world and dreaded the wages of sin, he was a stranger to the sorrow after God, and never knew repentance. After forgiveness and righteousness he did not yearn. The kingdom of God he could not see. In the world he found his delight. And the things that are above he did not seek, neither did he perceive them. When sin said *yes*, he said *yes*. Where sin led, he followed. And it was his delight to indulge in iniquity. Such is the old man of sin.

But that old man is dead. He that is in Christ Jesus is a new creature. "Old things are passed away; behold, all things are become new" (2 Cor. 5:17). It is true that the motions of sin are still in his members. But he hates those motions of sin. He still sins, but he is sorry for his sin and repents, and the cry for forgiveness is on his lips daily. He does not live in sin, dwell in sin, abide in sin. He does not find his proper sphere in sin anymore.

On the contrary, where formerly he agreed with sin, there is now in his inmost heart a deep, a radical disagreement between sin and him. Whereas formerly he found his delight in sin, he now abhors it, eschews it, hates it, opposes it, and takes God's side in the judgment of his own iniquities. And, on the other hand, he has an inner delight in the precepts of his God. He hears his word, he tastes that the Lord is good, he seeks God's fellowship, and he is a companion of all them that fear him. He is crucified unto the world, and the world is crucified unto him. He seeks the things which are above, where Christ sits at the right hand of God (Col. 3:1).

It is true that he often finds himself doing what he would not; but fact is that he does not will it. He frequently must confess that he does that which he hates; it is nevertheless true that he hates it. He delights in the law of God after the inward man; but he also sees another law in his members, warring against the law of his mind and bringing him into captivity to the law of sin which is in his members. And he exclaims with the apostle Paul in Romans 7:24, "O wretched man that I am! who shall deliver me from the body of this death?" But to this question he has nevertheless an answer. And that answer is: "I thank God through Jesus Christ our Lord" (v. 25).

In hope he longs for the day when he shall be delivered from the body of this death and be like unto the Lord in everlasting perfection, that he may offer himself forever unto God, a sacrifice of thanksgiving. And all this is the fruit of the death of the Son of God, the fruit of the living faith that confesses: "I believe in Jesus Christ, his only begotten Son, our Lord; who was conceived by the Holy Ghost, born of the Virgin Mary; suffered under Pontius Pilate; was crucified, dead, and buried." "Thanks be unto God for his unspeakable gift!" (2 Cor. 9:15).

Chapter 20

THE DESCENSION
INTO HELL

The last part of the fourth article of the apostolic creed speaks of the descension of Christ into hell.

This part of the article is not found in the older copies of the Apostles' Creed. Although the matter itself was believed by the church and the expression occurs in some isolated confessions, in our Apostles' Creed it was not introduced until the beginning of the sixth century. When in many of our American churches the Apostles' Creed is recited, the words "He descended into hell" are usually omitted. And, if this part of the article is explained to mean that Christ suffered hellish agonies on the cross, the words have no special meaning, and may just as well be left out. For in that case they merely are a repetition of what was already expressed before in the same article, when it confessed that Jesus was crucified and died.

However, this part of the article has been explained in more than one way. One explanation gives to it the meaning that Christ was in the state of the dead. The Greek word for hell is *hades*, a word that is translated, and that, too, usually correctly, in our English Bible by hell, but which may signify the same as the grave, the state of the dead before the resurrection. Hence, the explanation is indeed possible: he descended into the state of the dead. However, the context in which this part of the article occurs would seem to be opposed to the idea that this was actually the meaning of the article historically, that is, according to the faith of the early church: for it occurs at the end of the series, "suffered, was crucified, dead, and buried." The last of these terms already declares that Christ descended into the place of the dead, that is, into the grave. And to add another article virtually expressing the same thing would appear to be a rather useless repetition.

Another explanation of this part of the fourth article of the Apostles' Creed is that it refers to an actual self-manifestation of Christ after the crucifixion to all the departed spirits. However, the explanation is rather vague, and it is rather difficult to see how the descension into hell in this sense could be a part of God's redemption through Jesus Christ our Lord. Why should Christ thus manifest himself to all the dead? And what could such a self-manifestation to the dead add to the revelation of Jesus Christ as the savior of his people? This interpretation, therefore, must also be discarded.

Nor need we seriously consider the view that our Lord after his crucifixion descended into the place of desolation in order to suffer the tortures of the damned. Neither can this have the meaning of the early church that inserted these words into the confession. Whatever the early church may have meant by Hades, it certainly cannot have been the place of eternal punishment, into which Christ was supposed to have descended after his crucifixion. The notion that the savior suffered the torments of hell after his death is contrary to the plain teaching of Scripture.

Evident it is, that the Lord after he gave up the ghost cannot have suffered the torments of hell in body and soul. For in the first place, his body rested in the grave of Joseph of Arimathea, and therefore certainly was not in hell. Besides, such a view would be in conflict with the words which our Lord addressed to the malefactor from the cross: "To day shalt thou be with me in paradise" (Luke 23:43). And immediately before the Lord gave up the ghost he announced triumphantly: "It is finished" (John 19:30). And surely, this triumphant outcry was uttered in the consciousness that the work of redemption, the sacrifice of reconciliation, had been completed and perfected, and that no more suffering remained to be endured, certainly not the suffering of hell. The wrath of God and his curse because of sin had been fully borne, and reconciliation had been accomplished.

The words of Psalm 16:10 as quoted by the apostle Peter on the day of Pentecost in Acts 2:27 are sometimes interpreted as meaning that Christ actually descended into the place of the damned. We read there: "Because thou wilt not leave my soul in hell, neither wilt thou suffer thine Holy One to see corruption." But it must be very evident that the reference in this text is certainly not to the place of the damned, the place of eternal desolation, but to Hades, the bodiless state of the dead. In that state, after the Lord gave up the ghost, his soul was in paradise, as is evident from his second utterance on the cross, and his body lay in the grave. And the meaning of the passage is that God would not leave Christ's soul in that disembodied state, neither would he allow his body to be swallowed up by the corruption of the grave; but he would surely glorify his holy one in the resurrection. In the light of Scripture, therefore, the view that Christ personally descended into the place of the damned, in order to suffer there vicariously the pains of eternal torture, cannot be maintained.

Roman Catholic theologians appeal to the well-known text in 1 Peter 3:19–20 to support their view that Christ descended into what they call the *limbo*, a portal of hell, in order there to deliver thence the Old Testament saints, to whom heaven was not yet opened until Christ's own ascent from death into glory. According to them, at the time when the Apostles' Creed was composed, the word *hell* was used to designate any state of existence lower than heaven. Now the text in 1 Peter 3:19–20 is supposed to mean that after his death our Lord's soul went to preach to those spirits that were in the *limbo*, that is, in prison. He joined those souls which were detained from the fullness of heaven and which were awaiting the opening of heaven to mankind by him. This descent of Christ's soul into hell was obviously not to the hell of eternal damnation, but only to a certain place of detention, where the souls of the just were detained, who lived prior to our Lord's coming into this world.

However, this explanation of 1 Peter 3:19–20 by Roman Catholic exegetes cannot stand for a moment, even though there may be room for difference of opinion as to the true meaning of this somewhat difficult passage. This well-known passage reads as follows: "By which also he went and preached unto the spirits in prison; which sometime were disobedient, when once the longsuffering of God waited in the days of Noah, while the ark was a-preparing, wherein few, that is, eight souls were saved by water."

Now if you will study this passage of Holy Writ, and look at it a little more closely, you will at once find, in the first place, that the apostle is not speaking here at all of a personal descent of Christ into prison after his crucifixion and before his resurrection. On the contrary, he speaks of Christ's going to preach to the spirits that were in prison after his resurrection and through the Spirit. This is the simple and plain meaning of the words, the introductory words of verse 19, "by which," refer back to the latter part of the eighteenth verse, "being put to death in the flesh, but quickened by the Spirit." And then follows: "By which also he went and preached unto the spirits in prison." The order of the phrases, therefore, demands that we conceive of this mission of Christ to the spirits in prison as having taken place after his resurrection. Moreover, he went not in his human nature or in his disembodied soul, but in the Spirit, by whom also he was quickened from the dead. And through this Spirit he is able to send his word down unto the spirits in prison without a personal descent.

In the second place, it is also plain that the apostle by the phrase "spirits in prison" certainly cannot designate the Old Testament saints, unto whom heaven was supposed to be closed until the coming of Christ. For these spirits in prison are described as those "which sometime were disobedient, when once the longsuffering of God waited in the days of Noah, while the ark was a-preparing." This cannot possibly refer to the Old Testament saints, but clearly refers to the ungodly of Noah's day, when the righteous were persecuted all the day long and God saved them by the waters of the flood and in the ark.

Moreover, in the third place, the apostle does not speak with one word or even suggest in any way that these spirits in prison were delivered and taken to heaven by Christ. Nor does the Bible know anything of such a *limbo*, in which the Old Testament saints were kept until heaven was opened for them by Christ. For all these reasons we must reject the Roman Catholic view of the descension into hell.

Nor does the Lutheran explanation that after his death and before his resurrection Christ descended into hell to proclaim his victory to the spirits in prison find support in the text from 1 Peter 3:19–20. Nor does it find support in any other passage of Holy Writ. It is indeed quite in harmony with the text in 1 Peter 3 to say that Christ announced his victory to those spirits that persecuted his people and mocked at his cause in the world. But this word of victory was proclaimed by Christ not between his death and resurrection, nor by a personal descent into hell, but after his resurrection and exaltation and through the Spirit that is given him.

We conclude, therefore, that whatever may have been the significance of the clause concerning the descension of Christ into hell in the mind of the early church, Scripture knows of no such descent to the place of the damned, nor of such a self-manifestation of Christ to all the departed spirits. And if the clause "He descended into hell" is to be maintained at all, the Reformed interpretation of this clause is no doubt to be preferred. That explanation is that Christ endured inexpressible anguish, pains, terrors, and hellish agonies in all his suffering, especially on the cross, and more especially still when he finally cried out: "My God, my God, why hast thou forsaken me?" (Matt. 27:46).

Christ indeed endured in all his sufferings the very agonies of hell. For he bore the wrath of God and the curse of God against sin. He endured these sufferings, of course, especially when he was nailed to the accursed tree. And even on the cross there is a gradual increase in his suffering of these hellish agonies. This is evident from all that occurs on and about the cross. During the first half of the six-hour period of the crucifixion, the sun still shed its light upon the awful spectacle on Calvary; the enemies had the audacity to mock and jeer at the Crucified One; and the Lord himself finds it possible to take interest in the things about him, praying for his enemies, committing his mother to the care of the disciples whom he loved, and assuring the penitent malefactor of final salvation.

But during the last three hours on the cross, the cross is completely taken out of men's hands. Darkness, that dreadful symbol of God's wrathful presence, descends on the scene. The enemies, amazed at the fearful omen, cease from mockery and grow silent. And for the space of three hours the Crucified One is completely wrapped up in his own suffering. Not a word is heard from his lips. Then, almost at the end of these last three hours of his passion, he makes it known that he has been descending into the depths, that he has indeed reached the very bottom of hell, in the question of amazement: "My God, my God, why hast thou forsaken me?"

What does it mean? It means nothing less than that there and then, at the very moment of that fearful outcry of amazement and agony, Christ descended into the depth of hell and tasted the wrath of God against sin to the very end. And in the consciousness that he had indeed borne the full burden of the wrath of God in his suffering, he could shout triumphantly a few moments later: "It is finished" (John 19:30). The measure of suffering and of obedience is filled. All that was to be borne of the wrath of God against the sin of all the elect had been endured even to the end. Nothing, emphatically nothing, remains to procure for us eternal righteousness and life. The Son of God had tasted all there is to be tasted in the agony of death as the expression of God's just wrath. Such is the meaning of Christ's descent into hell.

By that descension of our Savior into hell, understood in this real, spiritual sense of the word, the believer may be assured that he is saved forever, delivered from the wrath of God and from the torments of hell. Or positively speaking, he may be assured that he is restored to God's everlasting favor, and worthy of eternal glory in the tabernacle of God with men. Many indeed may be the temptations that assail the believer, to move him from his sure ground of confidence in Christ. There are temptations from without and temptations from within. His own conscience accuses him. Sin from within would bring him into doubt. "The valley of the shadow of death" (Ps. 23:4) appears to testify that God's wrath is still upon him. The world laughs at his confidence. The devil assails his assurance of faith.

But in all these temptations he clings by faith to the death of the Son of God, that finished it all, which was a suffering of hellish agonies in his stead and in his behalf. And from the darkness of this present death and from the depths of his greatest temptations, contemplating that death of the Son of God, that death even into the bottom of hell, and clinging to that Son of God who died and was raised, he knows that nothing remains to be done, and that he is forever delivered from the torments of hell. The death of the Son of God, who descended for us into hell, is the sole ground of the believer's confidence. And nothing can separate him from his love.

Article 5

The third day he rose again
from the dead

Chapter 21

CHRIST IS RISEN

W e now approach the fifth article of the apostolic creed: "The third day he rose again from the dead." And to this article we wish to devote at least three or four sermons. We do this not because we consider it necessary that the minister of the word defend the truth of the resurrection of our Lord Jesus Christ over against various forms of modern philosophy and so-called theology, that either deny the reality of the bodily resurrection outright or give the term a new content, that deprives the resurrection of Christ of its significance and of its power. The truth needs no apology. The church does not need to defend the resurrection of the Lord Jesus Christ. It rather proceeds from the faith in the risen Lord, whose Spirit she receives and of whose life she partakes. Therefore, apart even from the abundant testimony of Holy Writ that Christ is risen indeed, it is true what a well-known hymn declares: "You ask me how I know he lives? He lives within my heart." And besides, the natural man receives not the things of the Spirit, for they are spiritually discerned.

But when we intend to devote a few sermons to this subject of the resurrection of Christ, we have in mind the great significance which Scripture attaches to this glorious wonder and the central place it gives to the resurrection of Jesus Christ in the economy of salvation. Without the resurrection of Christ the cross is vain and remains the darkest page in history. For thus we read in 1 Corinthians 15:14–19,

14. And if Christ be not risen, then is our preaching vain, and your faith is also vain.

15. Yea, and we are found false witnesses of God; because we have testified of God that he raised up Christ: whom he raised not up, if so be that the dead rise not.

16. For if the dead rise not, then is not Christ raised:
17. And if Christ be not raised, your faith is vain; ye are yet in your sins.
18. Then they also which are fallen asleep in Christ are perished.
19. If in this life only we have hope in Christ, we are of all men most miserable.

The resurrection of Christ the crucified one, that indeed is the heart of the gospel.

And therefore the apostles, in obedience to their charge to preach the gospel to every creature, do indeed proclaim Christ, and him crucified, but always as the one whom God raised from the dead on the third day. On the day when the Holy Spirit was poured out in the church, the apostle Peter preached unto the amazed multitude the Christ whom according to the determinate counsel and foreknowledge of God they had "crucified and slain," but "whom God hath raised up, having loosed the pains of death: because it was not possible that he should be holden of it" (Acts 2:23–24). Again: "This Jesus hath God raised up, whereof we are all witnesses" (v. 32).

When the impotent man, sitting daily at the gate of the temple, was healed, and the multitude that witnessed this miracle were filled with wonder and amazement at that which happened unto the man, and ran together unto Peter and John, the apostle Peter once again preached unto them Jesus, whom the Jews had killed, but whom "God hath raised from the dead; whereof we are witnesses" (Acts 3:15). And when, on the following day, the rulers of the Jews called the apostles to account for what they had done, Peter boldly testifies: "Be it known unto you all, and to all the people of Israel, that by the name of Jesus Christ of Nazareth, whom ye crucified, whom God raised from the dead, even by him doth this man stand here before you whole" (4:10). And when they were released from prison, the same apostles "with great power gave...witness of the resurrection of the Lord Jesus" (v. 33).

The same is true about the preaching of the apostle Paul. Also in this gospel the resurrection of Jesus Christ occupies a central place. At Antioch he proclaims that the Jews condemned and slew Jesus,

30. But God raised him from the dead:
31. And he was seen many days of them which came up with him from Galilee to Jerusalem, who are his witnesses unto the people.
32. And we declare unto you glad tidings, how that the promise which was made unto the fathers,
33. God hath fulfilled the same unto us their children, in that he hath raised up Jesus again; as it is also written in the second psalm, Thou art my Son, this day have I begotten thee. (Acts 13:30–33)

Notice that here the resurrection of the Lord is presented as the fulfillment of the promise of the gospel, and even as the realization of that significant word from the second psalm: through the resurrection of Christ God has begotten his Son.[1]

In the synagogue in Thessalonica "Paul, as his manner was, went in unto them, and three sabbath days reasoned with them out of the scriptures, opening and alleging, that Christ must needs have suffered, and risen again from the dead; and that this Jesus, whom I preach unto you, is Christ" (Acts 17:2–3). On the Areopagus in Athens Paul proclaims: "Because he hath appointed a day, in the which he will judge the world in righteousness by that man whom he hath ordained; whereof he hath given assurance unto all men, in that he hath raised him from the dead" (v. 31). Before King Agrippa the apostle witnesses "that Christ should suffer, and that he should be the first that should rise from the dead, and should shew light unto the people, and to the Gentiles" (26:23). In the well-known fifteenth chapter of the first epistle to the Corinthians, from which we already quoted, the apostle writes: "Moreover, brethren, I declare unto you the gospel which I preached unto you," and this gospel is briefly summarized in the words "how that Christ died for our sins according to the scriptures; and that he was buried, and that he rose again the third day according to the scriptures" (1 Cor. 15:1, 3–4).

---

1 Hoeksema is referring to Psalm 2:7, "I will declare the decree: the Lord hath said unto me, Thou art my Son; this day have I begotten thee."

Now what is the meaning of that resurrection of the Lord Jesus Christ on the third day? What happened on that marvelous first day of the week that was able to raise the spirits of the disciples of our Lord from the slough of despondency to the height of jubilant and triumphant faith, expressed in the shout: "The Lord is risen indeed"? To answer this question, we can do no better than first of all to turn our attention to the gospel narratives concerning the resurrection of Jesus, and to let the word of God speak to us through the first witnesses and evidences of that marvelous event.

First of all, then, there is the testimony of many faithful witnesses, who declared what they had seen and heard of the resurrection of Jesus Christ. In the second place, there is the important testimony of the vacated grave and of the place where the Lord lay. This testimony of the empty grave was very necessary, and at the same time, extremely important. That the grave had been vacated certainly assured the witnesses, especially when taken in connection with the later appearances of the risen Lord to them, that Christ had really risen, that he was not merely alive in the spirit, but that his body had been quickened and raised. But the testimony of the empty sepulcher was not only negative; it did not only leave with the eyewitnesses the indelible impression that their Lord had left the grave. But the sepulcher contained also a positive testimony: it spoke clearly of the otherness, the altogether transcendent nature of the resurrection. Of this we will speak later. And lastly, there is the testimony of the angels that appeared on the morning of the first day of the week in the empty grave, to bring to the disciples the joyful message that the Lord had risen indeed.

Many are the eyewitnesses of the resurrection of Jesus Christ. There were, in the first place, the women, who in the early morning of that first day of the week went to the sepulcher to finish the embalming of their Lord's body. There was Mary Magdalene, to whom the Lord appeared separately at the sepulcher. There were Peter and John, who upon the first report of Mary went to inspect the grave. In the late afternoon of that first day the Lord appeared to the sojourners at Emmaus through the word which he spoke to them and through the breaking of the bread. And in the evening of that same day the

Lord manifested himself to the disciples without Thomas, as they were gathered with closed doors for fear of the Jews.

A week later he appeared again to the disciples, now particularly to Thomas, who was with them. Still later there was the appearance to seven disciples at the Sea of Galilee, at which occasion Peter was restored to his place among the apostles. There were the appearances to Peter alone and to James the brother of the Lord. There was the manifestation on the mount of Galilee to more than five hundred brethren at once. And at the end of those marvelous forty days he appeared unto them for the last time when he was taken up from them on the Mount of Olives. And the apostle Paul writes in 1 Corinthians 15:8, "And last of all he was seen of me also, as of one born out of due time."

In all Scripture there is perhaps nothing more marvelous and exquisitely beautiful than these Gospel reports concerning the resurrection. They are clearly the testimony of faithful witnesses, wholly unprepossessed[2] as to the testimony they bear, simply reporting what they could not fully understand, but which they saw and heard and believed. All the attacks of unbelieving critics upon this testimony of the Gospel record concerning the resurrection of Jesus Christ are as silly and wicked as the story the Roman soldiers were bribed to tell, that, namely, the disciples had stolen the body of Jesus and that too, mark you, while they, the soldiers, were sleeping. If these narratives had been invented by the imagination of the witnesses, we would have had something entirely different. No human artist, were he of the most consummate skill, could possibly have designed them. There is only one possible adequate explanation for them: the testimony of these witnesses had its source only and wholly in the fact that the Lord had risen indeed.

For, in the first place, let us remember that all the witnesses were wholly unprepared for the revelation of the risen Lord which on that first day and after they received, and of which they became the faithful witnesses. Not one of them looked forward to the resurrection on the third day. In spite of the fact that the Lord had repeatedly assured them that he must suffer, and be delivered to the elders of the people,

---

2   Unbiased or unprejudiced.

and on the third day rise again, they did not believe and did not expect the resurrection of their Lord on that third day whatsoever. When that third day dawned, they all stood in the gloomy darkness of the cross. The women went to the sepulcher, not indeed to meet the risen Lord, but to perform a last act of loving service upon the body of their dead Master. When they reported to the apostles what they had seen and heard at the grave and how the Lord met them on the way back, their words were to them as idle tales. Not one of them, therefore, expected the resurrection of their Lord. Yet, presently they one and all believed, and gave testimony of their faith that the Lord had risen indeed.

Secondly, let us also consider the contents of their testimony. How wonderfully it bears witness of the fact that they simply reported what they saw and heard. They could not possibly have invented their testimony. Let us not forget that the resurrection of Jesus Christ from the dead was not a return to us: he did not again appear in his earthly body. He went into the grave from the earthly side; but he came out on the other, that is, on the heavenly side.

Had the Lord been raised as were the young man of Nain and the daughter of Jairus and Lazarus, the matter would have been simple, and the narratives of the resurrection would have been quite different from those we now have in the gospel. At the grave of Lazarus there were eyewitnesses that could and did see the dead become alive again and descend out of the grave. Besides, they could produce the living Lazarus, who had been dead, at any time, as evidence of the fact of his resurrection. He had returned to his former earthly life. Men could have fellowship with him again, eat and drink and speak with him. Not so the resurrection of Christ: his resurrection was no return into the sphere of our earthly life. It did not consist in a resumption of his former mode of living, in the earthly house of his tabernacle, but in an advance into the glory of immortality and incorruption. A mortal and incorruptible body had been sown, but it was raised in immortality and incorruption (1 Cor. 15:42). A natural or psychical body had been stored away by Joseph and Nicodemus in the former's sepulcher; but it was raised as a spiritual body.

And therefore, the reports by the witnesses of the resurrection must testify to two facts. In the first place, it must establish the fact of the bodily resurrection of Christ. The Lord was not simply glorified in the spirit; but his body was raised into the state of immortality. The Lord is risen indeed! But, in the second place, the testimony of the witnesses must also bear record of the wholly otherness of the risen Lord, or of the wonder of the resurrection of the third day. And it is precisely these two elements that make the reports by the first witnesses so marvelously beautiful.

It is undoubtedly because of the fact that the resurrection of Christ was so wholly unlike the resurrection of Lazarus and of others that no one was eyewitness of the fact of the resurrection as such. No one was present. No one saw the Lord issue forth from the grave. Closest to the moment of the resurrection approaches the narrative as given in the gospel according to Matthew. He tells us: "There was a great earthquake: for the angel of the Lord descended from heaven, and came and rolled back the stone from the door, and sat upon it" (28:2). Yet, even this narrative remains silent about the moment of the resurrection of the Lord. The angel did not descend from heaven to aid the Lord of glory in breaking the bonds of death. He did not roll away the stone from the door of the sepulcher to make it possible for him to issue forth from Hades. It is in fact quite probable that the Lord had risen before the angel descended from heaven. But the angel rolled away the stone "and sat upon it" to open the sepulcher for inspection to the expected witnesses, and to guard it against profane intruders that might destroy the wonderful testimony of the empty grave.

We will have more to say in our next sermon about this marvelous aspect of the resurrection of our Lord Jesus Christ. For this time I will close with the remark that our glorious resurrection in the day of Christ will be like the resurrection of our Lord. Even as he was raised into glory, so we shall be raised with our glorified bodies. Even as Christ was raised into immortality, so we shall be raised even with our bodies into the glory of eternal life. For thus the apostle writes: "So also is the resurrection of the dead. It is sown in corruption; it is raised in incorruption: it is sown in dishonour; it is raised in glory: it is sown in weakness; it is raised in power: it is sown a natural body; it is raised a spiritual body" (1 Cor. 15:42–44).

"Flesh and blood cannot inherit the kingdom of God" (vv. 50), for flesh and blood are carnal, but that kingdom is spiritual. Flesh and blood are temporal, but the kingdom of God is eternal. Flesh and blood are earthy, but the kingdom of God is heavenly. And it is only in our glorified nature, body and soul, clothed with immortality, that we shall be able to see and to hear, to taste and to touch the things of the kingdom of God, see him face to face in our Lord Jesus Christ, and dwell in his tabernacle forevermore.

Chapter 22

THE POWER OF
CHRIST'S RESURRECTION

We are still speaking of the fifth article of the Apostle's Creed: "The third day he rose again from the dead." In our previous sermons we spoke of the fact of the resurrection, as well as of its wonder, as supported by the testimonies and evidences of many witnesses. And the last time, as you will remember, we spoke on the significance, the meaning of the resurrection of our Lord Jesus Christ from the dead. In that resurrection we see the beginning of the new creation of God. For according to God's counsel he is the firstborn of every creature, and all things consist by him and for him. In the present sermon we must speak of the power of that resurrection of our Lord Jesus Christ.

That power is threefold. In the first place, by the power of the resurrection of Jesus Christ death is swallowed up principally and vanquished forever. In the second place, by the power of the resurrection of our Lord Jesus Christ we are assured of everlasting righteousness before God, and in fact become partakers of his righteousness: for we already are raised with Christ to a new life. And finally, the resurrection of Christ is a pledge of our own glorious resurrection: for Christ was raised up the firstfruits from the dead. Through his resurrection the Lord Jesus Christ became the living Lord, who is able to impart all the blessings of salvation which he merited for his church to all whom the Father gives unto him.

Christ conquered death in himself. He therefore is the ever-living head of his body, the church. Therefore as the living Lord he is able to make us partakers of all the blessings of salvation which he has purchased for us by his perfect obedience. For we must remember that Christ is not only the mediator of our redemption in the juridical sense of the word. But he is also the mediator of our deliverance, through whom righteousness and life are actually bestowed upon and realized in us.

As the mediator of our redemption he purchased all things for us. For he represented us in all his suffering and death. He took our place in the judgment of God. Our sins he took upon himself. He assumed responsibility for all our guilt. In that capacity he became obedient unto death, yea, unto the death of the cross (Phil. 2:8). And by his perfect obedience he, the Son of God in the flesh, blotted out the guilt of our sin, and merited for us eternal righteousness and life. This part of the work of salvation is finished. All that are in him have redemption in his blood, the forgiveness of sins, the right to eternal life, the right to all the blessings of salvation.

The question arises, however: how do we obtain the salvation which he has purchased for us? Does the finished sacrifice of Christ and his perfect obedience mean that all his work is accomplished? Does God bestow the blessings of salvation upon his people without Christ's meditation? By no means. Christ is the mediator through whom God accomplishes his whole purpose and counsel of salvation, not only with respect to our redemption, but also as regards our actual deliverance from all the power of sin and death and our ultimate perfection.

Just as within the holy Trinity God's eternal covenantal life of friendship is of the Father, through the Son, and in the Holy Ghost; and just as the work of creation is likewise of the triune God, but so that it is of the Father, through the Son as the eternal *Logos*, and in the Spirit; so the work of salvation is of the triune God, but again so that it is through the Son in the flesh, and in the Holy Spirit as the Spirit of Christ. All the benefits of salvation are literally in Christ. Out of him we receive grace for grace. He must impart himself to us, incorporate us into himself, quicken us, make us partakers of his death and resurrection, bestow upon us his righteousness and life, preserve us unto the final redemption, and receive us into his glory.

For that purpose he must be the living Lord. Suppose it had been possible that by his perfect obedience in suffering and death Christ had merited for us the fullness of salvation, but that in doing so he himself had been swallowed up by death, then the purchased redemption could never have become ours: there would be no channel through which the blessings of grace could reach us. But Christ is risen. He overcame death. The bonds of death and hell could not hold him. He broke through the gates of hell into the glory of his resurrection-life. And as the Risen One he ascended up on high, leading captivity captive, that he might bestow all the gifts of salvation upon men.

Unto that end, namely, unto the end that he, the glorious Lord, might impart himself and all the benefits of grace to his people, the church, he received the promise of the Holy Spirit. And in that Spirit he returned unto and into his church, to dwell with her, quicken her, and abide with her forever: "The first man Adam was made a living soul; the last Adam was made a quickening spirit" (1 Cor. 15:45).

Christ is the living Lord. From this fact follows a threefold benefit. There is, first of all, the benefit that he makes us partakers of his righteousness, of the righteousness which he purchased for us by his death and perfect obedience. This is first, because the blessing of righteousness is fundamental, basic for all the other blessings of salvation. God loves the righteous, but his face is against them that do evil. His favor is upon them that are righteous in his sight, even as his wrath is upon the wicked. Righteousness, therefore, is our great and fundamental need. For we are by nature, and in ourselves, sinful, corrupt, and guilty. And for that very reason "we are children of wrath," worthy of damnation, that is, eternal death (Eph. 2:3). We have no right to be set at liberty, to be delivered from the power of corruption and death as long as our position before the tribunal of the righteous Judge of heaven and earth is the position and state of guilt. Before all things we must certainly have righteousness. Our position before God's bar of justice, our legal status, in God's judgment must be changed from that of guilt and condemnation into that of righteousness and justification.

This righteousness Christ purchased for us by his perfect sacrifice on the cross; by all his obedience as our Lord and head, he merited for us the forgiveness of sins, perfect justification in God's judgment, the adoption unto children and heirs, the right also to be delivered from the dominion and corruption of sin and to be made ethically, spiritually righteous, and the right also to eternal life. Let us note that this righteousness which Christ purchased for us is not the same as the righteousness of Adam in the state of rectitude. Adam's righteousness was his own as long as he obeyed. The righteousness Christ bestows upon us is never our own; it is always the righteousness of Christ, a gift of grace. It is not based on our obedience, but on Christ's perfect work. It never rests in us, but always in Christ and in him alone. The righteousness of Adam was admissible, liable to be lost. The righteousness which we have in Christ, having its ground and source only in Christ, the Son of God in the flesh, crucified and died, is established forever: it can never be lost.

Adam was created in the state and condition of righteousness, and it was sufficient to sustain him in his earthly position and life. It could never make him worthy of anything higher. It certainly could not make him worthy of eternal life in the scriptural sense of the word. The righteousness of Christ, however, is light out of darkness, justification out of condemnation, life from the dead. And it makes us worthy of that higher glory which Scripture calls eternal life. For it is a righteousness which the Son of God merited for us by descending into the deepest death and lowest hell.

Now, of this righteousness the resurrection of Jesus Christ from the dead is, first of all, a proof, a divine revelation, the testimony of God. For Christ is "delivered for our offences, and…raised again for our justification" (Rom. 4:25). We must remember that Christ is risen, but he is also raised. When the Scriptures declare that he is risen, it denotes the resurrection as an act of his own, of the divine Son, who by and through his resurrection is powerfully set forth as the Son of God, the resurrection and the life. When, however, the Bible teaches us that Christ is *raised*, it denotes the resurrection of our Lord as an act of God with respect to Christ in his human nature. As such, it is the testimony of God concerning our justification: he "was raised again for our justification" (Rom. 4:25).

If Christ had not been raised, we would never have had a testimony of God that by his death and perfect obedience we were justified. Remember that Christ had assumed the responsibility for our sins, though he was personally without sin and guilt. According to that responsibility of our mediator and head, he was worthy of death, though again, as far as his personal relation to God was concerned, he was the object of God's favor. With the load of this responsibility for our sins upon his mighty shoulders he stood before the tribunal of God in the hour of judgment, and willingly descended into the darkest depth of death and hell, where he suffered all the pain and agony in body and soul that is caused by the wrath of God against the workers of iniquity.

Out of that depth there was only one way: such perfect obedience that God could declare him as mediator and head of his church, and therefore with regard to all our sins, perfectly righteous. For just as sin and death, so also righteousness and life are inseparably connected in the judgment of God. When, therefore, God raised him from the dead, he thereby declared him, and that too as mediator and head of his church, worthy of eternal life. God set his seal upon the perfect sacrifice of Christ, and declared that he, the mediator, had perfectly satisfied for all the sins that he had borne upon the cross, that is, for our transgressions. He was raised for, on account of, our justification. The resurrection of Jesus Christ from the dead is the gospel of God declaring us righteous and worthy of eternal life.

Christ paid the price for our justification, the price that was demanded by God's unchangeable justice applied to the guilty. That price was death, eternal death. And the price must be paid. For God cannot deny himself. Righteousness must be purchased. The suffering of death must be a voluntary act of love, just as sin is wanton rebellion and disobedience. And such an act of perfect obedience was the death of Christ. Hence, he purchased righteousness for us by his death. And the resurrection of our Lord is God's testimony, God's revelation, God's declaration that the price was paid in full, that Christ did indeed obtain righteousness for all his people.

But as has already been stated, Christ not only merited righteousness for us by his perfect obedience, but he also actually makes us righteous and bestows the gift of righteousness upon us as the living Lord. The living Lord effects that change in us whereby we lay hold upon the righteousness he obtained for us, and ourselves become righteous before God.

Of ourselves we never could and never would lay hold upon that righteousness of Christ. We are dead in sin, perverse of heart, darkened in our understanding, rebellious of will, polluted and defiled in all our desires and inclinations. In that state we are not for righteousness, not even if it is freely offered us. We do not want righteousness. We have no desire for it in our hearts, we do not seek it. We love unrighteousness, and the way of sin and iniquity we will pursue, even though we are quite aware of that fact that it leads us to destruction. "For the wages of sin is death" (Rom 6:23). Even though the gospel of a free righteousness were preached to us by men all our life, and though a thousand preachers would warn us of our peril and urge us to accept righteousness before it is too late, we would only despise and reject it. Christ indeed purchased righteousness for us, but there is no connection between that righteousness and us, nor is there any possibility that we on our part can establish such a connection.

But Christ is the risen Lord. He is living. And he that has overcome death, who is the righteousness and the life, is able to make us partakers of his righteousness, to establish the living link between that righteousness and our soul. The living Lord is able so to change us, that instead of hating and despising and rejecting the gift of righteousness, we seek it and are able to lay hold upon it and to appropriate it when it is bestowed upon us as a free gift.

This change is effected in us by that marvelous gift of grace which the holy Scriptures call faith. Faith is the living bond between our soul and the Christ of the Scriptures, between the righteousness he purchased for us and our inmost heart. Faith is the spiritual power whereby we are ingrafted into Christ, the spiritual power whereby our whole soul, with mind and will and all our desires, yearns for Christ and his righteousness, seeks him, hungers and thirsts after his righteousness, cleaves to him, knows him as no faithless soul is able to know him, wants him as above all things precious, and appropriates him and all his benefits. By the accomplishment of that change in us, by the bestowal of that spiritual gift of faith upon us, we become partakers of the righteousness which he purchased for us by his death and perfect obedience on the cross. We are justified out of faith.

This faith is the gift of the living Lord, who overcame death. He works it in us by his Spirit and by his own effectual calling through the preaching of the gospel. And even that faith for its continued existence presupposes the living Lord. For mark you well, it is not so that this faith as a gift is once bestowed upon us, and that ever after its first bestowal we possess it in ourselves, apart from Christ. On the contrary, it is a continuous gift, the fruit in us of the constant operation of the living Christ. It is the union of our soul with the living Lord.

Never can we have any connection with the righteousness of Christ except through the operation of the living Lord continuously in our hearts. Just as the branches of the vine have life and can bear fruit only as they are in the vine, so also can we have faith and righteousness only in union with the living Lord. It is through that living faith in the living Lord that we are ever sorry for our sins, that we ever cry out again: "God be merciful unto us, sinners." It is through that living union with the living Lord that we ever again hunger and thirst after righteousness, that we behold him as above all things precious. For he is the fullness of our emptiness, the righteousness of our unrighteousness, the light in our darkness. And it is also through the living faith in the living Lord that we come unto him, that we appropriate him, and say: Jesus is mine, he is mine forevermore. Such is the power of the resurrection of Jesus Christ from the dead.[1]

---

1   See Appendix 2 for an additional message on the same subject.

Chapter 23

THE WONDER
OF THE RESURRECTION

We are still speaking on the fifth article of the Apostles' Creed: "On the third day he rose again from the dead." The last time we called your attention to the fact that the resurrection of the Lord Jesus Christ is established by many and faithful witnesses.

This testimony we now will continue.

And first of all, I must call your special attention to the evidence of the empty grave. As I said last time, that evidence bears not only a negative testimony, but it also speaks rather clearly of the wonder of the resurrection, of the altogether transcendent nature of the resurrection of our Lord. The angel that awaited the women that had come to the grave to embalm the body of Jesus not only preached to them the first resurrection gospel but also invited them to inspect the sepulcher in the words: "Come, see the place where the Lord lay" (Matt. 28:6).

Now, why should the angel issue this particular invitation? Was it merely his intention to impress deeply upon their minds that this was indeed the grave in which Joseph and Nicodemus had stored away the body of the Lord? This was quite unnecessary. The women had no difficulty whatsoever to identify the sepulcher of their Lord. They had followed in the sad funeral procession of that late Friday afternoon before the Sabbath. They had watched the two friends of Christ bury the body. They had seen how the great stone was rolled before the entrance of the tomb. They needed no special verification that this was indeed the sepulcher where the body of Jesus had lain.

But what then? Was it the purpose of the angel to render them doubly sure that the grave was empty? But this is absurd. They stood in the grave, spices ready for the last service of love they intended to perform upon the body of their Lord. And their first glance assured them that the grave was vacated, and that they could not accomplish their purpose. What then was the special significance of this invitation of the angel: "Come, see the place where the Lord lay"?

In order to answer this question we must pay attention to two other witnesses who later in the day inspected the sepulcher of Jesus. Mary Magdalene had accompanied the other women on their journey to the grave early in the morning. But it is evident that she did not go with them to the grave and that she was not present when the angel preached to them the first gospel of the resurrection of Christ. When even in the distance the women had noticed that the heavy stone that somewhat belatedly had become an object of anxiety to them was rolled away from the door of the tomb, Mary had at once with characteristic inconsistency drawn the conclusion that the body of Jesus had been taken away by human hands. And no sooner had she drawn this conclusion than she turned about to report both her experience and her erroneous inference to the disciples.

Peter and John are at once aroused by this report of the Magdalene, and hasten to the sepulcher. John, being the younger of the two, outruns Peter, and coming to the tomb first stoops down to inspect it, and is at once struck by the position of the linen clothes. Peter, the more impetuous, as soon as he reaches the grave enters into it, and he too pays special attention to the linen clothes in which the body of Jesus had been wrapped. And as a special detail, he notices that the napkin that had been wound about Jesus' head was lying somewhat apart from the linen clothes in a place by itself. Evidently the two disciples did the very thing to which the angel had invited the women: they saw the place where the Lord had lain. And we read: "Then went in also that other disciple, which came first to the sepulchre, and he saw, and believed" (John 20:8).

What did John believe? It is evident that his faith was based on what he had seen in the sepulcher. The answer to the question, what did the disciple believe after he had inspected the grave, is not that he believed the report of Mary that they had stolen the body of the Lord. But it is very evident that he believed that Jesus had risen from the dead. To be sure, they did not as yet understand the Old Testament prophecies concerning this marvelous resurrection. Hence, we read in the same report of this narrative: "For as yet they knew not the scripture, that he must rise again from the dead" (John 20:9). For a clear understanding of these Scriptures they must wait until the promise of the Spirit had been fulfilled in them. Had they understood these Scriptures as Peter did the sixteenth psalm on the day of Pentecost, John would have had no need of the sight of the empty grave and the linen clothes to convince him of the resurrection. Now he saw and believed. Somehow the linen clothes reminded him of what the Lord had spoken concerning the resurrection on the third day.

But why should the position of the linen clothes have this faith-producing effect upon the apostle John? Must we answer that the apostle found the grave in perfect order, and that the linen clothes were neatly folded and piled up, even the napkin that had been around the Savior's head in a place by itself, and that John concluded that this was the work of the Savior's hand and that he had risen from the dead? This would hardly have been sufficient evidence for the resurrection, for the simple reason that any human hand might have unwrapped the body of the Lord, and folded the linen clothes. There can be only one answer to the question why the position of the linen clothes was sufficient to make John believe, and that is that they were found in the exact position and shape in which they had been wrapped around the body of the Lord.

We must remember that on that gloomy Friday evening when the body of our Lord was stored away in the sepulcher of Joseph even though the Sabbath drew nigh, the burial of Jesus had been completed. About this fact the apostle John informs us:

38. And after this Joseph of Arimathaea, being a disciple of Jesus, but secretly for fear of the Jews, besought Pilate that he might take away the body of Jesus: and Pilate gave him leave. He came therefore, and took the body of Jesus.

39. And there came also Nicodemus, which at the first came to Jesus by night, and brought a mixture of myrrh and aloes, about an hundred pound weight.

40. Then took they the body of Jesus, and wound it in linen clothes with the spices, as the manner of the Jews is to bury. (John 19:38–40)

What was the manner of the Jews regarding burial? It implied that the body was wrapped limb by limb in separate swaths of cloths. It is these cloths that mark "the place where the Lord lay" on the resurrection morning. This drew the special attention and excited wonder of the apostles that were to inspect the grave upon the report of Mary Magdalene. What else can it mean than that these linen clothes still lay there in the empty grave in the very shape in which they had been wrapped around his body? They had not been disturbed at all.

In the light of this explanation we can understand why the angels call special attention to the place where the Lord had lain. That place was clearly marked by the position of the linen clothes. Then too we can understand why the separate place of the napkin that had been around Jesus' head received attention and was considered worthy of special mention. For in case this explanation is adopted, that napkin would naturally lie by itself, somewhat apart from the rest of the clothes. And then only are these linen clothes significant. They testify to the wonder of the resurrection on the third day. Lazarus had come forth from the grave still bound in the linen clothes in which he had been buried. But Jesus had truly risen. And in his glorified, spiritual body he could leave his burial garments in the very position and shape in which they had been wrapped around his body limb by limb. That is the testimony of the linen clothes.

But it is not only the evidence of the empty grave and the wonder of the linen clothes that convinced the disciples of the truth of the resurrection of Christ, so that they became faithful witnesses of the risen Lord.

There is also of course the message of the angels that waited for the women in the vacated grave. The spoken word of God always accompanies the word that comes to pass. It was so at the incarnation of the Son of God: heavenly messengers point to the wonder of Bethlehem. How otherwise could men have recognized the fulfillment of the promise in the babe in the manger? Angels appear when immediately after the ascension of our Lord the amazed disciples still stare into the heavens. And the same occurs at the resurrection of Jesus from the dead on the third day.

Had the resurrection of Christ been similar in character to that of Lazarus and others, there would have been no need of this message from heaven. Jesus himself might have awaited the arrival of the women, and convinced them that he was alive. But now the Lord had risen, and yet he was with them no more. He had advanced into the sphere of the spiritual, of the incorruptible, and of the immortal. The wonder must be explained, must at least be announced, before the Lord could even appear to the disciples. They must become prepared for the glorious gospel of the risen Lord. Unto this preparation serves the evidence of the vacated grave.

But added to this in a sense negative evidence is the resurrection gospel that was preached by the angel at the grave. In the gospel according to Matthew chapter 28 we read:

5. And the angel answered and said unto the women, Fear not ye: for I know that ye seek Jesus, which was crucified.
6. He is not here: for he is risen, as he said. Come, see the place where the Lord lay.
7. And go quickly, and tell his disciples that he is risen from the dead; and, behold, he goeth before you into Galilee; there shall ye see him: lo, I have told you. (vv. 5–7)

And according to the gospel according to Luke chapter 24:5–7,

5. And as they were afraid, and bowed down their faces to the earth, they said unto them, Why seek ye the living among the dead?
6. He is not here, but is risen: remember how he spake unto you when he was yet in Galilee,
7. Saying, The Son of man must be delivered into the hands of sinful men, and be crucified, and the third day rise again.

That brief message in connection with the evidence of the empty sepulcher and connecting itself too with the words of Jesus himself which he had spoken to them while he was still with them certainly prepared the hearts and minds of the witnesses for the wonder of meeting the risen Lord as he would appear unto them.

And these several appearances on many different occasions and in different forms constitute the final link in this chain by which the first witnesses became convinced both of the reality and the wonder of the resurrection of the Lord. Even on that first day of the week he showed himself to his disciples several times. He appeared to Mary Magdalene, to the women returning from the grave, to Simon Peter, to the travelers to Emmaus, and to the gathering of the disciples without Thomas. A week later he appeared again to the disciples, as they were gathered behind closed doors, and manifested himself particularly to Thomas. Sometime later he was seen by seven of the apostles at the Sea of Tiberias, he showed himself to a large number of the disciples on a mountain in Galilee, to James alone, and finally to the disciples on the Mount of Olives, whence he departed from them into heaven.

All these manifestations no doubt had their special significance. Each of them revealed its own aspect of the risen Lord. But at any rate, these manifestations, for manifestations they certainly were, convinced the disciples of the reality of the bodily resurrection of the Lord, but also of the otherness of that resurrection. He was real. He had a very real body. He could show them his hands and his feet and his very imprints of his crucifixion. He could invite them to touch him. He even could and did eat in their presence, to convince them that he was no mere ghost.

And yet, he was altogether different from the time before the crucifixion. He was no longer with them in earthly fellowship. He evidently suddenly manifested himself to them in some form or other, communed with them, and spoke to them for a while, in order then to disappear as suddenly as he came. No one knew where the Lord was and where he dwelt during that marvelous forty days between the resurrection and the ascension. Mary Magdalene is warned not to touch him, for he has not yet ascended and did not yet return. Only occasionally he appeared from his resurrection sphere to manifest himself to the disciples. Suddenly he would stand in their midst while they were assembled behind closed doors. Surely, the risen Lord was altogether different from their master before the crucifixion.

And also this otherness of the risen Lord the disciples faithfully recorded exactly as they experienced it. They thought that they saw a ghost. At the Sea of Tiberias "none of the disciples durst ask him, Who art thou? knowing that it was the Lord" (John 21:12). On the mount in Galilee "they worshipped him: but some doubted" (Matt. 28:17). Through all this experience, an experience which, when they had received the Holy Ghost, was sealed in them and also clearly understood in the light of the Old Testament Scriptures, so that the last vestige of doubt was removed, the disciples became fully prepared to become witnesses of the resurrection and to proclaim to all men: "The Lord is risen indeed!"

And this is indeed the heart of the gospel of Jesus Christ. If the Lord had not been raised, if he had simply died on the accursed tree, there would have been no gospel of atonement and reconciliation, there would have been no answer of God from heaven to the triumphant shout of the Son of God in the flesh immediately before he gave up the ghost: "It is finished" (John 19:30). Then indeed our faith would be vain, and would still be in our sins. But now Christ is delivered for our transgressions and is raised for our justification. In the resurrection of Jesus Christ from the dead God set his seal upon the perfect obedience of his servant, upon his atoning sacrifice for the sins of his people. And therefore, through the resurrection of Jesus Christ from the dead we have the sure testimony of God that our sins are blotted out forever and that we have an everlasting righteousness, the righteousness of God which is by faith in Jesus Christ our Lord.

Chapter 24

THE MEANING OF THE RESURRECTION OF CHRIST

"On the third day he rose again from the dead." Such is the article of the Apostles' Creed we are discussing in our present sermons. We somewhat explained the fact of the resurrection, as well as its wonder, as testified by many evidences, such as the vacated grave, the place where the Lord lay, the message of the angels, and the manifold appearances of the Lord during that marvelous forty days between his resurrection and his ascension into heaven. In the present sermon we will meditate on the meaning of the resurrection of Christ from the dead, a question that is closely connected with the other question: who is he that was raised from the dead on the third day?

As we have already emphasized, we must always insist on the fact that the resurrection of Christ was real. It was a resurrection of the body. It was not a mere glorification of the spirit; nor was it a new creation. The empty grave, the place where the Lord lay, the linen clothes, and the brief resurrection message from the angel's mouth are sufficient evidence of this truth. He is not here, for he is risen. Such was the gospel of the resurrection that was proclaimed by the heavenly messenger to the women that visited the grave in the early morning of that marvelous third day.

What took place in the resurrection of Christ cannot be divorced from that empty grave, cannot be correctly explained without taking cognizance of the fact that the body of the Lord was in the grave no more. His body had been stored away in the sepulcher of Joseph, carefully embalmed, though in haste, wrapped in linen clothes. But on the third day it was there no more, for the simple reason that he was raised. The resurrection of Christ, therefore, was bodily resurrection. God's holy one did not see corruption in Hades. His body was snatched from the power of corruption and death by the resurrection. The human spirit of Christ, which at the moment of his death he had committed into the hands of the Father, united with a very real, though altogether different, body.

Besides, even though the body through the wonder of the resurrection was changed, it was essentially the same body in which he had been crucified and that had been stored away in the grave in Joseph's garden. In other words, the wonder of the resurrection was performed upon that body in which our Savior had walked among us in the days of his flesh. That this is true is evidenced by the fact that the disciples recognized him when he appeared to them during those wonderful forty days between his resurrection and ascension. It is evidenced also by the fact that he bore the signs of his suffering and crucifixion even in his resurrection body. And therefore, it is not a resurrection apart from the grave and apart from the body that was buried, which Scripture teaches, but very clearly a resurrection of and in the body. Thus we must conceive of the resurrection on the third day.

However, as was mentioned in the preceding sermons, after due emphasis has been given to the reality of the bodily resurrection, it is no less important that we try to conceive, in as far as this is possible in the light of Scripture, of the complete wonder, of the complete otherness, of the resurrection of our Lord. For Christ's resurrection is not a return to the old; it is something strictly and absolutely new. It is the revelation of the last Adam, of "the second man…the Lord from heaven" (1 Cor. 15:47). It is the realization of the image of the heavenly.

In his birth from the virgin Mary the Son of God assumed the likeness of sinful flesh, though without sin. In that likeness of sinful flesh he was "of the earth, earthy" (1 Cor. 15:47). He lived our earthly life and moved about in all our earthly relationships. He had earthly needs. He could hunger and thirst and grow weary. He came eating and drinking. He was born as a child, increased in stature and power of soul and body, grew up as a child into adolescence and manhood. Moreover, he was subject to suffering, sorrow, and death. He was tempted in all things even as we are. All that the word of God teaches us concerning that which is buried of man at his death is true of Christ in his human nature, "in the likeness of sinful flesh" (Rom. 8:3). When Christ was buried, all that is said of the human body in 1 Corinthians 15:42–44 is applicable: "It is sown in corruption…in dishonour…in weakness…it is sown a natural body."

But through the resurrection he became entirely different. All that belongs to the likeness of sinful flesh is removed. No longer is he subject to corruption, sorrow, suffering, death. And he is become immortal, not in the sense in which philosophy is wont to speak of the immortality of the soul, but in the far deeper and richer sense, that death has no more dominion over him. Through his resurrection Christ entered into eternal life in the qualitative sense of that scriptural term. He is above death. Death can no longer reach him. He is the resurrection and the life, the Living One.

But even this does not fully describe the wonder of the resurrection. For through that resurrection also the image of the earthly was removed, to be replaced by or changed into the image of the heavenly. Christ assumed in his incarnation the image of the earthly. He was of the earth earthy. But through his resurrection he became revealed as the Lord from heaven. And all that the apostle writes in that glorious chapter of 1 Corinthians 15 about the resurrection of the dead is true first of all, centrally and principally, of Christ: "It is raised in incorruption…in glory…it is raised a spiritual body" (vv. 42–44).

Christ's resurrection was not only no return to his former state in the likeness of sinful flesh. But through his resurrection the risen Lord became transcendent in glory and power, was raised far above the first man in his original state of righteousness, yea, even far above any state that first Adam might have attained, or might not have attained. Adam, even in the state of rectitude, was of the earth, earthy. Moreover, although he was not under the actual dominion of death, he was not immortal, but most emphatically mortal. He could die. But with the resurrection of Christ death is completely "swallowed up in victory" (1 Cor. 15:54); and this corruptible has put on incorruption, this mortal has put on immortality (v. 53).

And in the Risen One the image of the invisible God has been raised to its highest possible perfection on the plane of heavenly glory.

This must be emphasized. The risen Lord is not for a moment to be compared to the first Adam, even in his state of original righteousness. Nor dare it be said that Adam could have attained to the state of glory that is now realized in the resurrection of the Son of God. It is necessary that this be emphasized in order to prevent the notion that in the resurrection of Christ from the dead God repaired what was spoiled and marred by the first man Adam, or that through the amazing, deep, and marvelous way of the death and resurrection of the Son of God nothing higher was attained than what might have been accomplished through the first man, had he only remained obedient.

Salvation, we must remember, is no repair work. God never repairs. But he executes his counsel. And his counsel implies that he intends to raise the first creation through the deep way of sin and death, and through the death and resurrection of the Son of God, to the highest possible level of glory in the new creation, where the tabernacle of God will be with men. The first world was indeed good on its own plane. But it was not the final realization of the counsel of God with respect to all things. And that counsel of God will not be fully realized until the new heavens and the new earth are formed, and the new Jerusalem shall come down out of heaven from God.

Of that new world the risen Lord is the firstborn. The resurrection of Jesus Christ from the dead is the realization and revelation of the firstborn of every creature. This truth is most clearly and beautifully expressed in Colossians 1:15–20,

15. Who is the image of the invisible God, the firstborn of every creature:
16. For by him were all things created, that are in heaven, and that are in earth, visible and invisible, whether they be thrones, or dominions, or principalities, or powers: all things were created by him, and for him:
17. And he is before all things, and by him all things consist.
18. And he is the head of the body, the church: who is the beginning, the firstborn from the dead; that in all things he might have the preeminence.
19. For it pleased the Father that in him should all fulness dwell;

20. And, having made peace through the blood of his cross, by him to reconcile all things unto himself; by him, I say, whether they be things in earth, or things in heaven.

Christ is the firstborn of every creature, and that too as the first-born from the dead and as the head of the church. You understand at once, of course, that this passage in the epistle to the Colossians does not speak of the Son of God in the divine nature, but of the incarnate Son of God. In his divine nature he is not born, but eternally begotten of God. In his divine nature he cannot be called the firstborn of every creature, for the Son of God as such cannot be ranked with the creature. And again, only as the incarnated Son of God he is the firstborn of the dead and the head of the church. And therefore, the incarnated Son of God, the head of the church, the risen Christ, is the firstborn of every creature.

You understand, of course, that this can apply only to the appearance of Christ in the counsel of God. Historically he is not the first, but the second man; not the first, but the last Adam. In time Adam is first, and he may be called the firstborn of every creature in relation to the first creation. But Christ is the firstborn of every creature, of all that was formed in the beginning, and of all that ever exists in time in heaven and in earth, angels and principalities and powers, good and evil, sin and death, and of the everlasting glorious world of the new creation, in the counsel of God, in his divine conception, will, and purpose.

In the eternal counsel of God the risen Lord is the firstborn of every creature. In that eternal counsel he stands first. In the divine decree he is conceived first. And he opens the womb for every creature. All the works of God are subservient to the glory of this image of the invisible God. They are conceived after him and unto him, so as to be adapted to him. And in the perfect, finished works of God as conceived in the divine good pleasure, he has the preeminence, is the firstborn among many brethren, their Lord, and the firstborn of every creature, their everlasting head. Hence, we can also read in Ephesians 1:10 of the good pleasure of God which he has purposed in himself "that in the dispensation of the fulness of times he might gather together in one all things in Christ, both which are in heaven, and which are on earth."

All things in time must serve the realization of the firstborn of every creature. They have their ultimate meaning in him, and in him alone, to the glory of the Father. And in the revelation of the risen Lord we see the light of the wisdom of God. The risen Lord is the solution of all things. In the light of the risen Lord and in relation to him all things must be seen and interpreted. Only when perceived and evaluated in that relationship can we rightly understand the first creation, the first paradise, the first tree of life, the first man, Adam, but also the tree of knowledge of good and evil, the probationary command, the temptation of the devil, the fall of our first parents, sin and death, the incarnation and the cross, the deep ways of God unto the realization of his everlasting covenant.

If we thus explain all things, also in the present world, we can understand that God works out his own counsel even unto the end. Apart from the risen Lord, and apart from the light he spreads over all things, we can only conceive of the first creation as a frustrated attempt on the part of God to reveal himself and to attain to his glory in the works of his hands. In that case sin and death, the devil and all the powers of darkness, can only be seen as so many forces over against the Lord of heaven and earth, existing and operating, perhaps, by his permission, yet really standing in opposition to him, and to an extent successful, though ultimately they are vanquished. Christ then becomes an afterthought, designed to repair the damage wrought by Satan and sin, to save whatever may be salvaged from the wreckage.

But in the light of the revelation of the risen Lord we see all things differently. Then we understand that when God created the first world good and finished, though it was in itself, he had in mind the second world, in which all things concentrate in the glorified Son of God. Then we see that first world as an image of things to come, the first paradise as an image of the paradise of God in the new creation, the first man Adam as a figure of him that was to come. Then we do not place the forces of darkness, the devil, sin, and death, dualistically in opposition to the Most High, but know that they are subservient to his purpose, and that God chose the deep way of sin and grace because he had "provided some better thing for us" (Heb. 11:40). Then we begin to understand that "it became him, for whom are all things, and by whom are all things, in bringing many sons unto glory, to make the captain of their salvation perfect through sufferings" (2:10).

For we see Jesus, the firstborn of every creature, and the first begotten of the dead "crowned with glory and honour" (Heb. 2:9). And in the light of that risen Lord we already see the beginning of the new creation, of the new heavens and the new earth in which all things shall be subservient to Christ, and through him to the living God, and by which the tabernacle of God shall be with men forever. Then the revelation of the risen Lord means that we are more than conquerors through him that loved us. And as nothing can separate us from the love of God in Christ as the risen Lord, so nothing can ever deprive us of the everlasting glory of the incorruptible and undefinable inheritance that never fades away, and that is reserved in heaven for us. That is the meaning of the resurrection of Jesus Christ from the dead.

Article 6

He ascended into heaven,
and sitteth at the right hand of God
the Father Almighty

Chapter 25

ASCENDED INTO HEAVEN

This time we speak on the sixth article: "He ascended into heaven, and sitteth at the right hand of God the Father Almighty." In the present lecture we speak on the ascension of our Lord Jesus Christ into heaven.

During those wonderful forty days between the resurrection and the ascension of the Lord Jesus Christ, he certainly was not with the disciples as he was before the cross. But several times he appeared unto them, spoke to them, and instructed them concerning the things of the kingdom of heaven. After every appearance, evidently, the disciples expected him to appear to them again. But finally there came a time when they expected to see him no more, because he departed from them and was taken up into heaven.

The fact of the ascension, as well as its great significance, is frequently mentioned in Holy Writ. The event is mentioned in Mark 16:19, "So then after the Lord had spoken unto them, he was received up into heaven, and sat on the right hand of God." In the gospel according to Luke, chapter 24, verses 50 and 51, we read: "And he led them out as far as to Bethany, and he lifted up his hands, and blessed them. And it came to pass, while he blessed them, he was parted from them, and carried up into heaven."

The gospel according to St. John does not speak of the ascension of the Lord into heaven on the fortieth day, but it mentions that ascension repeatedly and definitely. So, for instance, to the murmuring Jews in Capernaum the Savior says: "Doth this offend you? What and if ye shall see the Son of man ascend up where he was before?" (John 6:61–62). To the unbelieving Pharisees in Jerusalem he spoke these words: "Yet a little while am I with you, and then I go unto him that sent me" (7:33). He comforts his disciples in the well-known words: "In my Father's house are many mansions: if it were not so, I would have told you. I go to prepare a place for you. And if I go and prepare a place for you, I will come again, and receive you unto myself; that where I am, there ye may be also. And whither I go ye know, and the way ye know" (14:2–4). And after the resurrection he spoke the remarkable words to the Magdalene: "Touch me not; for I am not yet ascended to my Father: but go to my brethren, and say unto them, I ascend unto my Father, and your Father; and to my God, and your God" (20:17).

But the most definite testimony concerning the event of the ascension as such is found in Acts 1:9–11,

9. And when he had spoken these things, while they beheld, he was taken up; and a cloud received him out of their sight.
10. And while they looked stedfastly toward heaven as he went up, behold, two men stood by them in white apparel;
11. Which also said, Ye men of Galilee, why stand ye gazing up into heaven?
12. This same Jesus, which is taken up from you into heaven, shall so come in like manner as ye have seen him go into heaven.

But even besides these references to the event of the ascension into heaven on the fortieth day after the resurrection, Scripture also mentions the truth of Christ's assumption into, and being in heaven, and that not only in connection with his sitting at the right hand of God, still less as a mere sign of his having all power in heaven and on earth, as some would have it, but as having significance in itself, and from the viewpoint of his having entered into the holiest of all as our intercessor. The book of Acts, as well as the epistles of the apostles, contain many such passages and I will not take time to quote them here.

About this ascension of our Lord Jesus Christ into heaven, we may remark, in the first place, that it was definitely a change of place. In the human nature Christ departed from the earth, and went into heaven, both in body and soul. After his ascension he is, according to his human nature, no longer on earth; he is in heaven only. In the ascension Christ did not become ubiquitous, or everywhere present, in the human nature. On the contrary, according to the testimony of

Holy Writ, his ascension consisted definitely in a change of place. He departed from one place, the earth, and entered into another, heaven.

For forty days the risen Lord had remained on earth, even though the relation between him and earthy things, as well as his fellowship with his disciples, were radically different from his sojourn among us in the state of his humiliation. After his resurrection the disciples had frequently seen the Lord. And, as I said before, during those forty days the disciples must have lived in the constant expectation of seeing him again. However, on the fortieth day of this wonderful period he led them out to the Mount of Olives, and from thence he was taken up from them in such a manner that they knew he had departed from them into heaven. Often during the forty days he had come and gone, had appeared to them and spoken to them, and disappeared again in a manner beyond their comprehension. This time, however, on the Mount of Olives, he not merely disappeared; he definitely departed from them, and went into heaven. After this they expected to see him on earth no more. They knew that he had gone away from them.

But when all this is duly established; when we have confessed that heaven is a place as well as the earth, and not a mere abstraction; and that the ascension of the Lord means that he departed from the one place and entered into the other, and is not a mere becoming omnipresent of his human nature; we must nevertheless warn against the danger of conceiving of the wonder of the ascension in an earthly manner. We shall have to remind ourselves that the ascension, as well as the resurrection of Christ, is a wonder. The ascension is not comparable to one's taking a journey from one earthly place to another. Nor is what the apostles observed on Mount Olivet, when their Lord was taken up from them, to be compared to what one sees when he visits an airport and watches the taking off of an airplane. We must never forget that also the last manifestation of the risen Lord to the apostles on Mount Olivet was an appearance of him who had already passed on into the resurrection-sphere, and who lived in his incorruptible spiritual body.

On Mount Olivet the disciples certainly could not behold the heaven of glory with their earthly eyes, and see the Lord enter into it. What they did see was that he was taken up from them, as a sign to them that he departed from them, to see them no more. We read that a cloud received him out of their sight. The meaning is evidently not that they saw him ascend up all the way into the clouds, but rather that as soon as he was taken up from them, at that very moment, some such cloud as had enveloped him on the mount of transfiguration hid him from their gaze.

We may ask the question: what is heaven, and where is it?

To be sure, as we said, heaven is not an abstraction or a condition, but a definite place. Nevertheless, heaven and the things that are therein differ radically from the earth and all earthy things. Flesh and blood cannot inherit the kingdom of heaven. With our present bodies we could not enter into heaven, nor live its life. Our earthy eyes cannot behold it. And the gaze of the disciples, though earnestly directed toward the firmament after their Lord had been taken up from them, could not follow him into the heaven of glory. A cloud received him out of their sight.

I think it is idle to speculate about the definite location of this heaven of glory in the present universe. It is true that the Scriptures speak of it as high, and even present it as the highest. Whether, however, this means that the glorious place of the exalted Christ and of the redeemed saints and the holy angels is above and beyond the starry heavens, as is often supposed, is a matter of speculation rather than of revelation. There may well be an element of symbolism in the language of the Bible when it speaks of the highest heavens.

At all events, we dare not speak of the distance of this glorious heaven from the earth in terms of our earthly laws of space and time. Scientists tell us that the most distant of the heavenly bodies are millions and even billions of miles distant from our earth. If then we would pursue the same line of figuring, and apply it to the distance of the heaven of heavens and to the ascension of our Lord, it would lead us to the conclusion that the Lord, after he was taken up from the Mount of Olives in the sight of the disciples, had to travel millions upon millions of miles before he reached his destination. According to the same way of figuring, it would also imply that when the earthly house of this our tabernacle is dissolved, we would still have to make a long journey before we would arrive in the building of God, the house not made with hands, eternal in the heavens. This I do not believe. We cannot possibly apply our earthly laws of space and time to heaven and to heavenly things.

Personally, I much rather conceive of heaven as interpenetrating our present world, as surrounding us on all sides, even though it is impossible for us to see it. We may never think of heaven as far away in the earthly sense of the word, so that there is no contact between heaven and earth, and so that it would actually take a long time to reach it. When the Lord was taken up from the earth on the Mount of Olives, he was at once in glory, in the highest heavens. The transition took place in a moment, in the twinkling of an eye. Proof of this is the fact that at the same moment, while the amazed disciples were still staring into heaven, two angels from that same heaven of glory stood by them to announce that their common Lord had been taken up from them into heaven and would so come again.

This heaven of glory is part of God's original creation, and as such it has a history as well as the world in which we live.

Originally it was the abode of the holy angels, the spiritual principalities and powers and dominions. It is not impossible, on the basis of Scripture, that the one who is now Satan and the devil originally was the head of the angel world. But this chief ruler of the heavenly principalities, together with a host of his fellow angels, fell away from God and became irrevocably the enemy and opponent of the Most High. God's election and reprobation made separation between the heavenly spirits, and the matter was at once decided.

After Satan seduced the king of the earthly creation, man, to fall away from the living God, and God maintained his covenant and established it in the line of continued generations, heaven also became the abode of the spirits of just men made perfect, of the church triumphant. The glorified saints in heaven throughout the old dispensation ever increased in numbers. They were saved in hope. It appears that Satan still had access to heaven, and acted as the accuser of the brethren. The promise was not yet realized. And with the saints on earth they looked forward in hope to its fulfillment.

In the fullness of time Christ came, brought the sacrifice of reconciliation, realized the justification of all the saints, was raised from the dead, and ascended up on high, leading captivity captive. For heaven and its inhabitants this ascension of Christ was of great significance. For the devil was cast out, and the accuser of the brethren could harass them no more. However, even now the history of the heaven of glory is not finished. When God shall create new heavens and a new earth, also the heaven of heavens shall be changed. For it is the good pleasure of God to unite all things in heaven and on earth into one glorious creation in Christ as the head over all, the glorious kingdom of heaven that is to be realized in the day of Christ.

Into this heaven of glory the Lord ascended forty days after his resurrection. He thus ascended in his human nature. We may indeed say that it was the person of the Son of God that ascended into heaven. But that ascension was realized only in his human nature. The Godhead is immutable, and in his divine nature the ascension of the Son of God did not effect a change. To speak of a change of place with regard to Christ's divine nature would be absurd. For God is immanent in all things, yet he is also the transcendent one. He fills all things, yet he is far above the world. He can neither descend nor ascend. But according to his human nature, he is no longer on earth, but is in heaven.

He was with us once when he was like us. Then we could meet him, see him in his earthly appearance, touch him, speak to him, have earthly fellowship with him. But now he is with us no more. In the flesh we know him no more. With our earthly eye we see him no more. All earthy associations are severed. As far as his human nature as such is concerned, he is definitely departed from us. In the sight of his disciples he was taken up.

However, the ascension of our Lord into heaven does not imply that in no sense of the word he is present with us who are on the earth. On the contrary, he is still with us. In fact, he is with us in a far higher and more intimate sense than he ever was with his disciples during his earthly sojourn. We must never express the desire that Jesus may still be with us as he was in his earthly sojourn with his disciples. He, the ascended Lord, whose human nature is in heaven, is present with us in his Godhead that is never separated from his manhood. He is therefore present with us not only as the Creator of all things, but as the God of our salvation, as the Redeemer who died for our transgressions and who was raised for our justification.

He is present with us as God that is for us. He loves us and favors us. He employs and applies all his divine power, his wisdom and virtues, his infinite love and mercy, in behalf of our salvation. Moreover, he is present with us in the glory of his sovereignty, in the authority of his lordship. All power is given unto him in heaven and on earth. He, the Christ of God, who loved us even unto death and who was raised for our justification, is present with us in his power constantly and forever. We know that he loves us, and that he employs his royal power and dignity unto our salvation. And being thus ever present with us as respects his glorious majesty, he makes us longing and willing to bow before him, to know and to do his will. Conscious of the constant presence of his power and glory, we work out our own salvation with fear and trembling, and become diligent to enter into his rest.

For do not forget that he is present with us and in us through his Spirit. Christ, as the mediator of our redemption and as the head of his church, received after his ascension the promise of the Holy Spirit. For he ascended up on high, leading captivity captive, in order that he might give gifts, glorious gifts of grace, gifts of forgiveness and righteousness, of holiness and love of God, of eternal life and glory, to men. Unto this end he received the Spirit. And in that Spirit he returned to his own, to dwell in them and be with them forever. This the apostle Peter proclaims on the day of Pentecost: "Therefore being by the right hand of God exalted, and having received of the Father the promise of the Holy Ghost, he hath shed forth this, which ye now see and hear" (Acts 2:33).

In that Spirit he is ever present with us. And he is present within us. He dwells with us and in us with his covenantal grace. Through the Spirit he is gracious to us, causes us to taste his grace, and makes us partakers of all the blessings of salvation which he merited for us. This presence is constant: he never leaves us, not for a moment. We may not be and are not always conscious of this blessed nearness of the God of our salvation in Christ Jesus our ascended Lord. But his presence never fails.

We may wander away sometimes, as sheep that go astray, so that we are quite oblivious of his presence. But he never forgets us, neither forsakes us. Nor does he ever fail to bring us back from our evil wanderings to the blessedness of his fellowship. But in the measure that we live by faith, hear his word, walk in his way, we also experience that Christ, the ascended Lord, is ever present with us by his Spirit and grace. And the consciousness of that presence is the joy of faith.

Chapter 26

THE FRUIT OF
CHRIST'S ASCENSION

C hrist is no longer on earth, but is ascended up to heaven. Nor do we desire him to return into the present world and be with us again on earth. He must not come back to us, but we must go to him. He certainly will return, but not into our world. In his final coming he will make all things new.

There is, according to Holy Writ, a threefold benefit of the ascension of Christ. In the first place, in heaven he is our advocate, or intercessor, with the Father. Secondly, his presence in heaven is an earnest and pledge of our future glorification. And thirdly, as we already remarked in our former lecture, from heaven he sent us his Spirit, so that principally we are even now in heaven and seek the things that are above.

In our present lecture we will make a few remarks about each of these three benefits. Christ is our advocate in heaven.

The idea of an advocate and that of an intercessor are closely related yet they may also be distinguished. An intercessor is one who prays for another; an advocate is one who pleads on behalf of someone. As our advocate, Christ pleads for us as in ourselves we are sinners and damnable before God, to obtain our justification before the bar of the Judge of heaven and earth.

Thus the term *advocate* or *paraclete* occurs with reference to our glorified High Priest in heaven in 1 John 2:1. The apostle had written about the message he heard of Christ: "That God is light, and in him is no darkness at all" (1:5). Hence, "if we say that we have fellowship with him, and walk in darkness, we lie, and do not the truth" (v. 6). But walking in the light "we have fellowship one with another, and the blood of Jesus Christ his Son cleanses us from all sin" (v. 7). Walking in the light we do not "say that we have no sin", for then we only deceive ourselves (v. 8). But "we confess our sins", and thus by faith lay hold upon the faithfulness and justice of God, according to which he forgives us our sins, and cleanses us from all unrighteousness (v. 9). Thus the apostle had written to the believers, in order that they might walk in the light and fight against sin. However, aware of the fact that our old nature is still with us, and that no matter how faithfully we "fight the good fight of faith" (1 Tim. 6:12), sin always cleaves to us and to the best of our works, the apostle continues: "And if any man sin, we have an advocate with the Father, Jesus Christ the righteous" (1 John 2:1).

This plea of Christ as our advocate in the presence of the Father concerns particularly his people in the world, for whom he died and obtained the forgiveness of sins and eternal righteousness, who also have been in principle delivered from the power and dominion of sin, who earnestly desire to be completely delivered from all corruption and unrighteousness and who walk in the light, but who find that they are still in the body of this death, so that there are still many sins against their will remaining in them. Any of these sins would make them damnable before God and would be sufficient to deprive them of the blessed fellowship with the Father, were it not for the fact that they have a Paraclete, an advocate with the Father in heaven, who constantly pleads their cause, defends them, and obtains from the Father the sentence of their perfect justification.

We must insist that this activity of Christ in heaven as our advocate is very real. It is not a mere figurative expression. It means that the Son of God, and that too, in his glorified human nature, is really in the presence of, before the face of God the Father. Secondly, that his plea in behalf of his still sinful people in the world is a real activity on his part, so that he appeals to the justice and faithfulness of God on the basis of his own work of atonement for their perfect justification. And finally, this work of Christ in heaven as our advocate with the Father constitutes a real element in the economy of redemption. Only in the consciousness of this function of Christ we approach God through him, and obtain the assurance of forgiveness of sin and perfect righteousness. However, we understand too that all that is earthy and imperfect must be eliminated from Christ's activity as our advocate with the Father. His plea in our behalf is not occasional, but constant. And as a constant plea it is also constantly perfect, both as to the plea and as to its results.

The plea of our mediator for the forgiveness of sins and for our perfect justification is always and constantly granted. It is not thus, that Christ must persuade God to refrain from his wrath and to bestow upon his people righteousness and life. On the contrary, even as the Mediator in heaven constantly pleads in behalf of his people, presenting to the Father the ground of his perfect work of atonement, so the Father is constantly delighted with this plea for forgiveness and righteousness and beholds his people in the light of this plea with an eye of everlasting mercy and eternal love. Hence, the first advantage, or benefit, of Christ's ascension is that he is our constant advocate in heaven before the face of the Father.

Secondly, the presence of Christ in heaven in his human nature is a pledge of our own glorification. As Christ is in heaven now, so we shall go to heaven, and ultimately dwell with him in the new heavens and the new earth.

We must remember that Christ in his incarnation assumed our human nature in the likeness of sinful flesh. As such, that nature was wholly unfit to enter into heavenly glory. For not only was it of the earth, earthy; but it was also corrupt through sin, that is, not in Christ, but in us. Nor did we have the right to be delivered from the corruption of our nature and to enter into heavenly glory. Heaven was closed to us. That nature, although without sin, yet as it was earthy and in the likeness of sinful flesh, Christ assumed. And in that nature he obediently suffered all that was required to satisfy God's justice, to merit for us righteousness, and to obtain the right to heavenly glory. And he, the Son of God, glorified that nature in himself. He took it through death into the glory of the resurrection. And having thus glorified it by his resurrection, he took it into heaven, into the sanctuary of God. For his ascension does not mean that he put aside that human nature. The human nature is not and never shall be separated from the divine in Christ Jesus our Lord.

Our human nature in Christ, therefore, is already in heaven. It is in heaven not as flesh and blood, but as glorified in the resurrection.

But it is nevertheless our nature which he took into heaven. And remember that Christ is our head. His entrance into heaven does not mean that someone succeeded to glorify his own human nature and to obtain for himself a place in glory. On the contrary, it is Christ that ascended up on high. He occupies a central position. His ascension is of central significance. He is the head of the body, the church. As such, he represents all the elect. As the head of his own in the forensic sense of the word he entered into death, bore all our iniquities on the accursed tree, blotted out all our sins, and obtained for us eternal righteousness. His righteousness is our righteousness. His death is our death. His resurrection is our resurrection. And so, in that legal sense of the word, his ascension is our ascension.

But there is still more. He is not only the head in a legal sense of all his elect. He is also the head of the body of the church in the organic sense of the word. We are members of his body. And we can never be separated from him, our head. That he went into heaven means that centrally we are in heaven. He will not return to us, but he will draw us unto himself, that we may also be where he is. And so we look up toward heaven by faith, in the consciousness of our inseparable union with Christ our head, and confess that in Christ we are already in heaven.

Of this benefit of Christ's ascension he himself assures us in his word. Said he: "And I, if I be lifted up from the earth, will draw all men unto me" (John 12:32). And again:

1. Let not your heart be troubled: ye believe in God, believe also in me.
2. In my Father's house are many mansions: if it were not so, I would have told you. I go to prepare a place for you.
3. And if I go and prepare a place for you, I will come again, and receive you unto myself; that where I am, there ye may be also. (14:1–3)

Thus we may and do lay hold upon the eternal hope that is set before us: "Which hope we have as an anchor of the soul, both sure and stedfast, and which entereth into that within the veil; whither the forerunner is for us entered, even Jesus, made an high priest for ever after the order of Melchisedec" (Heb. 6:19–20). And thus, "Our conversation is in heaven; from whence also we look for the Saviour, the Lord Jesus Christ: who shall change our vile body, that it may be fashioned like unto his glorious body, according to the working whereby he is able even to subdue all things unto himself" (Phil. 3:20–21).

That in our ascended Lord our human nature is in heaven is to us a sure pledge that he shall take us with him into his own glory. And that pledge shall be fulfilled first when the earthly house of this tabernacle shall be dissolved, and we shall have an house of God "not made with hands, eternal in the heavens" (2 Cor. 5:1). And this benefit of the ascension of Christ shall accrue to us finally when he shall come again in the glorious resurrection, in the heavenly creation, where "the tabernacle of God" shall forever be "with men" (Rev. 21:3).

But there is still more. In a sense we may also say that we are already present with him in heaven. For God, who is rich in mercy, "hath raised us up together, and made us sit together in heavenly places in Christ Jesus" (Eph. 2:6). This is true because from heaven Christ sent us his Spirit as an earnest of our final salvation. He himself received that Spirit, in order that through him he might bestow all the blessings of salvation upon his people. And on the day of Pentecost he dwells in them and works in them the firstfruits of salvation. Through that Spirit we become in principle partakers of his heavenly life. All that are regenerated by the Spirit of Christ partake of the life of their heavenly Lord. That life is resurrection life. It is the life of heaven. In virtue of that life we are even now citizens of the heavenly Jerusalem, not only because we have the rights of citizens, but also because in principle we partake of the life of that heavenly city.

Because of this principle of heavenly life wrought in the people of God by the Spirit of their heavenly Lord, they even now "sit together in heavenly places in Christ Jesus" (Eph. 2:6). The result is that the life of believers in this world is a continuous tension. It is the tension of hope. In hope they groan. For not only the whole creation,

> 23. But ourselves also, which have the firstfruits of the Spirit, even we ourselves groan within ourselves, waiting for the adoption, to wit, the redemption of our body.

24. For we are saved by hope: but hope that is seen is not hope: for what a man seeth, why doth he yet hope for?
25. But if we hope for that we see not, then do we with patience wait for it. (Rom. 8:23–25)

And again:

2. For in this we groan, earnestly desiring to be clothed upon with our house which is from heaven:
3. If so be that being clothed we shall not be found naked.
4. For we that are in this tabernacle do groan, being burdened: not for that we would be unclothed, but clothed upon, that mortality might be swallowed up of life. (2 Cor. 5:2–4)

And therefore, our life, our present life in this world, because of the firstfruits, the earnest of the Spirit in us, is in a constant tension. On the one hand, we are of the earth, earthy. We have our earthly house, our earthly body and soul, our earthly relationships and friendships. And we are strongly, with a thousand ties, attached to the earth and to the things that are earthy. We do not desire to be unclothed. Yet on the other hand, there is our heavenly Lord, who gave us his heavenly Spirit, and who made us partakers of his own heavenly life, ever drawing us unto himself, so that we are strangers in the earth, and even now our conversation is in heaven. In virtue of this drawing power of our heavenly Lord through the Spirit he has given us, we long to be with him, to be clothed upon with our house which is from heaven.

Thus the presence of Christ in heaven through his Spirit is to us an earnest of our heavenly glory. The ascended Christ is the firstfruits of the final harvest. Just as the firstfruits which Israel brought to the Lord in the temple were part of the harvest and a pledge that the full harvest should presently be reaped and gathered into the barns, so the firstfruits of the Spirit are an earnest of our final salvation, when we shall receive the full adoption unto children, and be forever with Christ our Lord in heavenly glory.

And by the power of that indwelling Spirit, we do indeed seek the things which are above, where Christ is sitting on the right hand of

God. His heavenly lordship we seek to realize even in our earthly life. For while we are still present in the body, and therefore absent from the Lord, yet longing to be present with him, we seek to be pleasing to him. We hear his voice. We love his good commandments. We fight against sin within and without. And we daily put on the new man, which after God is created in righteousness and true holiness. We labor to enter into the rest. And while confessing that we are sojourners and strangers in the earth, we declare plainly that we seek a country, the heavenly country of our heavenly Lord, the city that has foundations, whose builder and artificer is God. And thus, in the sound sense of the word the ascension of our Lord means that the life of those that are his is, even while they are still in this world, otherworldly: their conversation is in heaven. And they pray with all the saints in the world, as well as with the saints in heaven: "Come, Lord Jesus, yea, come quickly."

Chapter 27

EXALTED AT
THE RIGHT HAND OF GOD

The last part of the sixth article of the apostolic confession confesses that Christ is exalted at the right hand of God.

This indeed is a very important confession, as is evident from all Scripture, which speaks of this exaltation of Christ at the right hand of God with great emphasis.

This is true of the Old Testament especially in the Psalms and in the prophets. Literally this is expressed in Psalm 110:1, "The Lord said unto my Lord, Sit thou at my right hand, until I make thine enemies thy footstool." But in a more general way this is expressed in many of the other Psalms, such as the second, the twenty-fourth, the forty-fifth, the seventy-second, the eighty-ninth, and others. They all speak of the glorification of the Servant of Jehovah, the theocratic King, the Christ of God.

But this is no less true of the prophetic books of the Old Testament, of which we will quote only Daniel 7:13–14. Daniel saw,

13. In the night visions, and, behold, one like the Son of man came with the clouds of heaven, and came to the Ancient of days, and they brought him near before him.
14. And there was given him dominion, and glory, and a kingdom, that all people, nations, and languages, should serve him: his dominion is an everlasting dominion, which shall not pass away, and his kingdom that which shall not be destroyed.

It is true that in this passage regard is had even unto the second coming of our Lord, but so that his exaltation at the right hand of God is included in the scope of this vision. And this is true of many passages in the prophetic books of the Old Testament.

It is hardly necessary to demonstrate that this truth is strongly emphasized in the New Testament. The Lord himself in the hour of his deepest humiliation mentions his coming exaltation before the high priest: "Hereafter shall ye see the Son of man sitting on the right hand of power, and coming in the clouds of heaven" (Matt. 26:64). The disciples saw his power and his coming when they "were with him in the holy mount" (2 Pet. 1:16, 18). And of that glory and majesty they speak very emphatically in their preaching of the gospel. Thus, on the day of Pentecost the apostle Peter proclaimed:

33. Therefore being by the right hand of God exalted, and having received of the Father the promise of the Holy Ghost, he hath shed forth this, which ye now see and hear.
34. For David is not ascended into the heavens: but he saith himself, The LORD said unto my Lord, Sit thou on my right hand,
35. Until I make thy foes thy footstool.
36. Therefore let all the house of Israel know assuredly, that God hath made that same Jesus, whom ye have crucified, both Lord and Christ. (Acts 2:33–36)

Also in the epistles the truth of Christ's exaltation at the right hand of God is repeatedly emphasized. In Romans 8:34 the apostle writes: "It is Christ that died, yea rather, that is risen again, who is even at the right hand of God." And in 1 Corinthians 15:25–27 he writes: "For he must reign, till he hath put all enemies under his feet. The last enemy that shall be destroyed is death. For he hath put all things under his feet. But when he saith all things are put under him, it is manifest that he is excepted, which did put all things under him." In Ephesians 1:19–21 the exaltation of Christ is presented as the revelation of God's great power, by which God has given him a name that is above every name. And the same truth is expressed in Philippians 2:9–11. Christ is "highly exalted" and is given "a name… above every name," so that every knee must bow before him, and every tongue must confess that Jesus Christ is Lord. Virtually the entire epistle to the Hebrews is devoted to the exposition of the theme that God

2. Hath in these last days spoken unto us by his Son, whom he hath appointed heir of all things, by whom also he made the worlds;

3. Who being the brightness of his glory, and the express image of his person, and upholding all things by the word of his power, when he had by himself purged our sins, sat down at the right hand of the Majesty on high;

4. Being made so much better than the angels, as he hath by inheritance obtained a more excellent name than they. (Heb. 1:2–4)

The sitting at the right hand of God is everywhere presented as a goal that has been reached. It signifies that the first begotten of the dead has assumed his position as the firstborn of every creature.

We all understand, of course, that the expression "sitting at the right hand of God" is a figurative expression. And all the passages that speak of this highly exalted position of Christ show plainly that by the figure of sitting at the right hand of God is meant a position of power and might, of authority and dominion, of majesty and glory, and that too, of universal and of the very highest power and authority and might and dominion. It denotes that Christ is Lord over all, that he is exalted over all created things in heaven, on earth, and under the earth. It signifies that he is raised to the very pinnacle of all created things. He received a name that is above every name.

In all the wide creation there is no creature over which the exalted Christ does not sway his scepter, which he does not hold in his power, and which he does not render subservient to his will and purpose. Brute creation as well as the rational creature; sun and moon and stars, rain and sunshine, fruitful and barren years, forest and field, hills and valleys, rivers and floods, the beasts of the forest and the cattle on a thousand hills, sickness and health, life and death, war and peace; but also men and angels, the wicked and the good, the powers of darkness as well as the glorious spirits in heaven; all things have been subjected under his feet. He has received from God the Father authority to exercise this dominion over all creatures to his will, to use them for his purpose, to judge and to execute judgment over all. But he has also received the power, the wisdom and might, the knowledge and ability, to realize this dominion. And no one and nothing escapes his power or can escape the sway of his scepter. All the powers and principalities in heaven are subject under him, and they willingly and gladly obey his command and wait upon his word; but also all the powers of darkness in spite of themselves are subject under him and can but execute his will. Even Satan and all the demons of his domain tremble at his word, and all their intended and attempted opposition against him is vain. Christ is Lord, the only Lord of heaven and earth!

This power, we must remember, is given unto Christ. It denotes an official position to which Christ is appointed and exalted. It does not refer, therefore, to the power of the Son of God in his divine nature. For in his divine nature no power could possibly be given unto him: he has all power. He is the omnipotent one. But this particular power is given unto Christ. As he said himself: "All power is given unto me in heaven and in earth" (Matt. 28:18). And therefore, the power that is given unto Christ at his exaltation he has received indeed as the person of the Son of God, but only in his exalted human nature. It is the person of the Son of God in human nature that tabernacled among us, that spoke to us face to face, that suffered and died on the cross, that was buried and raised from the dead. That same person of the Son of God, who in the human nature ascended into heaven, is exalted to his glorious position at the right hand of God. Not the divine nature, but the human nature was glorified and endowed with power.

As to the significance of this exaltation of Christ at the right hand of God, it is important that we clearly distinguish between a twofold exercise of Christ's supreme lordship, namely, that of his power and that of his grace.

Christ is king of his church. And in and over that church he rules by the power of his grace, by his Spirit and word.

Many in our day deny that Christ is king over his church. Christ, say they, is king of Israel, of the Jewish nation. But he is the head of his church. Israel is the kingdom of Christ; the church is his body. They deny, therefore, the kingship of Christ over his church. But this is an error plainly contrary to scripture. For God set his king upon his holy hill of Zion (Ps. 2:6). And in the new dispensation it is said to the church: "But ye are come unto mount Sion, and unto the city of the living God, the heavenly Jerusalem, and to an innumerable company of angels, to the general assembly and church of the firstborn, which are written in heaven, and to God the Judge of all, and to the spirits of just men made perfect" (Heb. 12:22–23). That church of the firstborn is the same as Mount Zion. And upon that Mount Zion God has set his anointed as king forever.

To be sure, Christ is also the head of the church in the organic sense of the word. The church is his body. He lives in them, and they live through and out of him. As the branches live in organic connection with the vine and bear fruit in that living connection, so the believers are ingrafted into Christ, and they have their life in him. Without him they can do nothing. But this does not alter the fact that Christ is also the head of the church in the juridical sense: he is her king. And that this is the meaning of the word in Ephesians 1:22 is evident not only from the context, which speaks of Christ's exalted lordship, but also from the fact that he is called "the head over all things," in relation to the church. Christ, therefore, is king of his church.

In the domain of his church he rules by the power of his grace, and therefore through his Spirit and word. It is there that he dwells with his brethren. For this mighty Lord, when he was exalted at the right hand of God, received the promise of the Holy Ghost. And in this Spirit he returned to his church, to dwell in her and to make her partaker of his wondrous grace. There it is that he opens, and no man shuts. There he diffuses his marvelous gifts of grace, of life and faith, of love and mercy, of wisdom and knowledge, of hope and confidence, of hunger and thirst after righteousness and satisfaction with the bread and water of life, of the forgiveness of sins and sanctification, and of all the fullness of spiritual blessings he has obtained for her by his obedience even unto death, his resurrection, and exaltation at the right hand of God.

Thus he makes us, the members of his church, his glad and willing servants, citizens of the kingdom of God. Thus we become willing to acknowledge him, and it becomes our only comfort in life and death that we are not our own, but belong to our faithful Savior Jesus Christ, who delivered us from all the power of the devil, and makes us sincerely willing henceforth to serve him.[1] Then we hear his word, obey it, and keep it. Then we represent the cause of the Son of God in the midst of the present world. For then we confess that Jesus is Lord over our whole life, in all its implications and relationships. He is Lord over our body and over our soul, over our mind and will and all our desires, our means and possessions, our wife and our children. As our Lord we are determined to acknowledge him in our home and family life, in respect to the relation between man and wife, parents and children, in all our relationships in the world, in society and shop and office, as employer or employee, in church and state. And we proclaim his word, keep his commandments, and hold fast that which we have, that no one take our crown.

However, his lordship is not limited to this. He is Lord over all things also in the world. All things in creation are at his disposal, to use them for his own end, for the salvation of his church. He rules over the brute creation, as well as over all the affairs of men. He rules over the secret intents of the hearts of men, and controls all their plans and counsels. He holds the keys of death and of hell. He rules over the devil and all his demons, over the wicked and all their devices. For Christ is the Lord! He rules not only within the domain of his church and by grace, but also in the realm of creation and over all the forces of darkness in this world by his power. All power is given unto him in heaven and on earth.

And this power he employs to preserve his church in the midst of the world, and to protect her over against all her enemies. For the church is in the world. And that world is in darkness and of the darkness. And the church is of the light, and witnesses of the light, and walks in the light. For that reason the world hates the church. This is inevitable. If believers are faithful, they cannot be friends of the world: for the friendship of the world is enmity with God. And whoever will be a friend of the world is the enemy of God (James 4:4). The world loves its own. But believers are not of this world. And therefore the world hates them (John 15:19). And the more faithful the church becomes in her confession and walk, and the more Christ becomes

---

1   The author is freely quoting from the first answer of the Heidelberg Catechism.

manifest in her, the more bitterly the world will hate her and set itself to destroy her and wipe out her very existence.

But in this it shall never succeed.

For Christ is the Lord of the church, who loved her and gave himself for her. And he is Lord of the whole world also. He defends and preserves the church against all her enemies.

Oh, he preserves them also by his grace: for he dwells in them by his Spirit and abides with them forever. He never forsakes them. He ever lives to make intercession for them. In the midst of all these subtle dangers he is able to preserve his church. No one can pluck the faithful out of his hand. He keeps them by his grace.

But he also defends and preserves them by his power. The enemies cannot touch them but by his will and direction. This preservation is not such that the enemy has no power to make them suffer and to persecute them even to the death. On the contrary, it is the will of our Lord that believers shall suffer with him, and that they fill the measure of his suffering.

But this defensive and preserving power of Christ does so operate that, first of all, the elect shall never be deceived and finally fall away. Secondly, the enemy can attack and realize his wicked devices of destruction against the church only under the direction of Christ and to the extent that he permits him. And thirdly, affairs of men and history are so directed that the world remains a house divided against itself, and cannot unite all its forces against the church until the very end of time. In wars and contentions, in economic strife and dissension, in strikes, boycotts, and revolutions, the world is fighting against itself, and cannot direct all its attention to the church of Christ in the world. But Scripture instructs us that toward the very end the world will for a little while unite under one head. The man of sin must come. And under him the forces of darkness will unitedly attack the true believers. However, he may not come before his time. Always there is something that withholds. And it is the power of Christ by which the world is ruled that antichrist can appear only in his own time.

But even in the days of antichrist he will preserve and defend his own. All the forces of the universe he shall marshal to fight for his own. And with the heat of the sun, the destructive elements of creation, hail, fire, locusts, wild beasts, earthquakes, pestilence, and the like, he shall oppose and harass the enemy, until he shall consume him by the sword that proceeds out of his own mouth.

Christ is Lord over all and forever. And when all things shall have been finished, and the eternal kingdom of heaven shall have come, he shall rule over all things with his saints under God as God's Servant-King. And God shall be all in all!

Article 7

*From thence he shall come
to judge the quick and the dead*

Chapter 28

THE COMING OF
THE LORD

T he seventh article of the apostolic confession reads as follows:
"From thence he shall come to judge the quick and the dead."

Two subjects are mentioned here that are indeed closely connected, but which require separate consideration. The first is that of the return of the Lord Jesus Christ. The second is the equally important subject of the final judgment.

In the present lecture we shall speak on the coming of the Lord.

Scripture very frequently speaks of the return of our Lord Jesus Christ as the final wonder of grace and the consummation of all things. That coming is the hope of believers. It is true that the word of God also comforts believers in this world with the hope of glory that shall be their portion immediately after death and before the resurrection. It is also true that Scripture speaks of the coming of Christ in more than one sense of the word. He came in the Spirit on the day of Pentecost. For in the gospel according to John, chapter 14:16–18, he promised his disciples that he would not leave them orphans in the world, but that he would come to them after his death and resurrection in the Comforter which he promised them, a promise that was fulfilled on the day of Pentecost.

It may also be said that Scripture speaks of a continual coming of the Lord in all the events of this present time. To this the Lord refers when, immediately before his death, he answered the high priest: "Thou hast said: nevertheless I say unto you, Hereafter shall ye see the Son of man sitting on the right hand of power, and coming in the clouds of heaven" (Matt. 26:64). In this answer the word that is translated by "hereafter" can be better rendered by "from now on" or "henceforth," meaning, therefore, that in this dispensation the exalted

Lord is constantly coming. He is coming in and through the preaching of the gospel; and he is coming through all the events of this present world, in wars and rumors of war, in unrest and revolutions, in earthquakes and famines, in all the tumult of the nations. For these events are so directed by his power that they lead up to the day of the Lord.

Yet, in last analysis Scripture always directs the eye of our hope to the final coming of Christ, the last wonder of grace, whereby the history of this world will be closed, and the ages of ages, the kingdom of heaven in all its glory and perfection, will be ushered in.

Of this coming the Lord spoke to his disciples when he was still with them in the flesh. He forewarned us that many things must still be accomplished before the end can come. They "shall hear of wars and rumors of wars" (Matt. 24:6). "Nation shall rise against nation, and kingdom against kingdom." They shall hear of "famines, and pestilences, and earthquakes" (v. 7). And "all these" things are but "the beginning of the end" (v. 8). Then too, he warned us to expect great tribulation and distress before the redemption of the end will come, tribulations so great that unless the days would "be shortened, there should no flesh be saved" (v. 22). And then we read:

29. Immediately after the tribulation of those days shall the sun be darkened, and the moon shall not give her light, and the stars shall fall from heaven, and the powers of the heavens shall be shaken:

30. And then shall appear the sign of the Son of man in heaven: and then shall all the tribes of the earth mourn, and they shall see the Son of man coming in the clouds of heaven with power and great glory. (vv. 29–30)

And throughout the New Testament the hope of the church in the world is fixed upon the return of our Lord in glory. At the occasion of the ascension of Christ from Mount Olivet, the angels that stand by the amazed apostles as they gaze up into heaven address them, and tell them that the same Jesus "which is taken up from you into heaven, shall so come in like manner as ye have seen him go into heaven" (Acts 1:11). The apostle Paul in the first epistle to the Corinthians, chapter 15, although he does not mention the return of Christ there, nevertheless speaks of the last moment: "In a moment, in the twinkling of an eye, at the last trump: for the trumpet shall sound, and the dead shall be raised incorruptible, and we shall be changed" (v. 52). According to Philippians 3:20, "Our conversation is in heaven; from whence also we look for the Saviour, the Lord Jesus Christ."

In 1 Thessalonians 4:15–17 the apostle comforts the believers in Thessalonica concerning those that fall asleep in Jesus before he comes again:

15. For this we say unto you by the word of the Lord, that we which are alive and remain unto the coming of the Lord shall not prevent them which are asleep.
16. For the Lord himself shall descend from heaven with a shout, with the voice of the archangel, and with the trump of God: and the dead in Christ shall rise first:
17. Then we which are alive and remain shall be caught up together with them in the clouds, to meet the Lord in the air: and so shall we ever be with the Lord.

In 2 Thessalonians 2 the apostle instructs believers concerning the coming of the "man of sin" (v. 3), "whom the Lord...shall destroy with the brightness of his coming" (v. 8).

The apostle James comforts believers, and exhorts them to be patient with a view to the coming of the Lord (James 5:7–8). At that coming believers shall receive the "salvation ready to be revealed in the last time" (1 Pet. 1:5). And "the end of all things is at hand" (4:7). And "the day of the Lord will come as a thief in the night; in the which the heavens shall pass away with a great noise, and the elements shall melt with fervent heat, the earth also and the works that are therein shall be burnt up" (2 Pet. 3:10). And therefore believers are exhorted to walk in sanctification and godliness, "looking for and hasting unto the coming of the day of God, wherein the heavens being on fire shall be dissolved, and the elements shall melt with fervent heat" (v. 12). And the entire book of Revelation is an exposition of the theme of the coming of the Lord, closing with the well-known words: "He which testifieth these things saith, Surely I come quickly. Amen. Even so, come, Lord Jesus" (Rev. 22:20).

It stands to reason that in one brief lecture we cannot possibly exhaust the subject of the coming of the Lord. But we will make a few remarks about it.

And then I wish to emphasize that we must expect a personal, definite, visible return of Christ, and that too, at one definite moment. We believe that the coming of the Lord is one. We do not expect different comings and different resurrections, separated by a period of years. On the contrary, we believe that the coming of the Lord is one. It shall take place in the final moment. And in that final moment the resurrection of the dead shall take place, both of the wicked and of the righteous. For thus we read in John 5:28–29, "Marvel not at this: for the hour is coming, in the which all that are in the graves shall hear his voice, and shall come forth; they that have done good, unto the resurrection of life; and they that have done evil, unto the resurrection of damnation."

Nor must believers be deceived by the false hope that the Lord will come for them in the rapture before the great tribulation shall come. For Scripture not only warns us to expect tribulation, but also rather than exhorting us to rejoice in the idea of escaping it, emphasizes that we shall consider it a great honor and privilege to suffer with Christ. The hope of escaping tribulation, therefore, is not spiritual, but carnal. And it is as dangerous as it is false, because it fills its followers with a false hope that will leave them unprepared for the evil day.

However, just as positively as we reject the premillennial view of the coming of the Lord, just as earnestly we must warn against what is called the postmillennial view. According to this conception, Christ and his kingdom may be expected in the way of gradual development and improvement. The world will gradually become Christianized, and change into the kingdom of God. Through the preaching of the gospel men will accept Christ, and apply the principles of the gospel to all life, till the knowledge of the Lord shall fill the earth as the waters cover the bottom of the sea. Swords will be beaten into plowshares, and spears into pruninghooks. And there will be universal peace and blessedness over all the earth before the Lord will come. And if Christ will come at all, in any real sense of that word, it will only be to take into possession that which is all prepared for him. His coming will be postmillennial.

In opposition to this view, we believe that Scripture presents the end of this world in connection with the coming of the Lord as catastrophic. Things will be cut off. As we read in Romans 9:28, "For he will finish the work, and cut it short in righteousness: because a short work will the Lord make upon the earth." Scripture very definitely presents the coming of Christ as marking the end of this present world. And that end will be catastrophic. By the second coming of the Lord Jesus Christ history will be cut off.

This does not imply, however, that the final moment is to be conceived as chosen quite arbitrarily, as if it could come at any time, today as well as tomorrow, a thousand years from now as well as after millions of years still to come. On the contrary, although the coming of the Lord will indeed cut short the history of this world, certain ends must be attained before this final catastrophe, in which the very fashion of this world will pass away and the elements shall burn with fervent heat, may occur. In every respect there must be a fullness. A fullness there must be of the measure of iniquity: sin must have become manifest in all its horrible implication of enmity against God. There must also be a fullness of the suffering of Christ: the measure of this suffering, that was filled principally by Christ himself in the days of his flesh, must still be fulfilled in the saints that are in the world unto the praise and honor and glory in the revelation of Jesus Christ. And finally, of course, all the elect must be born and gathered into the body of Christ. For God will not that any should perish, but that all should come to repentance before the coming of the Lord.

A second observation that must be made concerning the coming of the Lord is that it is the final wonder of grace. The confession that we believe in a literal, personal return of our Lord Jesus Christ must not tempt us to overlook the equally important truth that it is a wonder, that therefore we dare not conceive of it and speak of it in terms derived from our present earthly life and existence. This is frequently done. We are inclined to picture the return of our Lord in earthly and carnal colors and forms, as if he were to return to us in his former earthy body, sitting on some cloud in the sky above us, and as if thus, with our earthly eyes, we shall see him.

That this is the conception many form of his second coming is evident from the irrelevant questions that are often asked concerning the possibility of such a universally observed advent, and the silly objections that are raised against it, as well as from the equally irrelevant answers that are given to such silly questions and objections. How, it is asked, is it possible that every eye, that all men, on the whole earth, shall see him when he comes on the clouds of heaven? Have we not definitely discovered that the earth is a sphere? If, then, men that live in the Western hemisphere shall see him at his coming, it must follow that those that live on the other side of the earth cannot possibly be witness of his coming.

We shall not even attempt to answer such silly questions. All attempts to explain the second coming of the Lord are oblivious of the fact that the *parousia*, the second coming, lies in the line of the wonders of grace. We believe that the Son of God assumed our human nature, soul and body, from the virgin Mary. But this does not mean that we can comprehend or demonstrate this wonder of wonders. We believe that on the cross it was the Son of God that laid down his life. We believe that he arose from the dead on the third day. We believe that he ascended from the Mount of Olives to heaven, and sits at the right hand of God. But all this does not imply that we conceive of these wonders in a carnal, earthly way, or that we can comprehend and demonstrate their possibility.

And the same is true of the wonder of the second coming. We believe that our Lord, who arose from the dead and ascended up on high into heaven, shall come again in person, at a definite moment, in the end of the world, and that this coming shall be witnessed by all men, that every eye shall see him. But no more than our modern airplanes explain the possibility of his ascension, no more do wireless and television demonstrate the possibility of his return. We should not forget that he ascended in his resurrection body, that in that body he appeared to his disciples on the Mount of Olives, and that in his appearance they saw him being taken up. So also he shall come again, not in an earthly, natural body, but in the heavenly, spiritual body of his resurrection.

The Bible therefore speaks of his second coming as an appearance. Our life is now hid with Christ in God, but when he shall appear, we shall appear with him in glory (Col. 3:3–4). And we look "for that blessed hope, and the glorious appearing of the great God and our Saviour Jesus Christ" (Titus 2:13). Or, it also speaks of the coming of Christ as his revelation (1 Pet. 1:7). Just as he appeared several times to his disciples during the forty days between his resurrection and his ascension, so he shall appear to all in the end of the world, then to be revealed in all his glory, and never to leave us again; or rather, to take us with him into his glory. His coming will be as the lightning flashing through the heavens (Matt. 24:27).

We would therefore conceive of this final wonder of grace as follows. First, and in the midst of great distress and dreadful signs, when the powers of the heavens shall be shaken, the "sign of the Son of man" shall appear in the heavens (Matt. 24:30). Whatever this sign of the Son of man may be, it shall be visible to all that are then living on the earth. And by that sign all shall know that he is come to judge. Secondly, thereupon shall follow the resurrection of the dead and the ingathering of the elect. In the third place, in their resurrection bodies all the righteous and the wicked shall behold him in the full revelation of his glory and power. And finally, all this shall be followed by the last judgment and the execution of its verdict.

The word of God always presents this final wonder as near.

When the apostles speak of the coming of the Lord as near, and at hand, and about to occur, we must not explain this as an error on their part, as if they expected the coming of the Lord in their own lifetime. It is true that in the time of the apostles believers often conceived of the time that must elapse before the Lord would come again as much shorter than it has actually proved to be. With the early believers there seemed to have been a general expectation that the Lord would come in their own day. But this does not mean that the current and definite testimony of the New Testament with regard to the nearness of the *parousia*, or second coming of the Lord, dare to be interpreted as due to the same mistaken expectation.

It is true that this nearness cannot be understood and expressed in terms of days and months and years. The apostle Peter reminds those that complain of God's slackness in fulfilling the promise that one day is with the Lord as a thousand years, and a thousand years as one day.

But first of all, believers must live in the constant consciousness of the ever-approaching coming of the Lord, and of all it implies. For them the *parousia* must be near, always near. In fact, they must live as in that day.

Secondly, that day is near in the sense that it is next: no other comings of the Lord, as in the flood, in the incarnation, in the resurrection, can be expected. It is the last hour. In this dispensation we are in the day of the Lord. Just as a traveler by train passes several stations on his long journey, but finally the conductor comes through the coaches announcing that the next stop is the terminal, where all get out, so we, in the new dispensation, have passed the last station-stop on the world's journey through time. And the gospel call is: the Lord is coming next!

And thirdly, the Lord is coming quickly, as fast as possible, so to speak. Tremendous things must still come to pass before the final coming. They must be finished. And they are being accomplished with amazing rapidity. This is especially evident in our day. We are flying toward the end. In view of all this, believers must take the testimony of Scripture very seriously, that the coming of the Lord draws nigh.

Do you live with the hope of his coming in your hearts? Then we must keep our garments clean. Otherwise this hope is impossible. We must walk in sanctification of life, be sober, and watch unto prayer. Then, in the midst of the tribulation of this present time, we may lift up our heads, and earnestly look for the coming of our Lord Jesus Christ and our final and complete redemption. That is the hope of his coming.

Chapter 29

GOD'S RIGHTEOUS JUDGMENT IN THE PRESENT TIME

A rticle 7 of the apostolic confession connects the final judgment with the coming of the Lord.

This is, of course, entirely in harmony with the word of God. Scripture speaks very frequently of the coming of the Lord for judgment. It teaches throughout that there will be such a final judgment, to bring to a definite close the history of our world and to serve as a revelation of God's justice as maintained in the everlasting state of the righteous and of the wicked. This is taught both in the Old Testament and in the New. In Psalm 96:10–13 we read:

10. Say among the heathen that the Lord reigneth: the world also shall be established that it shall not be moved: he shall judge the people righteously.
11. Let the heavens rejoice, and let the earth be glad; let the sea roar, and the fulness thereof.
12. Let the field be joyful, and all that is therein: then shall all the trees of the wood rejoice
13. Before the Lord: for he cometh, for he cometh to judge the earth: he shall judge the world with righteousness, and the people with his truth.

A very similar passage you may find in Psalm 98:7–9.

The same note is sounded in all the prophets of the Old Testament. I will quote only one passage:

12. Let the heathen be wakened, and come up to the valley of Jehoshaphat: for there will I sit to judge all the heathen round about.

213

13. Put ye in the sickle, for the harvest is ripe: come, get you down; for the press is full, the fats overflow; for their wickedness is great.

14. Multitudes, multitudes in the valley of decision: for the day of the LORD is near in the valley of decision. (Joel 3:12–14)

In the New Testament, as might be expected, this day of the Lord is more clearly defined. It is connected with the coming of Christ: "For the Son of man shall come in the glory of his Father with his angels; and then he shall reward every man according to his works" (Matt. 16:27). Christ shall

31. Sit upon the throne of his glory:

32. And before him shall be gathered all nations; and he shall separate them one from another, as a shepherd divideth his sheep from the goats:

33. And he shall set the sheep on his right hand, but the goats on the left.

34. Then shall the king say unto them on his right hand, Come, ye blessed of my Father, inherit the kingdom prepared for you from the foundation of the world.

41. Then shall he say also unto them on the left hand, Depart from me, ye cursed, into everlasting fire, prepared for the devil and his angels. (Matt. 25:31–34, 41)

For the Father has committed all judgment unto the Son, and has given him authority to execute judgment also, because he is the Son of man (John 5:22, 27).

The apostle Paul speaks of "the day of wrath and revelation of the righteous judgment of God, who will render to every man according to his deeds" (Rom. 2:5–6). And "we must all appear before the judgment seat of Christ; that every one may receive the things done in his body, according to that he hath done, whether it be good or bad" (2 Cor. 5:10). To Timothy he gives the charge to preach the word "before God, and the Lord Jesus Christ, who shall judge the quick and the dead at his appearing and his kingdom" (2 Tim. 4:1–2). And "the Lord knoweth how to deliver the godly out of temptations, and to reserve the unjust unto the day of judgment to be punished" (2 Pet. 2:9).

In Revelation 20:11–15 a vision is recorded which was given to the seer on Patmos:

11. And I saw a great white throne, and him that sat on it, from whose face the earth and the heaven fled away; and there was found no place for them.
12. And I saw the dead, small and great, stand before God; and the books were opened: and another book was opened, which is the book of life: and the dead were judged out of those things which were written in the books, according to their works.
13. And the sea gave up the dead which were in it; and death and hell delivered up the dead which were in them: and they were judged every man according to their works.
14. And death and hell were cast into the lake of fire. This is the second death.
15. And whosoever was not found written in the book of life was cast into the lake of fire.

And in the last chapter of this book the coming of the Lord for judgment is solemnly emphasized in these words: "And, behold, I come quickly; and my reward is with me, to give every man according as his work shall be" (Rev. 22:12).

Various notions were developed in the course of the history of doctrine concerning this final judgment. We shall not weary you with them all in this lecture. However, in modern times a conception of this final judgment was developed, which, although fundamentally wrong, nevertheless contains an important element of truth to which we wish to call your attention in this present lecture. Under the influence of German theology the idea of a distinct and final judgment, that will terminate this age and the history of the world, has been rather generally denied. There will be no final judgment as a distinct and separate event in the end of time. Such a final judgment, according to them, is not necessary: for the world is always in judgment, and God executes his judgment constantly. History itself is judgment, and every man always receives according to his work, and God inscribes his judgment in the consciences of men. As I say, there is in this modern conception of the judgment of God an element of truth that dares not be denied or overlooked with impunity.

It is to be feared that many believers look upon the last judgment as an isolated event, a mere momentary act of God by which he will for the first time and forever judge the affairs of men and set straight whatever was permitted to be crooked in the history of the world. The only judgment is that which is to come at the end, according to them. In the course of the present history of the world God does not appear as the judge of heaven and earth. He judges, to be sure, all the moral acts of men and of nations in the sense that he evaluates them as to their moral worth, and writes them all in his book. And, occasionally he reminds the world of his wrath and just judgment by sending special catastrophes, such as world wars, earthquakes, famines, and pestilences on the earth. But for the rest, he does not in this present dispensation execute a righteous judgment. Every man is not rewarded according as his work is in this world. Many things are left crooked. For God is tolerant, forbearing, longsuffering. In fact, in the affairs of the world it appears as if force rather than justice prevails, and has the victory. The wicked prosper, especially if, as they generally have, they have the power. And the righteous suffer and are oppressed. And it seems as if there is no Judge in heaven, and no knowledge in the Most High.

Nevertheless, according to them, God remembers. He writes all these things in his book. And although for the present he permits injustice to prevail and to triumph, he has appointed Christ to judge the world, and in his day God will open the books and execute a righteous judgment. Although in this world iniquity is often victorious, and the wicked are in power, in the day of Christ the righteous shall be justified and the wicked shall be condemned forever. The last judgment is the only and final act of God whereby he will rectify and set straight whatever was unjust in the present government of the world.

It is partly, at least, because of some such conception of God as the final judge in respect to the affairs of the present world that many find room for the erroneous notion of common grace. The prosperity of the wicked must be considered a token of God's gracious disposition and attitude toward them. The wicked hate God and blaspheme his name. They commit iniquity in the world, and oppress the righteous. Yet, God blesses them in that he bestows upon them all the bounties of this present life. Does he not send rain upon the evil and upon the good? And does he not cause his sun to shine upon the righteous and the unrighteous? It is true that in the end God will execute a righteous judgment upon them, and they shall be damned forever in the pool that burns with fire and sulfur. But for the present God is gracious to everybody in his common grace. Particularly is he gracious to the wicked, as well and even more as to the righteous. And recently some speaker suggested that those who denied this theory of common grace answer against God, and even quoted the text: "O man, who art thou that repliest against God?" (Rom. 9:20).[1] This he said, although at the same time he did not appeal to Scripture to prove his own false theory.

In this connection we would emphasize that this entire notion is false and unscriptural, simply because it implies an erroneous conception of God as the judge of heaven and earth.

God always judges. He always executes a righteous judgment. It is not thus, that during the present history of the world he permits the affairs of men to run their own course, carefully noting them in his book, in order at the end of the world to ascend his throne of judgment. He always sits on the throne as judge. Constantly he judges. And all his moral creatures stand always before him in judgment. Moreover, all the works of God are perfect, and all his judgments are just. Even though the final and everlasting reward of the righteous in glory and the retribution of the wicked in hell cannot be realized in this present time, nevertheless with both of them God always deals according to strictest justice.

---

1 Cornelius Van Til (1895–1987) says something similar in "Common Grace and Witness-Bearing," *Torch and Trumpet* 4, no. 5 (December 1954–January 1955): 5. Hoeksema delivered this speech on January 16, 1955. Considering that *Torch and Trumpet* was published in Grand Rapids and that Hoeksema was living in Grand Rapids at the time, it is possible that Hoeksema was referring to Van Til in his sermon.

It is true that we cannot always understand and discern this righteous judgment of God in detail in this present time. To us it often appears as if God's dealings with men are unjust. But this appearance of things is due only to our limited understanding and to the fact that we often fail to discern the meaning of the present time for man's eternal state. If we could always understand the ways of God, we would no doubt also clearly discern that God always judges righteously, and that he executes a righteous judgment upon men, both upon the righteous and upon the wicked. Never would we then complain anymore that he favors the wicked and that he assumes an attitude of common grace in relation to them. Constantly God rewards the good with good, and never does the sinner advance one step on the way of iniquity that is not visited with evil on the spot.

We do not answer against God when we speak thus. But we speak the language of Holy Writ.

The curse of the Lord is always in the house of the wicked, though that house may be a veritable palace, and though it is filled with the riches of this world. And he blesses "the habitation of the just," no matter how poor a hovel that habitation may be (Prov. 3:33). Asaph in Psalm 73 also relates how, before he entered into the sanctuary of God, he was inclined to think that God favors the wicked. Says he in verse 3: "For I was envious at the foolish, when I saw the prosperity of the wicked." He saw that "their strength is firm," and that "there are no bands in their death;" that they were "not in trouble as other men; neither [were] they plagued like other men…Their eyes stand out with fatness; they have more than heart could wish" (vv. 4–5, 7). Yet, "they are corrupt," and they "speak wickedly concerning oppression: they speak loftily" (v. 8). They even "set their mouth against the heavens, and their tongue walks through the earth" (v. 9). On the other hand, God's people often have the experience that waters of a full cup are wrung out to them. And then they are inclined to ask: "How doth God know? and is there knowledge in the most High?" (v. 11).

But all this changed as soon as the psalmist had entered into the sanctuary of God and beheld the end of the wicked. For that end could not be dissociated from the present. Their present way leads to the end. And the end is destruction. Then the poet saw that God with all this prosperity certainly did not show any favor or common grace to the wicked, but that he "set them in slippery places," and cast "them down into destruction" (v. 18). On those slippery places of their present way they are brought into desolation as in a moment, and they are utterly consumed with terrors. And on the other hand, God is always gracious to the righteous, no matter how their way may be a way of suffering and distress and persecution, and even death. For in the sanctuary he understood that God guided him with his counsel, in order afterward to receive him to glory (v. 24). No more than there is a common wrath upon the righteous and the wicked alike, no more is there a common grace for the wicked.

This is also evident from Psalm 92, from which we quote the following: "O LORD, how great are thy works! and thy thoughts are very deep. A brutish man knoweth not; neither doth a fool understand this. When the wicked spring as the grass, and when all the workers of iniquity do flourish; it is that they shall be destroyed for ever" (vv. 5–7). The prosperity of the wicked leads to and is intended by the Lord to lead to destruction. And that certainly cannot be grace. A brutish man, or a foolish, does not understand this work of the Lord. But the righteous do, in the light of God's own revelation.

The same truth is revealed in that dreadful first chapter of the epistle to the Romans. For there we are taught that not grace, but the wrath of God is revealed from heaven over all the ungodliness and unrighteousness of men, who hold the truth in unrighteousness. This is true throughout all the history of this present world. The wicked know that God is. And they are aware that he is to be thanked and glorified. But they refuse to acknowledge him. And God executes a righteous judgment upon them even in this present time. For he makes them foolish. He causes them to grope in the darkness of idolatry, so that they foolishly bow before four-footed beasts and creeping things. He punishes sin with sin. He casts them into the mire of sin, so that they become more corrupt all the time. And thus they hasten to their own destruction.

From this and many other passages of Holy Writ, it is very evident that God also in this present world is the judge of heaven and earth, and executes a righteous judgment all the time. All things are so made and so governed that they must work together for good to them that love God, and that they must work together for evil to them that hate him. There is no common grace.

God is the Lord! He cannot be mocked, even for a moment.

And not only does he deal with his moral creatures righteously in this world. Not only does he execute judgment constantly, both upon the righteous and upon the wicked. But he also inscribes his righteous judgment in the conscience of every man. Man's conscience is his awareness of God's judgment of his every act. It is because of this judging act of God that men have the work of the law inscribed in their hearts, and that their conscience witnesses with the testimony of God's law, so that they accuse or excuse themselves and one another (Rom. 2:15).

This, and not any false philosophy of common grace, is the plain language of Holy Writ. And this, and not any erroneous common grace theory, is the comfort of all that live godly in the world, and expect the coming of our Lord Jesus Christ to judge the quick and the dead.

Chapter 30

THE FINAL JUDGMENT

In our last lecture we emphasized that God is judge throughout the history of the world, and also always executes a righteous judgment in the present time.

We may add that according to Scripture there is also an individual, preliminary judgment, immediately after death that will be executed in the damnation of the wicked and the intermediate glory of the saints that die in Christ.

Yet, in distinction from God's present just government in the world, and also from that preliminary judgment that will be passed upon every soul that departs from this present life, the church on the basis of Holy Writ confesses that she looks for a final judgment, when Christ shall come again to judge the quick and the dead.

We may ask the question, first of all: what is the idea of this last judgment by which all the affairs of this present world, especially as they are concerned with the moral creatures, will be terminated, and their eternal state will be decided?

To this question we answer, in the first place, that the central idea of this final judgment is that of the theodicy, the justification of God in the consciousness of all his moral creatures. That final judgment will be the *revelation* of the righteous judgment of God. As we have said, in this world too God's government is characterized by strictest justice. But the justice of God's judgments is not clearly revealed. Many things are hid. We judge only according to that which is apparent. The hidden things of the heart, for instance, the reasons and motives that lie behind the outward deed, we cannot judge. Moreover, there are many things done in secret, words that are spoken in secret, secret counsels that are never revealed, secret abominations that are committed in darkness. Besides, we do not clearly discern the dealings of God with men in relation to their moral deeds.

But in that final day all will be revealed. Then it will be made manifest not only that God will finally reward every man according to his own deeds, but also that he always did execute a righteous judgment in his government of the world. It will be the revelation of the righteous judgment of God also in this respect, that he will be clearly revealed as the judge, so that the moral creature can no longer deny him. Here, in this present world, the fool may say and actually does say in his heart that there is no God. The ungodly ascribe the righteous judgments of God, especially when they become manifest in great upheavals and special calamities, to the inevitable laws of nature, or to fate, or to man's own folly and weakness. Always he sets himself against God, and vows that he will overcome him in judgment. He will make a good world out of it all, and establish peace and prosperity without God and without his Christ. But in that day God will so reveal himself that all must acknowledge that he is the Lord of the universe, and that he is the righteous judge of heaven and earth.

We must not forget that this final judgment is the last wonder of grace. We cannot conceive of it in the present world.

For it implies that this final judgment will be strictly public, in the sense that the righteousness of God's judgment will be clearly revealed to all the moral creatures. It will not be merely individualistic, so that each one will be convinced of the justice of his own sentence. But it will be given unto all in that day to behold the whole of the works of God, of his righteous government and his just judgment with regard to all his moral creatures. Christ and his cause shall be publicly justified. And his saints shall share in this public justification, so that even the wicked, that here condemned and persecuted them, will have to acknowledge that they, the people of God, are the rightful heirs of all things. And, on the other hand, they shall behold the retribution of the wicked, and acknowledge that the Lord of all is just in consigning them to eternal desolation.

This judgment is final. By it the history of the entire world will come to a close. The ethical fruit of the moral creature will be ripe. And the final judgment will be the everlasting separation of the chaff from the wheat, of the wicked from the righteous, of the reprobate from the elect. And all will receive their final, their everlasting reward.

It is in harmony with this idea of the final judgment as the revelation of the righteous judgment of God that Christ will be the judge. For he is the revelation of the Father. This is the teaching of Holy Writ, as we have already shown. We must all appear before the judgment seat of Christ. He will come quickly, and his reward is with him, to give to every man according as his work shall be.

This means, of course, that the Son of God will appear in his glorious human nature as the visible representative of the invisible God as judge, and that too, in such a way that all the moral world will recognize him as the revelation of the Lord of all, receive his judgment as the revelation of the righteous judgment of God. All the power of judgment will be delivered into the hands of Christ, the Son of God in glory. Every knee shall bow before him. Every tongue shall confess that Christ is the Lord Judge, to the glory of God the Father (Phil. 2:10–11). And all things will be naked and open before him whose eyes are like a flame of fire, whose feet are like burnished brass, and out of whose mouth proceeds "a sharp, twoedged sword" (Rev. 1:14–16). Him whom they despised and condemned and crucified all shall then behold and recognize as the representative of God in his final judgment.

This last judgment will concern all moral creatures, angels and men, the righteous and the wicked, small and great.

Especially under Pelagian influence this is often denied. It is claimed that only those can be brought into judgment that have been in contact with the gospel, and had the opportunity to accept or to reject Christ. All others, heathen and small children, must be excluded. This is an individualistic conception of the judgment of God, and is to be condemned in the light of Scripture. The word of God always proceeds not from the individualistic, but from the organic idea. The world is to be judged; and the sin of the world, and not of a few individuals, has already been revealed through the crucifixion of the Son of God.

Besides, this view is based on the erroneous supposition that one can be brought into judgment and condemned only because of his rejection of the Christ. It is true that "this is the condemnation, that light is come into the world, and men loved darkness rather than light, because their deeds were evil" (John 3:19), and that therefore "he that believeth on him is not condemned: but he that believeth not is condemned already, because he hath not believed in the name of the only begotten Son of God" (v 18). But this can only mean that through the coming of the Son of God in the world, and his rejection by men, the sin of the world is clearly manifested as sin. Even before, and apart from the coming of Christ, however, the whole world lies in sin and under condemnation in the first Adam. And therefore all men, the whole world, will be brought into judgment in that final day.

Not only the wicked, but also the righteous shall stand before the throne of Christ in that day. For the purpose of the final judgment is not only the condemnation of the wicked; but, as has been said, its chief purpose is the theodicy, the justification of God, the revelation of the righteous judgment of the Most High. And this will be revealed not only in the condemnation of the ungodly, but also in the public justification of the righteous in Christ.

The whole world, therefore, all God's moral creatures, angels as well as men, adults as well as children, that is, those that were children in this world, will appear in the righteous judgment of God before Christ. The angels will be judged, both good and bad: for also the good angels must be publicly justified, and the fallen angels still await their final judgment and punishment. Therefore the apostle writes to the church of Corinth: "Know ye not that we shall judge angels? how much more things that pertain to this life?" (1 Cor. 6:3). And in 2 Peter 2:4 we read that the angels that sinned are "delivered...into chains of darkness, to be reserved unto judgment."

It is also evident from Scripture that all nations will appear before the judgment seat of Christ. And before that judgment seat they shall at once be separated into the righteous and the wicked (Matt. 25:31–46). And that also the people of God shall appear before Christ in judgment is evident from 2 Corinthians 5:10, "For we must all appear before the judgment seat of Christ; that every one may receive the things done in his body, according to that he hath done, whether it be good or bad." The only ones that probably will not even have the honor to appear in judgment before Christ are the persons of Satan and those of the false prophet and the antichrist. For we receive the impression from the book of Revelation that they will be cast into the lake of fire without any form of judgment.

As to the judgment itself, Scripture teaches that it shall be according to the works of those that are judged. For the Lord comes quickly, and his reward will be with him "to give every man according as his work shall be" (Rev. 22:12). And when we appear before the judgment seat of Christ, it will be in order that "every one may receive the things done in his body…whether it be good or bad" (2 Cor. 5:10).

We must remember, however, that these works include not only the outward deeds, but also the inner thoughts, the desires, the intentions, the purposes, the motives of those deeds. We shall be made manifest. We shall be turned inside out. And our works shall be evaluated in the light of God's perfect law. The secrets of men shall be exposed in their true value. Nothing shall be hid. Our personal works in connection with our talents and powers, with our position in the world, with the age in which we lived, and with our circumstances and means, as well as with relation to the light of revelation we possessed, will then be manifest in their proper meaning, in their ethical worth. It will "be more tolerable for Tyre and Sidon" than for Capernaum and Chorazin and Bethsaida in that day (Luke 10:14). And there is nothing hid that will not be made public in the day of the Lord (12:2).

Nor can one possibly maintain in the light of Scripture that this universal and complete exposure and manifestation of all our works must necessarily exclude the sins of the people of God. Scripture is far too explicit on this point to leave any room for doubt. It is exactly of believers that the apostle writes in 2 Corinthians 5:10 that we must *all* be made manifest before the judgment seat of Christ. In fact, we may well accept that in that day we shall see our sins as we have never seen them before, in the present world.

Only, it must never be forgotten that in that day Christ and our belonging to him will be our only, but also our perfect, comfort. That is why believers can look forward in hope and with uplifted head to that final day of the judgment of God in Christ Jesus our Lord. It is only because we look in that day for the very same person who sacrificed himself for us on the accursed tree, and who has removed all curse from us, to come as judge from heaven. And therefore it is certainly true that all the sins of the people of God shall be exposed in judgment in that final day. But those sins shall be manifested only in the light of the everlasting love wherewith God loved us in Christ Jesus our Lord. And we shall see our sins, shall see them as we never saw them before, but only to adore all the more the perfect righteousness of God in Christ Jesus, whereby we are justified forever. We shall see our sins, but only as they are blotted out in the blood of the Lamb.

Because of Christ, and because of our living part with him, we shall have no fear in the day of judgment. Even in respect to our own sin we shall be of God's party in that day, take his side in the condemnation of all iniquity, even our own, only to cling in the perfect confidence of faith to Christ Jesus our Lord, and to adore forever the wondrous grace whereby we have been redeemed from so great a darkness of death, and become worthy of eternal life and glory. Also in that day, and especially then, it shall be our only comfort in life and death and in the day of judgment that we are not our own, but belong to our faithful Savior Jesus Christ, in whose death and resurrection we have our perfect justification.

Thus the end of all things and the final judgment will be the perfect theodicy, the perfect justification of God. All will acknowledge that God is good. The damned in hell will forever have to confess that their damnation is just. And the saved in glory will everlastingly behold themselves in Christ, and boast in God's wondrous grace only, and in that alone. No flesh shall ever glory in God's presence.

Article 8

I believe in the Holy Ghost

Chapter 31

THE HOLY GHOST

The entire apostolic confession of faith is evidently based on the Trinity.

The first article speaks of God the Father, who distinctly appears as the Father first of all in the work of creation, and who, of course, is our Father for Christ's sake. Articles 2 to 7 speak of God the Son, the only begotten of the Father. But he appears as God the Son as he is revealed in Christ Jesus our Lord, who came in the likeness of sinful flesh, died on the accursed tree for our sins, was raised on the third day for our justification, ascended up on high in heaven, where he sits at the right hand of God the Father Almighty, and is expected to come again to judge the quick and the dead.

Article 8 speaks of God the Holy Ghost: "I believe in the Holy Ghost." It would appear that this article is very brief indeed. But we must not forget that in the apostolic confession the Holy Ghost also appears as the Spirit of Christ, who applies all the blessings of salvation unto his people. Taken in this sense, all the rest of the apostolic confession, which speaks of the holy catholic church, the communion of saints, the forgiveness of sins, the resurrection of the body, and the life everlasting, deals with the subject of the Holy Spirit as the Spirit of Christ.

In the present lecture we must briefly treat the subject of the holy third person in the holy Trinity.

Although, as we said, the apostolic confession of faith is concerned especially with the Spirit of Christ, who applies all the blessings of salvation to us, nevertheless we must begin our confession concerning the Holy Ghost by setting forth who and what he is in himself, as the third person in the holy Trinity, in relation to the Father and to the Son. And I wish to emphasize especially three elements in this connection.

First of all, the church confesses that the Holy Spirit is God. He is not inferior to, but co-equal with the Father and the Son. All the divine virtues belong to him as well as to the Father and the Son. As the Father and the Son are self-existent, so is the Holy Ghost. As the Father and the Son are independent, so is the Holy Ghost. As the Father and the Son are eternal and infinite, so is the Holy Ghost. As the Father and the Son are omniscient and almighty, so is the Holy Ghost. And all the other attributes of the divine essence, such as love and grace and mercy, belong to him as well as to the Father and the Son. He is God.

It is by no means superfluous to make special mention of this truth. We are perhaps easily inclined to ascribe to the Holy Spirit a subordinate position, as, in fact, many have done. That the Father is God is never a question with us: he is the almighty creator of heaven and earth. That the Son is co-equal with the Father we also have little difficulty to believe and to maintain: is he not our mighty redeemer that overcame sin and death for us? But the Holy Spirit is often a vague idea to us. At any rate, he seems to occupy a position of inferiority and subordination to the Father and to the Son. Does not the Bible speak of him as a means, or as an instrument by whom God works all things? And is, after all, an instrument not inferior to him that employs it? And therefore it is by no means superfluous to remind ourselves that also the third person of the holy Trinity is very God, not subordinate to, but co-equal with the Father and the Son.

We have no time to refer to all the passages of Holy Writ that definitely speak of him as God. But I will give you the references, and you can look them up for yourselves. He is called God (Acts 5:4; 1 Cor. 3:16–17). Besides, all that is ascribed to the Holy Spirit proceeds from the truth that he is very God, co-equal with the Father and the Son. He is the author of God's eternal counsel and good pleasure with regard to all things in time (Isaiah 40:13–14). He searches the depths of God (1 Cor. 2:11). The work of creation, as well as the work of providence, is ascribed to him (Gen. 1:2; Ps. 33:6; 104:30). Together with the Father and the Son he is the author of our salvation, and applies unto us all the blessings of salvation, filling the church with spiritual gifts (1 Cor. 12:3–11).

Moreover, the Spirit is said to be omnipresent (Ps. 139:7–8). He is omniscient (1 Cor. 2:10). He is the eternal Spirit (Heb. 9:14). The name of the Holy Ghost is mentioned in one breath and on a par with the name of the Father and the Son (Matt. 28:19). And with the Father and the Son he is the source and author of all blessings bestowed upon the church (2 Cor. 13:14). In the light of all these passages there can be no doubt but that the Holy Ghost is God, co-equal with the Father and the Son.

It is equally important, however, and perhaps more imperative, that the personality of the Spirit is maintained and emphasized. He is a distinct person. This is often denied, and the Holy Ghost is presented as a vague, indefinite power. It is denied by all forms of unitarianism. But if his personality is denied, his essential Godhead cannot be maintained: the two stand and fall together. If the Spirit is not a definite person, then what is called Spirit in Holy Writ either refers to the one God, one in essence and one in person, in the sense in which Scripture teaches that "God is a Spirit, and they that worship him must worship him in spirit and in truth" (John 4:24). Or else it simply refers to a power, an effluence of God. If the Holy Spirit is not a distinct person, then he is not God, but merely a mode of divine revelation or operation of power or gift; but he certainly is not God.

Those that deny the personality of the Holy Spirit even appeal to Scripture. They refer to passages that seem to speak of the Holy Ghost merely as a power, or as a gift, rather than as a person. He is a gift to believers. He is bestowed upon men, rests on them, fills them with wisdom and knowledge in a way that might leave the impression that he is an operation and power of God, rather than a person. This power is given unto men even by the laying on of hands by the apostles. Besides, it is argued by those that deny the personality of the Spirit that we never read in the Bible that the Spirit is worshiped. The Father is the object of prayer. The Son too is addressed in worship. But the Holy Spirit never.

However, though these passages teach us that we must indeed distinguish between the Holy Ghost as the third person of the holy Trinity and as the Spirit of Christ, and though many passages of Scripture emphasize the gifts that are bestowed by the Spirit rather than his personal subsistence, yet there can be no question that the Scriptures teach also that the Holy Spirit is a definite person. Even though some passages of Holy Writ refer by the term "Holy Ghost" to the very special gifts that were bestowed on the early church, such as the gift of tongues, the gift of healing, the gift of prophesying, yet the fact remains that there can be no doubt at all that the Scriptures clearly speak of the Holy Ghost as a definite person, subsisting with the Father and the Son in the divine essence.

He thinks as a person, he wills as a person, he acts as a person. He searches "the deep things of God" (1 Cor. 2:10). He teaches the apostles to speak (v. 13). He prays for the believers "with groanings which cannot be uttered" (Rom. 8:26). He leads them that are children of God, and witnesses with their spirit that they are sons of God (Rom. 8:14–16). He is "the Spirit of the Son" that cries "Abba, Father" (Gal. 4:6). He commands Philip to join himself to the chariot of the Ethiopian (Acts 8:29). And when the apostles want to go to Mysia, the Spirit suffers them not (16:7). He leads Christ "into the wilderness to be tempted of" Satan (Matt. 4:1). He gives life (2 Cor. 3:6). He bears witness, because the Spirit is truth (1 John 5:6). And as to spiritual gifts, we read: "All these worketh that one and the selfsame Spirit, dividing to every man severally as he will" (1 Cor. 12:11). Moreover, he moves "upon the face of the waters" (Gen. 1:2). He strives with men (6:3). And he sends the prophets and servants of Jehovah (Isa. 48:16; Ezek. 3:12).

All these passages, and many others, teach us plainly that, like the Father and the Son, the Spirit too is a person, and not a mere power or gift or effluence of God. He is the third person of the holy Trinity.

In this connection we might ask, perhaps, what is a person. My person is what I call my *I*, my ego. It is the subject of all my actions. It remains the same through whatever changes I may pass in life or in death. I think, I desire, I will, I speak, I see, I hear, I eat and drink, I rejoice and am in sorrow, I love and hate, I sing and weep, I suffer and die, I am raised from the dead. In all these actions and experiences my person is the subject that performs and experiences and that remains the same throughout.

From infancy to old age we pass through many changes; yet we know quite well that we remain the same individual subjects. Even in death, when the earthly house of this tabernacle is dissolved (2 Cor. 5:1), it is the same person that passes through death into the eternal home. When, therefore, we say that the Holy Spirit is a person, we mean that together with the Father and the Son he is a distinct subject in the divine essence and nature. He is distinct because in the divine nature he always acts and thinks and speaks as Spirit, never as Father and Son. He is the third person in the holy Trinity.

He is third, not in the sense that in any way he is subordinate to the Father and the Son: for all the three persons are equally divine. But he is third in order. He is the Holy Ghost; that is, he is the Spirit of the Father and of the Son. The name Spirit is also applied to the Godhead, to the divine essence. God is a Spirit, and they that worship him must worship him in spirit and in truth. But with reference to the Holy Ghost, the name *Spirit* denotes the third person of the holy Trinity in relation to the Father and to the Son. He is breathed forth by the Father and by the Son. He proceeds from the Father to the Son, and from the Son to the Father.

This is plain from all Scripture. In John 15:26 the Spirit is said to proceed from the Father: "But when the Comforter is come, whom I will send unto you from the Father, even the Spirit of truth, which proceedeth from the Father, he shall testify of me." However, he is also called the Spirit of the Son. In Galatians 4:6 we read: "And because ye are sons, God hath sent forth the Spirit of his Son into the hearts, crying, Abba, Father." Now there can be no doubt that as the Spirit of the Son he proceeds from him. Besides, of the Spirit the Lord declares: "He shall testify of me" (John 15:26). And again: "He shall glorify me: for he shall receive of mine, and shall show it unto you. All things that the Father hath are mine: therefore said I, that he shall take of mine, and shall show it unto you" (16:14–15). And lastly, I may say that in the indwelling Spirit, sent into our hearts, we have fellowship with the triune God. In the Spirit, through the Son, the Father makes his abode with us: "If a man love me, he will keep my words: and my Father will love him, and we will come unto him, and make our abode with him" (14:23).

On the basis of these and other passages of Holy Writ, the church confesses that the Spirit is not subordinate, but co-equal with the

Father and the Son, and that he proceeds from the Father to the Son, and from the Son to the Father. In the Spirit the Father knows and loves the Son. And in the same Spirit the Son knows and loves the Father. While in himself, searching the deep things of God, the Spirit knows and loves the Father, and the Son. In the Spirit the Father eternally says to the Son: "Thou art my Son, this day have I begotten thee" (Acts 13:33). And in the same Spirit the Son cries eternally: "Abba, Father." Of the Father, through the Son, in the Holy Spirit, the three persons of the Holy Spirit live an eternal life of friendship in infinite perfection.

For God is the living God. And as the living God he lives a covenantal life of perfect and everlasting friendship. For the idea of the covenant is not that of an agreement, pact, or alliance. It is a bond of friendship and living fellowship. Friendship is that bond of fellowship between persons according to which, and by which they enter into one another's life in perfect knowledge and love, so that mind is knit to mind, will to will, heart to heart, and each has no secrets from the other.

It presupposes a basis of likeness, of equality. For only like know like. And on that basis of equality it requires personal distinction. For without this there is only sameness: there can be no fellowship. And both the equality and the personal distinction are in God. For he is the Triune. The most absolute equality exists between Father, Son, and Holy Spirit. For these three are one in being. And in him there is the personal distinction between the three persons subsisting in the one being.

And so the three persons of the holy Trinity completely and perfectly enter into one another's life. Their fellowship is infinitely perfect. They have no secrets from one another. There is no conflict between them. Their relationship is one of perfect harmony. The Father knows and loves the Son in the Spirit. The Son knows and loves the Father in the Spirit. The Spirit knows and loves the Father through the Son in himself. The living God is the covenantal God. That is the great significance of the truth that God is triune, and that these three distinct persons are the one, only true and eternal God.

And that is also the significance of the confession of the church: "I believe in the Holy Ghost."

And when that Spirit is sent into our hearts, and makes his abode with us, it is in that Spirit that we too have covenantal fellowship with the living God, and that the word of our Lord is realized: "I in them, and thou in me, that they may be made perfect in one" (John 17:23).

Chapter 32

THE SPIRIT OF CHRIST

B efore we turn to the article concerning the church, we must still elaborate on the confession of the church concerning the Holy Ghost. And this time we must speak of the Holy Ghost as the Spirit of Christ.

It is possible, and also strictly necessary, to make a distinction between the Holy Ghost as such, as the third person of the holy Trinity, and that same Holy Ghost as he is become the Spirit of Christ. Just as concerning the person of the Son of God the distinction must be made between the only begotten Son as such, as the eternal Son, as the second person of the Trinity, and the incarnated Son, Jesus Christ, who tabernacles with us in the human nature; so we must also distinguish between the Spirit of God and the Spirit of Christ. Even as the only begotten Son and Jesus Christ are the same person, so the Holy Ghost and the Spirit of Christ are the same person. Again, just as the only begotten Son, the second person in the Trinity, is the eternal Word, through whom all things are made, so the Holy Ghost is the Spirit of all creation, in whom all things are made, giving life to all things.

But once more, even as the only begotten Son from before the foundation of the world is ordained to be the mediator of salvation, the head of the elect church and the head over all things in the new creation, so the Holy Ghost in God's eternal good pleasure is promised to Christ, ordained to be the Spirit of regeneration and sanctification and perfection, that he might dwell in the church and make us partakers of all the benefits and blessings of grace. And finally, even as the eternal Son became Jesus Christ our Lord and redeemer in the fullness of time through his incarnation, his death and resurrection, and his exaltation at the right hand of God, so the Holy Ghost became the Spirit of Christ after his exaltation, and as such came to dwell in the church on the day of Pentecost.

This is no doubt the teaching of Holy Writ. In John 7:39 we read (according to the original): "But this spake he of the Spirit, which they that believe on him should receive: for the Holy Ghost was not yet: because that Jesus was not yet glorified." I say that this is the reading of the original text, because the word "given" does not occur there. The text simply reads: "The Holy Ghost was not yet; because that Jesus was not yet glorified." This, of course, is very important. The meaning cannot be, of course, that the Holy Spirit as such, as the Spirit of God, did not yet exist. For, as we said before, he is very God, coeternal with the Father and the Son. Nor can it mean that there were no operations of the Spirit of God at all in creation and providence, or even with regard to the work of redemption. For all the works of God are of the Father, through the Son, and in the Holy Ghost.

But evidently it means that the Holy Ghost as the Spirit of Christ, who makes us partakers of all the fullness of Christ, was not yet. This is evident from the context. On the last day of the feast of tabernacles Jesus stood in the temple and loudly proclaimed himself as the fountain of the water of life. And he gave the promise: "He that believeth on me, as the Scripture hath said, out of his belly shall flow rivers of living water" (John 7:38). However, all this could not be realized at that moment. The fountain of living water must first be opened. Jesus must first suffer and die, be raised to glory, and be exalted at the right hand of God.

Moreover, he must receive the promise of the Spirit after his exaltation, and in that Spirit return unto his own and dwell in his church. Only through that Spirit that would be given, the Spirit of Christ, could his own come unto him and drink, and could the promise be fulfilled that out of their belly should flow rivers of living water. Hence, it is added: "But this spake he of the Spirit, which they that believe on him should receive." And as a further explanation it is said that "the Holy Ghost was not yet; because that Jesus was not yet glorified" (John 7:39). Just as before the fullness of time and the incarnation it could be said that Jesus Christ was not yet, so before the exaltation of our Lord it is said that the Holy Ghost was not yet.

This does not mean, of course, that the saints of the old dispensation were not saved even as we. For although Christ was not yet, the Son of God had been ordained as the mediator of his people in God's eternal counsel. And even before his incarnation he operated and became revealed as such in the promise and through the shadows. And although the Spirit of Christ was not yet, the Holy Ghost had been eternally ordained to be the Spirit of redemption, and as such he operated in the prophets and led the people through the shadows to the hope of the reality that was to come.

But the saints of the Old Testament, even with respect to the spiritual blessings of salvation, which now are fully ours, were saved by hope. Even as we in the new dispensation still look forward to the final realization of the promise and can but dimly apprehend the glory of the heavenly kingdom that is to come in the day of Christ; so the saints of the old dispensation were indeed saved, yet the reality of atonement, of redemption, of justification and life, the fullness of the revelation of Jesus Christ and of the blessings of salvation in him, had not yet been realized. They could only dimly apprehend them through the shadows, and by the promise of him that was to come.

That we must distinguish between the Holy Ghost as such and the Spirit of Christ is taught in many other passages of Scripture. Repeatedly the Lord speaks of the Spirit in his final addresses to his disciples, spoken to comfort them concerning his departure from them through the cross and the resurrection, and preserved for us in chapters 14–16 of the gospel according to John. This we read, for instance, in John 14:15–17, "If ye love me, keep my commandments. And I will pray the Father, and he shall give you another Comforter, that he may abide with you for ever; even the Spirit of truth; whom the world cannot receive, because it seeth him not, neither knoweth him: but ye know him; for he dwelleth with you, and shall be in you." Especially these last words are significant in the connection. Upon the prayer of Christ the Father will send the Spirit to his disciples. And in the Spirit Christ himself shall return to them. The Spirit, therefore, that will be given to the church at the departure and exaltation of Christ is his Spirit, the Spirit of the exalted Lord, through whom he himself will dwell in his people and abide with them forever.

In John 15:26 the Lord promises his disciples that after his exaltation he will send "the Spirit of truth" from the Father. And that Spirit of truth will testify of him. In the sixteenth verse of chapter 14 the Lord had presented the sending forth of the Spirit as an act of the Father: he will pray to the Father, and upon the prayer of the Mediator the Father would send the comforter unto them. In this passage, however, he definitely declares that he will send the Spirit of truth unto them from the Father. If we combine these two statements, we will understand that the Spirit is to be given to Christ as the mediator and exalted Lord, and from and through him as the Spirit of Christ he is to be sent into the church. The promise of the Spirit is to be fulfilled in Christ. And in that Spirit he will return to his own.

More clearly still this is explained in John 16:7–15. In this passage the Lord speaks of the comforter whom he will send to them after his departure into heaven. And when that comforter, which is the Spirit of truth, is come, he will guide them into all the truth: "For he shall not speak of himself; but whatsoever he shall hear, that shall he speak: and he will shew you things to come. He shall glorify me: for he shall receive of mine, and shall show it unto you. All things that the Father hath are mine: therefore said I, that he shall take of mine, and shall show it unto you" (vv. 13–15).

All through this passage the Spirit of God is presented as the Spirit of Christ. He cannot come unless Christ goes away, that is, through his death and resurrection and exaltation. And this is impossible, first of all, because through his suffering and death and perfect obedience Christ must merit the promise of the Spirit; and secondly, because only after his death and exaltation can he receive the Spirit, that as the exalted Christ he may return to and dwell in his own. All the work of this Spirit proceeds from and is concentrated in Christ.

This is true of his work in the world that must be judged by Christ. And this is equally true of his saving operation in the believers. He is the Spirit of truth. He serves the truth. He reveals the truth as it is in Christ. Of the truth he witnesses, but not in the sense that he ever speaks directly, without Christ, who is the truth and the life. On the contrary, what he hears, that is, of Christ, that he speaks. Christ he glorifies. Of Christ he receives the contents of his testimony. And of Christ he witnesses in the church. He is the Spirit of Christ.

This is very important. It is important from a practical viewpoint, because it teaches us that the Spirit and the Word always belong together. The Spirit never speaks of himself. He takes it out of Christ. And this means for us, who have no other Christ than the one that is revealed to us in the gospel, that the Spirit of Christ never witnesses without the word of Christ in the Bible. He takes it out of the Scriptures, and reveals it unto the church.

Equally true, of course, it is, that without the Spirit the Scriptures are dead. There is no access to the word of God, to the Christ of the Scriptures, to the gospel, except through or in the Spirit. In this sense it certainly must be maintained that Christ must and does speak his own word, and that through his Spirit. And again, this is true whether the word is a savor of life unto life or a savor of death unto death: "No man knoweth the Son, but the Father; neither knoweth any man the Father, save the Son, and he to whomsoever the Son will reveal him" (Matt. 11:27). And again: "And that no man can say that Jesus is the Lord, but by the Holy Ghost" (1 Cor. 12:3). The word is the contents; the Spirit is the life and the power of the revelation of God. Spirit and word, therefore, never dare to be separated.

Thus it is regarding the revelation of Christ unto salvation. Through the Spirit of Christ the word becomes a savor of life unto life. Nor does that word as we have it in the Scriptures become a savor of death unto death by itself. Also this power is of the Spirit. For it is the Spirit that convicts the world of sin and of righteousness and of judgment. Of sin, because they believe not on him. Thus Christ is and remains the sovereign Lord also in respect to his own word. He reveals the Father unto whomsoever he will. And whom he will he hardens. No flesh dare glory in the presence of Jesus Christ who is the Lord.

The preacher must understand this. And what is more, he must be willing to submit his own ministry to the sovereign will and purpose of the Lord, who is the Lord of his own word, whether it be unto salvation or unto damnation. Never may he act or leave the impression that he has power over the word of Christ, that by force of argument or by the power of persuasion he can make the word he speaks, even though it be according to the Scriptures, either a savor of life unto life or a savor of death unto death. He preaches the word. He preaches the same gospel to all. But whether the effect will be unto salvation or condemnation depends not at all on him, but on Christ himself, who makes his word powerful through his Spirit.

This promise of the Holy Spirit, as we understand, was realized on the day of Pentecost. As the apostle Peter proclaims on that day: "Therefore being by the right hand of God exalted, and having received of the Father the promise of the Holy Ghost, he hath shed forth this, which ye now see and hear" (Acts 2:33). And through that outpouring of the Holy Spirit on the day of Pentecost, let us understand, the church was delivered from the bondage of the law and was set in perfect liberty. Jerusalem is now above. She is the mother of us all. And she is free. Not only is there no longer any external law of precepts, prescribing to us just how and when to worship, and enjoining us to keep days and months, to pay tithes and to bring sacrifices. But the church is no longer inseparably bound to any institution, nor dependent on anyone except Christ himself to exercise her religious life.

It is true, also in the new dispensation after the Spirit was poured out, the Lord has instituted his church. And for the upbuilding of the saints he gave unto her apostles, prophets, evangelists, ministers, elders, and deacons. But although these are given to the church for the edifying of the body of Christ, this does not mean that believers are now wholly dependent upon an institution of men for the knowledge of the Lord and for the proper functioning of their spiritual life. They are free; all have the Spirit. All have the unction of the Holy One. And they need not that anyone teach them. And they no longer teach every man his neighbor and every man his brother, saying, "Know the Lord" (Jer. 31:34). For all know him, from the least to the greatest. And if a certain institution of the church in the world would become deformed, wicked men are in high places, the truth is corrupted, and the holy things of God's covenant are profaned, the church, the true spiritual remnant, is in a position to exercise the office of believers, separate themselves from that false church, and institute the true church anew. From the state of bondage under the law the church has passed on into the state of freedom. For she has not received the Spirit of bondage again to fear, but the Spirit of adoption, whereby she cries, "Abba, Father."

This, then, is the meaning of the distinction between the Spirit of God as such, and the Spirit of Christ. This is the meaning of Pentecost. That the Spirit of God has become the Spirit of Christ, of the exalted Lord, and that through this Spirit Christ himself came to dwell in his church, to make her partaker of all the blessings of salvation he purchased for her by his perfect obedience even unto death, that is the glorious significance of the day of Pentecost. And through that Spirit the everlasting covenantal communion of God with his people is realized: "I in them, and thou in me, that they may be made perfect in one" (John 17:23).

Article 9

I believe an holy catholic church;
the communion of saints

Chapter 33

THE CHURCH:
THE BODY OF CHRIST

"I believe an holy catholic church." This is the ninth article of the apostolic confession.

Notice that the church is here presented as an object of faith. We believe an holy catholic church. We do not believe *in* the church. We believe *in* God the Father, Almighty, Maker of heaven and earth. We believe *in* Jesus Christ, his only begotten Son. We believe *in* the Holy Ghost. But we do not believe *in* the church. Hence, the confession merely has it: "I believe an holy catholic church." And this means: I believe that there is such a church which is both holy and catholic.

The nature, the attributes, and the calling of the church are not to be determined empirically, by that which we observe of the church as she historically exists in the world. They are not to be determined philosophically, in the way of human contemplation, but only from God's own revelation in the Scriptures. The church is not a human institution. Men do not bring her into existence. God alone determines her being, nature, purpose, and calling, even as he alone gathers and preserves her. And therefore, it is from the word of God alone that we can derive our knowledge concerning the church. And whatever men may postulate about her nature and calling that is contrary to the word of God must be rejected. Only on the basis of Scripture can one say: "I believe an holy catholic church."

This truth becomes immediately apparent as soon as we compare the contents of the faith of the church and of the individual believer as expressed in the ninth article of the apostolic confession with the actually existing church in the world. Thus, for instance, according to the confession, the church is catholic. This, of course, we understand, does not refer to the Romish church in distinction from the

Protestant church, but designates the true church, as she exists in the whole world, and is one in faith.

It is evident that this confession cannot possibly rest on experience. For where does this unity and catholicity reveal itself in the world? Hopelessly the church appears to be a house divided against itself. There seem to be many Christs, many faiths, many baptisms, many hopes of our calling. The church is not one and catholic, but split up into many denominations and sects, all clamoring to be the true church. Nevertheless, in spite of the division manifest in what is called the church on earth, the believer maintains that the church is one and universal, agreeing in true faith. For "there is one body, and one Spirit, even as ye are called in one hope of your calling; one Lord, one faith, one baptism, one God and Father of all, who is above all, and through all, and in you all" (Eph. 4:4–6). The faith of the church concerning itself is based on the word of God.

We also confess that we believe an *holy* catholic church. But in the world the church never appears as a holy communion. Fact is that she is polluted with sin, and that frequently in her historical manifestation she appears more corrupt than the world out of which she is called. Strife and dissension, hatred and envy, bloody persecution, the killing of the prophets, lust for power and filthy lucre, these and many other corruptions mar her appearance. Nevertheless, on the basis of the word of God, not on the basis of experience, the church confesses that she believes an holy catholic church. For according to Scripture, the church is a communion of saints, "a chosen generation, a royal priesthood, an holy nation, a peculiar people," in order that she should show forth the praises of him who hath called her out of darkness into his marvellous light (1 Pet. 2:9).

What, then, in the light of Scripture, is the church? The Bible describes the church in various terms and by means of different figures. But they all refer to the church as one organic whole, the people of God in Christ, redeemed and called out of the world, living in fellowship with the triune God through Christ in the Spirit, and reflecting the glory of the grace of God in Christ Jesus our Lord.

This is already implied in the well-known figure which the Bible uses, that of the body of Christ, which perhaps more than any other term offers us a rather concise and comprehensive denotation of the idea of the church. She is the spiritual body of Christ, that is, the body of which Christ is the head, and believers are members. For God has revealed his exceeding great power in that he raised Christ from the dead, set him at his own right hand in heavenly places, and "put all things under his feet, and gave him to be the head over all things to the church, which is his body, the fulness of him that filleth all in all" (Eph. 1:22–23).

The same is expressed in that marvelous and profound passage of Colossians (1:15–20). There Christ is described as the "firstborn of every creature" (v. 15), and that too, as the first begotten of the dead, by whom and unto whom all things are created, "and he is the head of the body, the church: who is the beginning, the firstborn from the dead; that in all things he might have the preeminence" (v. 18). And lastly, in 1 Corinthians 12:12–13 the apostle Paul writes: "For as the body is one, and hath many members, and all the members of that one body, being many, are one body: so also is Christ. For by one Spirit are we all baptized into one body, whether we be Jews or Gentiles, whether we be bond or free; and have been all made to drink into one Spirit." The church, therefore, according to Scripture, is the body of Christ.

It is entirely in harmony with this idea that the Bible uses similar figures to describe the idea of the church. She is compared by our Lord to the vine and its branches. Christ is the vine; believers are the branches. And even as the branches live out of the vine, so believers have their life in Christ. And only when they abide in him can they bear fruit (John 15:1–5). In the well-known eleventh chapter of the epistle to the Romans, the church of all ages is compared to an olive tree, on which branches are grafted in that represent the elect from Jews and Gentiles.

From a slightly different viewpoint the church is presented as the temple of God, or, as the city of God, the new Jerusalem, or Mount Zion (1 Cor. 3:16–17; 2 Cor. 6:16–18: Eph. 2:19–22; Heb. 12:22–23). From the above cited passages, to which many more might be added, may be deduced with regard to the idea of the church, first of all, that she is not a mere crowd, but a harmonious whole, a unity dominated by and expressing one idea: the glory of God in Christ. Secondly, they teach that the church is not a society, that comes into existence by men banding together to realize a common purpose, but a living, spiritual organism, developing from and dominated by a common principle of life, the life of Christ. In the third place, these passages of Holy Writ teach us that the nature and scope of the church are not at all determined by the will of her members, but only by the will of God in Christ her head.

We must constantly bear in mind that we are not discussing the church as she appears on earth, but as she is revealed in Scripture, as an object of our faith. Even though the church is in the world, and becomes manifest on earth as the gathering of believers and their children through the institute and through the confession and walk of the believers, yet the church is a spiritual organism, and is as such essentially invisible. We cannot see the church. Moreover, on earth we never see more than the manifestation of a very small part of the church, as she is being gathered throughout the ages from generation to generation. Ideally, however, the church is the body of Christ as she exists eternally in the counsel of God, and of which all the elect are members, those that have already gone into glory, those that are still in the world, and those that must as yet be gathered from future generations. The whole church, as once she shall be presented to the Father without "spot or wrinkle" (Eph. 2:25), to dwell in the tabernacle of God forever, is the object of our faith.

That church, then, is a perfect unity, a harmonious whole, consisting of a definite number of parts or members, each of which occupies its own place and serves its own purpose in that whole. The church is not a mere crowd of redeemed people, consisting of an arbitrary number of individuals, to which one may add as many as you like and the result remains the same, you still have a pile of one thousand bricks. You may remove one-third or one-half, or you may add as many as you like: and the result remains the same, you still have a pile of bricks. But this is not the case with a temple or any other edifice. A temple is not a pile of building material, wood and steel, brick and mortar, but is a well-ordered, beautiful, harmonious whole, representing one dominating idea, and serving a common purpose.

The same is true of the members of a body. The human body is not an arbitrary number of members, but a complete and perfect unity, a well-organized whole; and every member derives its significance from the fact that it occupies its own place in the whole, and serves its own purpose in the body. This is also true with respect to the church of God. It is a spiritual temple, the dwelling place of God with men. It is a well-organized body, the body of which Christ is the head and all the elect are members. It does therefore not consist of an arbitrary number of individual believers without any connection or organization; but it is a well-organized, harmonious whole.

The number of individual members that must constitute this whole is no more determined by the members themselves or by the will of men than the number of stones that constitute the masonry of a beautiful temple is determined by the stones or by the will of the dealer in building material. The whole and its parts, as well as the place of each part and the purpose each part must serve in the spiritual temple which is the church of Christ, are determined by the Architect before the world was. And the purpose of this harmonious whole is that it may be a dwelling place of the living God, in which God through Christ and in the Spirit exercises fellowship, the fellowship of friendship with his people. They taste that the Lord is good, and reflect his glorious grace, showing forth the virtues of him that called them out of darkness into his marvelous light.

This is the implication of the words of our Lord in John 6:37, "All that the Father giveth me shall come to me; and him that cometh to me I will in no wise cast out."

However, the church is not a mechanical, but an organic unity. It is a spiritual organism. The difference between a mechanism and an organism is that, while both are constituted of parts through which the whole functions, the former is assembled from a previously prepared number of parts, but the latter grows from a common principle of life. Thus, for instance, a watch is a mechanism; a tree, however, is an organism.

The church is the spiritual body of Christ. It is the olive tree of which Christ is the root. Believers are branches of the vine, which is Christ; members of his body, of his flesh and of his bone (Rom. 11;

John 15:1–5; Eph. 5:30). The saints, therefore, must grow up in him in all things, which is the head, even Christ (Eph. 4:15). And from Christ "the whole body fitly joined together and compacted by that which every joint supplieth, according to the effectual working in the measure of every part, maketh increase of the body unto the edifying of itself in love" (v. 16). Christ is first. He is the head. In him is all the life of the whole body, of every one of its members.

Even though it is true that the church is gathered out of the whole world, and though its gathering through the preaching of the gospel calls individual men into the fellowship of the church, the fact is that this is accomplished only through Christ's entering by his Spirit and word into the hearts of those that are given him by the Father. From him, from Christ as the head of the body, the members receive their life. And in virtue of his abiding in them they continue to live. Even as the branches live in and out of the vine, so believers live only in fellowship with Christ. His mind is their mind; his will is their will; his resurrection-life is their life; his glory is their glory. Apart from him they are nothing and they can do nothing. By him their existence as members of the church is determined as truly as Adam's existence was determined by God's act of creation.

Thus the whole church, in all its parts and through all its organs, is adapted to serve its purpose. That purpose is indicated in Scripture by such terms as the temple of God, the city of God, the people of God, a royal priesthood, a kingdom of priests. They express that the church is designed to be the dwelling place of the living God and that she must serve the purpose of reflecting the glory of God's grace in Christ. The church is the reflection of God's own covenantal life of friendship. With her the triune God establishes his most intimate fellowship, that she may know him, taste that he is good, be consecrated to him in holy service, walk in the light, and show forth the praises of him that called her out of darkness into his marvelous light.

Let me remind you once more that I am speaking of the church not as she actually exists in the world, but as an object of faith, based upon the revelation of the word of God. As such the church now exists and eternally exists in the divine conception and counsel. But that same church shall once be revealed and presented to the Father without spot or wrinkle, when the new Jerusalem shall come down from heaven. Outside of that church there is not salvation. Of that church you must be, and must forever remain, a living member in order to be saved. And always, in every generation, that church is also in the world. Hence, if you are of Christ, you will love that church, join her, seek her wellbeing, diligently attend her gatherings, worship with her, confess the Christ in fellowship with her, suffer with her in the world, and with her hope for the final manifestation of that body of Christ in eternal perfection and glory.

Chapter 34

THE CHURCH CHOSEN TO EVERLASTING LIFE

In our former sermon we mentioned repeatedly that the members of the church as to their number are not determined by the will of man, but by the sovereign determination of God. It is God alone who determines the number of those that are gathered out of the old organism of the human race into the new organism of the church of Christ, as well as the individuals that are privileged to belong to this number.

This is the heart of the doctrine of Calvinism, over against Arminianism. This touches the heart of the difference between the Reformed conception of the church and the view of those who make the work of salvation and the number of those that are to be gathered into the church of Christ dependent upon the will of man.

Arminianism, no matter what form it may assume, is essentially humanistic. It teaches that the idea and the scope of the church, the number of its members and the individuals that enter into the fellowship of the body of Christ, are determined by the will of man. God is dependent in his choice on the choice of man. For the Arminian does indeed speak of divine election, but to him it means that God chose those that he foresaw as believers and faithful in Christ. God saves those that are willing to be saved. He rejects those that reject Christ.

Arminianism is man-centered. Man's freedom must be maintained, and that too, at the expense of God's sovereignty. His salvation, rather than the glory of God, is the purpose of all things, the important thing that matters. Hence, according to Arminianism the church is a mere multitude of individuals called into existence by the efforts and will of man. Those that become members of the church cannot be conceived as component parts of a pre-conceived, predetermined, and well-planned whole. For it is the will of individual men that determines the scope and the number of the members of the church.

When not the architect, but the dealer in building materials, determines how much and what kind of building material shall go into a structure, the result can hardly be a harmonious whole. According to the Arminian conception, the matter is even worse with respect to the house of God. For it is the building material itself that determines its idea and size. Hence, the church on earth is really a society for the salvation of as great a number of men as possible—possible, that is, through the efforts of men.

Radically different from this Arminian view is the truly Reformed conception of the church and of salvation.

I say, the *truly* Reformed conception: for there are, and always have been, many so-called Reformed preachers that camouflage this truth, between whose preaching and that of the Arminians one can detect no difference whatsoever. There are those who teach and preach that the gospel is a well-meaning offer of salvation, well-meaning on the part of God to all men. And there are those who proclaim from the pulpit that God promises salvation to all on condition of faith. There are those who preach that instead of God's sovereign act of regeneration, it is our act of conversion that is condition to enter into the kingdom of God. But by thus teaching and preaching they corrupt the Reformed truth in the name of Calvinism.

Hence, I speak of the truly Reformed conception. That conception revolves around the proper conception of God as revealed in the holy Scriptures. The purpose of all things, also the calling of the church, is the glory of God in his self-revelation. It is, moreover, organic, so that the whole is not determined by the individual members, but the latter are determined by the former. The whole church very really exists, the idea of the church is there, before she is gathered out of the whole human race.

She is, namely, in the mind and will of God. She is in his eternal counsel. With God the church is eternally. He has engrafted her in both the palms of his hands. Her "walls are continually before" him (Isa. 49:16). "For whom he did foreknow, he also did predestinate to be conformed to the image of his Son, that he might be the firstborn among many brethren. Moreover whom he did predestinate, them he also called: and whom he called, them he also justified: and whom he justified, them he also glorified" (Rom. 8:29–30). The whole of the redeemed, sanctified, and glorified church is with God eternally. He determined the idea of the church, the purpose and scope of the church.

And he alone determines who shall enter into the church, into the blessed fellowship of his covenant. And he also determined with equal freedom and sovereignty who shall not enter into the fellowship of Christ, but perish in the way of sin and death. And this eternal determination he also executes in time. Those whom he gave to Christ in his sovereign counsel he also draws to him in time: "All that the Father giveth me shall come to me; and him that cometh to me I will in no wise cast out" (John 6:37).

It is this truth which our fathers in the seventeenth century maintained over against the Arminians and expressed in the well-known Canons of Dordrecht. In these Canons we read, for instance:

> That some receive the gift of faith from God, and others do not receive it, proceeds from God's eternal decree. 'For known unto God are all his works from the beginning of the world' (Acts xv. 18; Eph. i. 11). According to which decree he graciously softens the hearts of the elect, however obstinate, and inclines them to believe; while he leaves the non-elect in his just judgment to their own wickedness and obduracy. And herein is especially displayed the profound, the merciful, and at the same time the righteous discrimination between men, equally involved in ruin; or that decree of *election* and *reprobation*, revealed in the Word of God, which, though men of perverse, impure, and unstable minds wrest it to their own destruction, yet to holy and pious souls affords unspeakable consolation.[1]

And again, in the same Canons:

> Election is the unchangeable purpose of God, whereby, before the foundation of the world, he hath, out of mere grace, according to

---

1   Canons of Dordt 1.6, in Schaff, *Creeds of Christendom*, 3:582.

the sovereign good pleasure of his own will, chosen, from the whole human race, which had fallen through their own fault, from their primitive state of rectitude, into sin and destruction, a certain number of persons to redemption in Christ, whom he from eternity appointed the Mediator and head of the elect, and the foundation of salvation.[2]

The same truth is expressed in other symbols of Reformed persuasion.

This truth is always called *the heart of the church.* And the doctrine of sovereign predestination is so thoroughly the current teaching of Scripture and so intimately related to the whole system of truth that the denial of it distorts the whole and every part of it.

In a brief sermon like this, I naturally have no time to quote Scripture at length in proof of this truth. A few passages must suffice.

In the first place, I may refer you to chapters 9 to 11 of the epistle to the Romans, which throughout refer to Israel of the old dispensation, as well as to the church of the new dispensation. Even in the nation of Israel, according to this chapter, God's sovereign predestination made distinction between the carnal and the spiritual seed. Always it was only the remnant according to the election of grace that were saved. They are not all Israel which are called Israel (Rom. 9:6). Not "the children of the flesh…but the children of the promise are counted for the seed," according to the apostle (v. 8).

And what determined whether, among the people of Israel, some were carnal, others were spiritual children? Only God's sovereign predestination. For

10. When Rebecca also had conceived by one, even by our father Isaac;

11. (For the children being not yet born, neither having done any good or evil, that the purpose of God according to election might stand, not of works, but of him that calleth;)

12. It was said unto her, The elder shall serve the younger.

13. As it is written, Jacob have I loved, but Esau have I hated. (Rom. 9:10–13)

---

2 Canons of Dordt 1.7, in Schaff, *Creeds of Christendom*, 3:582.

God is and remains free and sovereign, not only to bestow his mercy and compassion on whomsoever he will; but he is equally the sovereign Lord in regard to reprobation. "For the scripture saith unto Pharaoh, Even for this same purpose have I raised thee up, that I might show my power in thee, and that my name might be declared throughout all the earth" (Rom. 9:17). More clearly and forcefully no mere human philosophy of predestination could possibly express it. Pharaoh in all his pride and rebellion against the Lord may not for a moment imagine that he is sovereign, and that even his opposition to the word of God and his refusal to let Israel go can possibly thwart God's purpose. On the contrary, in his vain rebellion he serves God's purpose. That purpose is that through Pharaoh's perversion and obduracy God might show his power and his name might be declared throughout all the earth. The apostle concludes this section: "Therefore hath he mercy on whom he will have mercy, and whom he will he hardeneth" (v. 18).

Consider also the remarkable words of our Savior in Matthew 11:25–27,

25. At that time Jesus answered and said, I thank thee, O Father, Lord of heaven and earth, because thou hast hid these things from the wise and prudent, and hast revealed them unto babes.
26. Even so, Father: for so it seemed good in thy sight.
27. All things are delivered unto me of my Father: and no man knoweth the Son, but the Father; neither knoweth any man the Father, save the Son, and he to whomsoever the Son will reveal him.

The Savior had been laboring in Galilee. He had preached the gospel of the kingdom of heaven, and had performed many wonderful works. And as he now surveys the field of his labors, and takes inventory of the fruit upon his work, he recognizes a twofold effect of his preaching: there were those that received the gospel and were impatient to enter the kingdom of heaven, and there were others who never entered in, no matter who preached and in what form the gospel of the kingdom was delivered unto them.

In this twofold result of his labors the Lord recognizes a word of his Father to him. And he replies in his thanksgiving to this word of the Father. While he preached and labored, there had been a twofold operation of God's power: a revealing and saving operation, but also a hiding and hardening operation of the Father. And for this the Savior gives thanks. And in this fruit upon his labors, this twofold fruit, the Lord traces the good pleasure of the Father, the sovereign dispensation of him who is the Lord of heaven and earth. For he says: "Even so, Father: for so it seemed good in thy sight." Ultimately it is the good pleasure of the Father that determines who shall enter into the kingdom of heaven.

Consider too John 6:37, which I already quoted: "All that the Father giveth me shall come to me; and him that cometh to me I will in no wise cast out." In the preceding verse the Lord had said to those that did not believe on him: "Ye also have seen me, and believe not" (v. 36). However, although they all leave him, their unbelief cannot have any effect upon the final fruit of his labors. For all that the Father gives him shall surely come, and will surely be received by him. The church in God's election is one whole, a completeness, a body. Not one of its members may be lost. Hence the Lord says "all that," not "all those" the Father giveth me. And the gathering of every last one of this whole depends not on the will of man, but on the good pleasure of the Father, who gives his own to Christ.

I have no more time to quote other passages of Holy Writ. I may refer you to passages like John 10:26–30, where the Lord speaks of his sheep, which the Father gave him and which no one can ever pluck out of his or out of the Father's hand. I also refer you to 1 Peter 2:8–9, which speaks on the one hand, of those who were appointed by God to stumble at the stone, and on the other hand of "a chosen generation, a royal priesthood, an holy nation, a peculiar people, that…should show forth the praises of him who has called them out of darkness into his marvellous light." I also may refer you to Ephesians 1:3–4, which teaches us that all the spiritual blessings in heavenly places are bestowed upon believers according as he has chosen them in him before the foundation of the world. But let it be sufficient.

This truth is fundamental, and is the very heart of the whole truth concerning our salvation. Only on the basis of this truth can the truth of vicarious atonement be maintained. Only when the truth of election is maintained can one also believe the plain teaching of Scripture that man is by nature nothing but an enemy of God, incapable of doing any good, incapable of coming to Christ, unless the Father draw him. Only if the truth of election is taught can one also teach that all the blessings of salvation are sovereignly applied by God to all the elect.

And once more, only on the basis of the truth of election can one maintain the truth of the preservation and perseverance of the saints. And only then can we have the true comfort in life and death, and triumphantly shout:

35. Who shall separate us from the love of Christ?...

37. Nay, in all these things we are more than conquerors through him that loved us.

38. For I am persuaded, that neither death, nor life, nor angels, nor principalities, nor powers, nor things present, nor things to come,

39. Nor height, nor depth, nor any other creature, shall be able to separate us from the love of God, which is in Christ Jesus our Lord. (Rom. 8:35, 37–39)

Chapter 35

THE COMMUNION
OF THE SAINTS

The confession concerning the communion of saints is appended to that of the holy catholic church in the same article. This is not surprising, for the two are most intimately related. The church is the communion of saints. And, it stands to reason that actual communion of saints is found only in the church. Yet, although they are intimately related to each other and cannot very well be separated, they can easily be distinguished. For the communion of saints is only one aspect of the holy catholic church, the aspect, namely, of fellowship between the members, and of their mutual relation to one another.

We must remark from the outset that the communion of saints is not established by the saints. It is of the Lord Jesus Christ. It does not spring into existence from the determination and act of the believers to realize a certain fellowship with one another, to create a certain society for mutual advantage and edification. On the contrary, the communion of saints is first, and the experience and exercise of it follows. In the apostolic confession the communion of saints is presented as an object of faith, "I believe...the communion of saints," that is, "I believe that there is such a communion."

That communion may not always be manifest to the earthly eye. It may not always be visible. Many influences in this world may often mar this fellowship. Nevertheless, I believe that the communion of saints is a reality. It exists now, in the gathering of believers and their children in this world. And it will exist and be fully and most gloriously revealed when the whole church shall have been gathered out of the world, and Christ shall present her to the Father without spot or wrinkle in heavenly perfection.

Now what do we mean when we confess, "I believe the communion of saints"?

All true communion requires a basic unity of the whole, but also diversity of the members of that whole. When a large chorus renders Handel's "Messiah," that chorus constitutes a communion of singers. Their unity rests in the fact that they all sing the same oratorio; their multiformity is found in the variety and diversity of many voices. Did they all sing different songs, there would be no bond of unity. Were all the voices identically the same, there would be no communion or fellowship possible.

This basic likeness and unity, as well as this individual difference, also applies to the communion of saints. The saints are one in Christ. There is one Christ, and he is the head of the whole church. That one Lord has received the Spirit. And through that one Spirit he dwells in the whole church, which is his body, and in all its members. And this indwelling Christ is the sole basis and fountain for the unity of the saints. Through that indwelling Lord there is in all believers a communion of nature, the spiritual nature of the Son of God; a communion of life, the life of their risen Lord, spiritual, heavenly life; and a communion of love, the love of God that is shed abroad in the hearts of all the saints, and that reveals itself as love to God in Christ and as love to one another.

Moreover, they have the same faith, the same knowledge of God, the same righteousness, the righteousness of God in Christ. They have the same hope, the hope of the glory of God. They speak fundamentally the same language, so that they know and understand one another. And they unitedly strive for the same purpose, the purpose of the glory of God in Christ Jesus their Lord. In them is the same mind, the mind of Christ; the same will, the will of their Lord. And they all speak the same thing, the word of Christ. This unity of nature, of life, of love, of faith, of hope, and of purpose is the ground of the communion of saints. It is not of themselves, but it is established by Christ through the one Spirit.

Moreover, we must emphasize that the confession speaks of a communion of *saints*. It does not speak of a brotherhood of men. Even though the believer does not deny that there is a certain natural affinity among men, rooted in the fact that God made all mankind of one blood, he denies that this affinity from a spiritual, ethical viewpoint is still a communion or brotherhood. Just as he denies the universal fatherhood of God in the modernistic sense of the term, so he repudiates the universal brotherhood of men in the same sense. For sin entered into the world. And sin is darkness. And in darkness there is no possible fellowship.

But out of that world that lies in darkness God through Christ gathers his church. And in the church he establishes a new communion, the fellowship of God in Christ, according to which we walk in the light and have communion with one another. This communion of saints, therefore, is a purely spiritual communion, which is particular and exclusive. It does not embrace all men. It is incapable of taking up into its fellowship mere men as such. And this is not due to any act or attitude on their part, or to some exclusive constitution which they adopt, or to a proud holier-than-thou attitude. It is simply due to God's election, and to the act of Christ whereby he gathers unto himself all whom the Father gave him out of the world.

The communion of saints, therefore, is a spiritual, ethical fellowship. It is not a communion of select friends, of men that are attracted to one another by common natural characteristics. It transcends all natural traits of character, and unites men of the most diversified and opposite type. Nor is this communion determined by or dependent on a certain likeness in social standing, or commonness in the pursuit of earthly ends. It draws together men of every class and social standing in the world, rich and poor, learned and uneducated, great and small, masters and servants, rulers and subjects. In the communion of saints they are all alike.

Nor is this communion a caste. It overcomes all differences between men, provided they are called out of darkness into the marvelous light of God. Only the fact that Christ is in them, and that by his grace they have been called unto new life, unites them into a common bond. It is the communion of saints. "There is one body, and one Spirit, even as ye are called in one hope of your calling; one Lord, one faith, one baptism, one God and Father of all, who is above all, and through all, and in you all" (Eph. 4:4–6).

However, there is in the body of Christ an endless diversity of individual members. And because of this multiformity of the members, they are interdependent. They supplement one another; they are in need of one another; and they constitute a real communion of saints.

If they were all identically alike, such a communion could not exist. Suppose it were possible that the whole of Christ dwelled individualistically in every saint, and that each one possessed in himself all the riches of Christ and was able to reflect all his fullness in himself alone. Then there would be no fellowship of the saints. Each believer would be sufficient unto himself. But this is not the case. The members of the body of Christ are diverse one from another.

This diversity is caused by more than one factor. There is, first of all, the natural difference in nationality and race and color, in character and temperament, in personality and ability and talents and gifts. It is true that this diversity is not spiritual, but natural. Nevertheless we may certainly assume that this natural distinction is made subservient to the communion of Christ, so that the grace of Christ does not destroy it, but rather uses it for its manifold reflection and glory. How different is David from Asaph, Amos from Isaiah, John from Paul, James from Peter. And also this difference is predestinated by God in his inscrutable wisdom, in order that through it the wonderful grace and knowledge of Christ might be reflected in all its manifold glory.

The same is true in respect to all the saints. The almighty and eternal God without doubt also predestinated the individual character, temperament, ability, capacity, and personality of every one of his chosen saints in such a way that in heavenly glory, when the entire multitude of the redeemed shall sing the praises of him that called them, each may do so in his own way, with his own voice, and together they may constitute one mighty and harmonious chorus, causing the new creation to rebound with its blessed "Hallelujahs."

But there is more.

There is also a diversity of spiritual gifts. Although all partake of the same Christ, and all have the same life and love and faith and hope, yet there is difference in the dispensation of special gifts. There are, of course, gifts of wisdom and knowledge, of instruction and exhortation, of comfort and consolation. And these are not the same in all.

One has one special gift, another has another, as Christ bestows these gifts upon every saint.

Thirdly, there is also diversity in regard to the measure of the gifts of Christ. They may all receive talents; but to the one is given five, to another two talents, to a third one talent. And all these differences are not restricted to the saints on earth only; they are also carried over into eternity. Also in the new creation the millions upon millions of saints will all have their distinct individuality. Christ will give them all a new name which no man knows saving he that receives it (Rev. 2:17). In heaven too, therefore, there will be diversity of spiritual gifts and of positions. The servant whose pound had gained ten pounds was put in authority over ten cities; and he that had gained five pounds was given authority over five cities. And shall not the apostles sit on thrones, judging the twelve tribes of Israel?

This indeed is the true nature of the communion of saints. That this is so, is plainly taught in Holy Writ. In Ephesians 4, after the apostle had written of the unity of the Spirit he adds: "But unto every one of us is given grace according to the measure of the gift of Christ" (v. 7). And a most beautiful description of this communion of the saints, both from the viewpoint of its unity and of its diversity, is given in the twelfth chapter of 1 Corinthians, where the apostle writes: "Now there are diversities of gifts, but the same Spirit. And there are differences of administrations, but the same Lord. And there are diversities of operations, but it is the same God which worketh all in all" (vv. 4–6). And then the apostle continues to show how different gifts are bestowed upon different saints, and he uses the illustration of a human body with its many members. And he shows that although the body is one, nevertheless its many members all have their own function in the body (1 Cor. 12:4–27).

This truth of the communion of saints is, of course, of the most important practical significance.

First of all, it stands to reason that the saint who lives from the faith and in the consciousness of this communion will feel himself irresistibly drawn to the assemblies of the people of God, and diligently attend them. This is true chiefly with respect to public worship, the gathering of the saints for the purpose of the ministry of the word and of the sacraments and of united prayer and praise. For more than one reason it is a sad sign when professed Christians leave their pews empty when the church is assembled for worship, and when they rather stay home or seek their pleasure elsewhere than to go up to the house of the Lord. It certainly reveals a most miserable lack of appreciation for the fellowship of the saints. But it also must be applied to all other gatherings of the saints as such, to those especially that are organized for mutual edification in the knowledge of Christ. Especially in view of the fact that the believer must needs live a large part of his life in the world, in which he is a stranger, he longs for the gatherings of the people of God and seeks them diligently.

Secondly, the believer, living in the consciousness of the communion of saints, will be deeply imbued with a sense of his own individual helplessness and insignificance, and understand that he can have significance only in the fellowship of the body of Christ. Even as in a human body all the members are interdependent and no member has any power or meaning by itself, in separation from the body, so each individual believer can have significance only in connection with and in dependence upon all other members. No member occupies an independent place. No matter how richly he may be endowed with spiritual gifts and talents, though he be a theological giant, a most brilliant preacher, the greatest reformer, still he does not stand and labor alone; but he can function only as a member of the body of Christ. In the grand oratorio that is sung by the church, the glory of God in Christ, there are no soloists.

The believer who lives from the faith of the communion of saints is no separatist or schismatic: "If the foot shalt say, Because I am not the hand, I am not of the body; is it therefore not of the body? And if the ear shall say, Because I am not the eye, I am not of the body; is it therefore not of the body?" (1 Cor. 12:15–16). Nor will the believer exalt himself above the other members, but he will heed the exhortation of the apostle Paul: "Let nothing be done through strife or vainglory; but in lowliness of mind let each esteem other better than themselves. Look not every man on his own things, but every man also on the things of others" (Phil. 2:3–4).

Finally, in the consciousness of the communion of saints all seek to know and to occupy their own place in the whole, to employ their Christ-given gifts of grace for the well-being of the whole and for the salvation and edification of all the other members. The church has but one purpose, the glory of God in Christ. To reflect that glory in word and walk is the communal purpose of the saints. They are of one mind to realize this calling. And in the realization of this calling is implied the salvation and spiritual edification and growth of the members. For if one member suffers, the whole body suffers.

Hence, no believer lives unto himself. Conscious of the fact that he has nothing that he has not received, he lives in humility before the face of God, not seeking his own glory. Yet, again, in a deep sense of his obligation to employ all his gifts to the realization of the high calling wherewith he is called, he will not hide them or bury them in a napkin, but be diligent in the service of his God. And again, knowing that he is not the body, but only one of its members, he will earnestly seek to know and to occupy his own place in the body, in order that in that position he may function to the glory of Christ and to the salvation of his fellow members.

What a glorious confession this is! I believe the communion of saints. How necessary it is clearly to understand this confession and by the grace of God to bring it into practice.

In the exercise of the communion of saints the church will flourish, the believers will be edified, the saints will rejoice, and God will be glorified.

In the communion of saints God will command his blessing.

Article 10

The forgiveness of sins

Chapter 36

THE FORGIVENESS
OF SINS

The church, and that too, in the communion of saints, and in that communion only, sings:

> How blest is he whose trespass
> Hath freely been forgiv'n,
> Whose sin is wholly covered
> Before the sight of heav'n.
> Blest he to whom Jehovah
> Imputeth not his sin,
> Who hath a guileless spirit,
> Whose heart is true within.[1]

However, we must never forget that only he who has become conscious of his sin and confesses his sin before the face of God can live in the consciousness of this blessedness whereof the psalm speaks. That is why the psalmist continues in the second stanza:

> While I kept guilty silence
> My strength was spent with grief,
> Thy hand was heavy on me,
> My soul found no relief;
> But when I owned my trespass,
> My sin hid not from Thee,
> When I confessed transgression,
> Then Thou forgavest me.[2]

---

1   No. 83:1, in *The Psalter*.
2   No. 83:2, in *The Psalter*.

This truth is confessed in the tenth article of the apostolic confession: "I believe...the forgiveness of sins." This article about the forgiveness of sins is part of the series that belongs to the third part of the apostolic confession, the part that speaks of the Holy Ghost. And let us note too that the article concerning the forgiveness of sins stands between that about the church and the communion of saints, on the one hand, and that which speaks about the resurrection of the dead, on the other. This means that of all the spiritual blessings that are in this life bestowed upon the believers by the Spirit of Christ, only the forgiveness of sins is mentioned in the apostolic confession. It is singled out.

We understand, of course, that this is not the only spiritual benefit that the saints have in Christ in this life. We might easily enlarge upon this part of the confession by adding, for instance: "I believe the new birth; I believe the efficacious calling; I believe the gift of faith; I believe eternal righteousness, sanctification, and preservation unto the end." All these gifts, and many other riches of grace, are bestowed upon the church in the world. But of all these blessings of grace the apostolic confession simply mentions the forgiveness of sin. Evidently it proceeds from the truth that this one blessing is fundamental, and of basic importance. The forgiveness of sins occupies a central place in the confession.

This presupposes that we are still in the body of this death. And as long as we are still in this world and in our sinful and carnal flesh, our sins rise up against us, prevailing day by day, unless something is done about them and they are taken away. The meaning is not that we sinned in the past, that we were delivered from the power of sin perfectly and completely, and that now we sin no more. On the contrary, we sinned, we still carry about with us our corrupt nature, and we do sin every day. In that state it is impossible that any blessings of grace and salvation should be bestowed upon us. First our sins must be removed. For if they are not, they form an impassable barrier between God and us.

Moreover, in the consciousness of our sins, the sins we have committed and do commit, and of our defiled and corrupt nature, we could not possibly have confidence to approach God to ask him for his favor. Remember: sin is guilt, worthiness of death and of the wrath of

God. And God is holy and righteous. He can have no fellowship with the sinner in his corruption. Nor can he acquit the guilty.

All this must be clearly understood even now. Only then can we see the basic importance of the forgiveness of sins. It must be clearly understood that we are by nature, in ourselves, in the state of sin and guilt and therefore under wrath and condemnation, and that as long as we are in that state before God, we can neither receive nor expect even the smallest token of his favor. Hence, above all, this state must be changed before we can hope for salvation. It is this fundamental and radical change that is effected by the forgiveness of sins.

Forgiveness of sins means that God does no longer remember our sins against us. In fact, it means that God never remembered our sins against us. No, this does not mean that God forgets that we are sinners. This would be quite impossible, of course. But it does mean that he does not remember our sins in his wrath and just condemnation, that he does not impute them to us. It means that he does not behold us simply as sinners, but as redeemed sinners, that have been perfectly justified, whose sins have been blotted out and that have fully satisfied for all their sins.

I said a moment ago that God *never* remembered our sins against us. You understand that the forgiveness of sins does not presuppose a change in God, as if he formerly remembered our sins against us, but now holds them against us no more, as if he formerly condemned us, but now condemns us no longer. The change is not in God, but in us, when through faith he translates us from the state of condemnation into that of forgiveness. In God it means that there was always forgiveness with him, that he eternally beholds his people, whom he chose in Christ before the foundation of the world, as redeemed sinners, or "whom he did predestinate...them he also justified" (Rom. 8:30). And therefore, "there is...no condemnation," and there never was any condemnation, for "them which are in Christ Jesus" (v. 1). Only when we lay hold upon this marvelous mystery and amazing wonder by faith, we know and have confidence in God as our redeemer, and we appropriate the forgiveness of sins.

We understand, of course, that the forgiveness of sins does not imply that God sets aside his righteousness and justice, and that he acquits the guilty. That would be impossible. On the contrary, the forgiveness of sins is a revelation of that abundant grace and mercy according to which he loaded the guilt of our iniquity on his only begotten Son, our Lord Jesus Christ, and that in him he realized our righteousness.

We must understand, too, that in God this act of forgiveness is eternal. In him this act of mercy and grace whereby he ordained his Son to be the head of the church, so that he might represent them in the hour of judgment and might bear their sins and iniquities and take them away forever, is from everlasting to everlasting. In God's eternal counsel Christ is "the firstborn of every creature," and that too, as the head of his church and as "the firstborn from the dead" (Col. 1:15, 18). And therefore there is, there eternally is, forgiveness with God. And there is no condemnation, and there never was with God condemnation for them that are in Christ Jesus. In Christ "we have redemption through his blood, even the forgiveness of sins" (v. 14).

That eternal mercy, the sovereign good pleasure of God, is the ultimate fountain of all the spiritual blessings we have in Christ. For

3. The God and Father of our Lord Jesus Christ...hath blessed us with all spiritual blessings in heavenly places in Christ:

4. According as he hath chosen us in him before the foundation of the world, that we should be holy and without blame before him in love:

5. Having predestinated us unto the adoption of children by Jesus Christ to himself, according to the good pleasure of his will,

6. To the praise of the glory of his grace, wherein he hath made us accepted in the beloved.

7. In whom we have redemption through his blood, the forgiveness of sins, according to the riches of his grace. (Eph. 1:3–7)

Deny the truth of sovereign, eternal election, and you must deny the truth of the atonement of Christ and of the forgiveness of sins. Deny the truth that the blessing of the forgiveness of sins is eternal in God, and you must also deny that there is remission of sins in time.

In time this act of God's mercy and grace whereby our sins are blotted out, so that they are never remembered and imputed to us, is realized through the death and resurrection of our Lord Jesus Christ. The death of Christ is, as far as its significance and power is concerned, vicarious satisfaction, that is: Christ satisfied the justice of God in respect to our sins in our stead. He might do so because he was from eternity appointed to be the head of his people. And as such he died on the accursed tree, blotting out forever all our iniquities.

The death of Christ, therefore, is the actual blotting out of our sins because it is the perfect satisfaction of God's justice. It is the ground of a perfect and everlasting righteousness because it is the infinitely precious death of the Son of God in the flesh. And the resurrection of Christ is God's own seal upon his atoning work. It is his declaration that by his death sin is blotted out, and perfect righteousness is obtained for all that are in him, a righteousness so perfect and so precious, that those that believe in him have eternal life. This righteousness of Christ God imputes to us. In him, therefore, we are not guilty sinners, but redeemed and righteous. And in him we are deemed worthy of all the blessings of salvation in Christ Jesus our Lord.

Thus it is objectively. That is, thus it is forever in God, as he has revealed himself in Jesus Christ our Lord. And subjectively, as far as our own knowledge and experience of this blessing is concerned, we lay hold upon it only by faith. For faith is an assured knowledge, a spiritual knowledge, of all the blessings of salvation which God has revealed in his word; and at the same time, faith is a perfect trust, an indubitable confidence, that I have the forgiveness of sins and everlasting righteousness and life, which are freely given unto me by God, merely of grace, only for the sake of Christ's merits.

This faith, you understand, is not of ourselves. The natural man has no faith. Faith is wrought in our hearts by the Spirit of Christ. It is a gift of grace. And by that spiritual power of faith we first of all know our sins, are sorry for them before God, confess them in dust and ashes, and do so day by day. Without this spiritual experience of sorrow over sin, one cannot possibly lay hold upon the mercy of forgiveness. And secondly, by that same faith we look upon the cross and resurrection of our Lord Jesus Christ as the only means of our salvation and the ground of our righteousness. Thus, finally, the church comes to write with indubitable certainty in her confession: "I believe the forgiveness of sins." And in the fellowship of the church, and therefore in the communion of saints, the believer lays hold upon this blessing and makes this confession.

This is the connection between the article concerning the church and the communion of saints, on the one hand, and that of the forgiveness of sins, on the other. Outside of the holy catholic church, that is, outside of the communion of saints, there are no spiritual benefits, and the forgiveness of sins cannot be appropriated. If, for some reason, the believer severs himself as far as his conscious life is concerned from that communion, the first effect of this error is always that he lacks the joy of forgiveness. Perhaps for a time he lives in hatred over against some of the brethren, or he evinces an unforgiving spirit, or he seeks the friendship of the world, or he lives in whatever other sin may sever his fellowship with the saints and disturb the exercise of the communion of saints. In that state of separation from the body of believers he forfeits the forgiveness of sins.

This truth is strongly emphasized in Scripture. For this

5. Is the message which we have heard of him, and declare unto you, that God is light, and in him is no darkness at all.
6. If we say that we have fellowship with him, and walk in darkness, we lie, and do not the truth:
7. But if we walk in the light, as he is in the light, we have fellowship one with another, and the blood of Jesus Christ his Son cleanseth us from all sin. (1 John 1:5–7)

This is the reason why the Lord teaches us to pray: "Forgive us our debts, as we forgive our debtors" (Matt. 6:12). The two parts of this petition are inseparably connected. You cannot pray for the one without being able to state the other before the face of God. This is also the teaching of the well-known parable of the unmerciful servant, which the Lord applies in the words: "So likewise shall my heavenly Father do also unto you, if ye from your hearts forgive not every one his brother their trespasses" (Matt. 18:35).

What do we mean when we confess, "I believe the forgiveness of sins"?

"I believe an holy catholic church. I believe the communion of saints. I believe the forgiveness of sins." These three elements of the apostolic confession are inseparably related to one another. Nor is it difficult to understand why this relation between our living in the communion of saints and in the joy of forgiveness exists and is so inseparable that the one cannot be enjoyed without the other.

Remember: it is never in our power to lay hold on the forgiveness of sins. That we are sorry for sin, repent, seek forgiveness, and obtain it, is the work of Christ himself. By his Spirit and grace he works the true sorrow after God in our hearts. By that Spirit he brings us to repentance, leads us to the cross, and assures us of redemption, even the forgiveness of sins, in his blood. But that Spirit, on whose constant indwelling and operation our appropriation of the forgiveness of sins continuously depends, is the Spirit of Christ, and therefore the Spirit of the body, that is, the church. For there is one Lord and one Spirit. And that one Spirit dwells in the one body. He does not dwell in you or in me individually apart from the body, but in the body as a whole and in the individual believers only in fellowship with the body. Hence, outside of that body the Spirit does not operate to bestow the blessings of salvation upon men. If, therefore, through some sin the believer separates himself as far as his consciousness is concerned from the body, and does not live in the communion of saints, he immediately forfeits the forgiveness of sins.

And as he loses the forgiveness of sins, he necessarily forfeits all the blessings and joy of salvation. For the remission of sin, as we have seen, is basic for all other benefits in Christ.

Hence, if we would enjoy the blessing of the forgiveness of sins, we must surely repent daily in dust and ashes, and must surely lay hold by faith upon the atoning blood and upon the resurrection of our Lord Jesus Christ from the dead. But we must also keep the unity of the Spirit in the bond of peace.

Article 11

The resurrection
of the body

Chapter 37

THE RESURRECTION
OF THE BODY

"I believe the resurrection of the body."

This is the eleventh article of the apostolic confession. In 1 Corinthians 15:35 we read: "But some man will say, How are the dead raised up? and with what body do they come?" To this the apostle answers: "Thou fool, that which thou sowest is not quickened, except it die" (v. 36).

This implies, in the first place, that essentially the same body that is buried will be raised up again. The resurrection body is no new creation. This is evident from the resurrection body of our Lord Jesus Christ. That in his case no new body was created is evident from the empty grave, as well as from the fact that he could show to his disciples the marks of his suffering in hands and feet and in his side. Although his body was completely changed and glorified, it was nevertheless essentially the very same body in which he had walked among us in the days of his flesh and in which he had been crucified and buried.

This is also the teaching of Scripture in 1 Corinthians 15:42–44, "So also is the resurrection of the dead. It is sown in corruption; it is raised in incorruption: it is sown in dishonour; it is raised in glory: it is sown in weakness; it is raised in power: it is sown a natural body; it is raised a spiritual body. There is a natural body, and there is a spiritual body." The identity of the body that is buried and the body that is raised is plainly taught in this passage. The same body that is sown is also raised. The very figure of the sowing is based on the same notion. When one sows wheat, he expects to harvest wheat, not oats or rye. And therefore we may say, in the first place, that essentially the resurrection body is the same as the body that was buried.

This, of course, is a profound mystery. It lies beyond, exactly beyond, the scope of our comprehension. It belongs to those things which "eye hath not seen, nor ear heard, neither have entered into the heart of man" (1 Cor. 2:9). When we consider what becomes of our bodies in physical death, how completely they are disintegrated, dissolved into their very elements, how literally they return unto the dust whence they are taken, even so that their substances become part of other bodies; if we contemplate how many bodies of the believers were never even buried, were drowned in the depth of the sea, cut to pieces, or burned at the stake and their ashes blown to the four winds of heaven, the resurrection becomes utterly inconceivable to us. It would seem easier, perhaps, to think of a new creation. Yet God will bring again all those bodies and unite them with their proper souls. He is the one that calls the things that are not as if they were, and that quickens the dead. He is God, and becomes known as God exactly in performing wondrous things. Always his way is in the sea; and the things that are impossible with man are possible with God.

The question therefore arises: what belongs to the very essence of our bodies? For it is only in essence, certainly not in form, that the resurrection body is like unto our present body.

We may call attention especially to three elements.

First of all, it belongs to the essence of a body, not only of our present body, but also of the resurrection body, that it is material. A spiritual substance is not a body. The resurrection body also will be material. When the apostle in 1 Corinthians 15:44 speaks of a spiritual body, he does not use the word in the sense of "immaterial": for the term there is used in distinction from "natural," or better, "psychical." When, however, we say that also the body of the resurrection is material, we must not be understood as saying that it will be of the same kind of matter as "flesh and blood." We must remember what the apostle teaches us in 1 Corinthians 15:39–41, where he tells us that "all flesh is not the same flesh," and all bodies are not the same bodies. There are heavenly bodies and earthly bodies, and their glory differs one from the other.

What is essentially the same matter may assume different forms. Ice may be melted into water: yet the ice and the water are the same matter. And when the water evaporates, the invisible and intangible vapor is still the same matter as ice. When you sow the seed of a tulip and you finally develop a bulb, the bulb and the seed you originally sowed are essentially the same. Thus the human body will no doubt assume a different form through the wonder of the resurrection. It will not be of "flesh and blood," for that cannot inherit the kingdom of God. Yet it will be a material body, and essentially the same as the body that was interred at death.

Secondly, we may say that the body of the resurrection, like the body we have now, will be a human body. Through the resurrection man will not be changed into a different being. Through all the changes to which he is subject—sin, death, regeneration, the intermediate state in heaven, and the final resurrection—he remains the same man. And this means that he is a rational creature. His nature is such that he is adapted to bear the image of God. This is true of man's spirit, his soul. But to that soul belongs a body that can serve as its instrument, that is capable of reflecting the image of God. Through the body of an animal the human soul could not possibly function. Hence, also the body of the resurrection, that will be reunited to the soul, will be an essentially human body, a body that is capable of serving as an instrument to express and effect the image of God in the new creation.

In the third place, we may no doubt assert that through death and the resurrection the body shall preserve its individuality, that which distinguishes it from all other human bodies. It is the glory of God that he is able to create millions upon millions of variations of the same nature. All men have the same human nature in common, and wherever you meet man you experience no difficulty to recognize him in distinction from other creatures. Yet, among the millions of men there are no two alike. Each has his own individuality. And those individual characteristics that distinguish men from one another belong to the body as well as to the soul. There can be no doubt that to each individual soul belongs its proper body, even so that the soul of the one could not possibly function in the body of another. And as the personal identity and individuality of the soul will be preserved through death and in the glory of our heavenly house, so in the resurrection of the dead the body will appear with its own individual characteristics: each soul will be united with its proper body.

Yet, although it will be essentially the same as our present body, in the resurrection it will nevertheless be radically different in form. This also is taught in 1 Corinthians 15:42–44.

The apostle teaches there that our present bodies are "in corruption" (v. 42). In the sphere of corruption they exist. By this is meant that they are corruptible from within and that they are subject to forces of corruption from without. In our present world, that is, under the curse, there are several forces of corruption that tend to destroy the organism of our body. All kinds of tiny bacterial organisms find their way into our lungs and bloodstream from without, and disintegrate the body. And the latter is subject for them, for the body is corruptible. It cannot successfully resist their destroying power. Even the science of medicine, bent upon discovering these disease germs and upon counteracting their corrupting influence in the body, in last analysis stands helpless over against them. No one can fight death.

The process of corruption has its inception already at birth: in corruption we are born. It continues during the whole of our earthly life, so that dying we die. In many different diseases it reveals itself in various ways. And it is finally completed when the body gives up the struggle against these forces of destruction and is entrusted to the grave.

However, "it is raised in incorruption" (1 Cor. 15:42). The body of the resurrection is subject to these powers of corruption no more. It is immune. It has the victory. Incorruptible it is. Nor is there in the kingdom of God any power of corruption from without. The inheritance reserved in heaven for us is "incorruptible, and undefiled, and that fadeth not away" (1 Pet. 1:4). The body of the resurrection will be made like unto the "glorious body" of Christ (Phil. 3:21). It is beyond the possibility of corruption. Death has no dominion over it.

Further, the apostle states that the body is sown in weakness. This really expresses that same idea, but from a slightly different point of view. It means that our bodies have but limited strength, and that they must succumb to death even apart from the forces of corruption that violently destroy them. The measure of that strength is "threescore years and ten," or "fourscore years" (Ps. 90:10). "As for man, his days are as grass: as a flower of the field, so he flourisheth" (103:15). For a while the flower blooms. But its vitality is limited. Soon it loses its beauty, and it withers away. Thus it is with man in his present state. The strength of his physical organism is limited, and there is nothing to renew it. He is like a candle that burns itself out. For a while he may appear in youthful strength, but soon he begins to bend under the burden of years, and he inclines toward the grave. Our earthly house collapses over our head. For "it is sown in weakness" (1 Cor. 15:43).

However, "it is raised in power" (v. 43). The body of the resurrection shall never be wanting in strength. It draws from a source of unlimited power and vitality. It will not gradually deteriorate. It shall renew its youth like the eagles. Always there will be strength for the task. In the resurrection no one will ever say that he is weary or exhausted. The source of this ever-renewed strength is the risen Lord. With him the risen saints are united. From him who is the Son of God they draw their power. In everlasting youth they shall stand in the house of God, to serve him day and night.

Then too, the apostle tells us that the body "is sown in dishonor" (v. 43). The present body is without its original glory and beauty. No longer is it an instrument for the reflection of the image of God. Sin and death, corruption and disease, have left their marks on its appearance. As an instrument of unrighteousness, it is in dishonor. It is fundamentally ugly. The truth of this becomes more and more apparent as old age approaches. By many artificial means men and women attempt to give their bodies a superficial beauty. And even the repulsiveness of the dead body in the coffin is covered to an extent by the undertaker's art. But all these attempts are vain. We know, and by all these superficial attempts to beautify the body we confess, that it is sown in dishonor.

However, through the wonder of the resurrection it will attain to glory. All the effects of sin and death will be erased from its appearance, and it will be clothed with perfection of beauty that is far greater than the glory it enjoyed even in the state of original righteousness in paradise. For it will be made like unto the most glorious body of our Lord Jesus Christ. The image of the heavenly it will effect as an everlasting instrument of righteousness and holiness. It will serve the manifestation of the likeness of the Son of God. It is "raised in glory" (v. 43).

But the apostle mentions still another difference between our present body and that of the resurrection. For he writes: "It is sown a natural body; it is raised a spiritual body. There is a natural body, and there is a spiritual body" (v. 44).

We said before that the phrase "spiritual body" must not be interpreted as standing in opposition to "material body." In the text it stands over against "natural." And the literal rendering of the word that is translated "natural" in the text is "psychical." Our present body is psychical. By this we understand that it is adapted to serve as the instrument of our present earthly soul. It is a "soul" body. For "the LORD God formed man out of the dust of the ground, and breathed into his nostrils the breath of life; and man became a living soul" (Gen. 2:7).

Through his present body man lives an earthly life. He is strictly limited to the earthly sphere of existence. He has an earthly eye, and perceives earthly things. He has an earthly ear, and hears earthly sounds. He is bound to the earth, and craves food and drink. Spiritual realities he cannot perceive, nor have direct communion with them. The heavenly things are hid from him.

Even in as far as he can know about them and apprehend them in his present, earthly, psychical state, he can do so only through the means of earthly symbols. Through the word that is heard with our physical ear we have knowledge of and fellowship with God, and apprehend spiritual and heavenly things. And that word addresses us in earthly terms. On the earthly plane of our present psychical existence God reveals himself to us. He speaks to us in human and earthly symbols. We cannot see him face to face. Even the risen Lord, in his glorious body, must "appear" to his disciples, in order to convince them of the reality of his resurrection. Angels and heavenly things lie beyond the scope of our present experience. We have an earthly soul, and in our psychical body we live an earthly life. And with regard to things spiritual and heavenly, which "eye hath not seen, nor ear heard" (1 Cor. 2:9), we "walk by faith" (2 Cor. 5:7), which is the evidence of things not seen, the substance of things hoped for (Heb. 11:1). We do not walk "by sight" (2 Cor. 5:7).

In death, therefore, the body "is sown a natural body" (1 Cor 15:44). But "it is raised a spiritual body." The body of the resurrection will be wholly subservient to our glorified spirit and to the indwelling Spirit of Christ. By it we will be able to "inherit the kingdom of God," which "flesh and blood" cannot inherit (v. 50). In that new and eternal kingdom we shall see God face to face. We shall behold Christ and always be with him. And we shall have direct contact and fellowship with the things that are heavenly. With new eyes we shall see the things that are now hidden from us, and with spiritual ears we shall apprehend the things that now lie beyond the scope of our hearing. For,

44. There is a natural body, and there is a spiritual body.
45. And so it is written, The first man Adam was made a living soul; the last Adam was made a quickening spirit.
46. Howbeit that was not first which is spiritual, but that which is natural; and afterward that which is spiritual.
47. The first man is of the earth, earthy: the second man is the Lord from heaven.
48. As is the earthy, such are they also that are earthy: and as is the heavenly, such are they also that are heavenly.
49. And as we have borne the image of the earthy, we shall also bear the image of the heavenly.
50. Now this I say, brethren, that flesh and blood cannot inherit the kingdom of God; neither doth corruption inherit incorruption.
51. Behold, I show you a mystery; We shall not all sleep, but we shall all be changed,
52. In a moment, in the twinkling of an eye, at the last trump: for the trumpet shall sound, and the dead shall be raised incorruptible, and we shall be changed.
53. For this corruptible must put on incorruption, and this mortal must put on immortality.
54. So when this corruptible shall have put on incorruption, and this mortal shall have put on immortality, then shall be brought to pass the saying that is written, Death is swallowed up in victory. (1 Cor. 15:44–54)

I believe the resurrection of the body.

What a glorious and comforting confession this is. For it means that in the resurrection the glorified spirits of the believers in Jesus Christ our Lord shall be reunited with their glorified bodies. And in those glorified, heavenly bodies the saints shall forever live in the sphere of incorruption, of power, glory, and immortality. And thus they shall forever inherit the kingdom of God, in which they shall see him face to face.

Article 12

And the life everlasting

Chapter 38

ETERNAL LIFE

"I believe the life everlasting."

This is what the believer and the church confesses in the last article of the so-called apostolic confession.

And about this we must stammer a few words in our present sermon.

I say "stammer," for this is really all we can do about the mystery of life, and particularly about the mystery of eternal life. It is only in as far as Scripture reveals something about this mystery that we can say a few things about life eternal.

Very often Scripture speaks of it, as we all know. "For God so loved the world, that he gave his only begotten Son, that whosoever believeth in him should not perish, but have everlasting life" (John 3:16). According to the Bible, this eternal life is a present state and condition as well as a future blessing: "He that believeth on the Son hath everlasting life" (v. 36). Christ is the bread of life, he is the living bread. And "if any man eat of this bread, he shall live for ever" (6:51). Eternal life is the blessing which the Good Shepherd bestows upon the sheep the Father gave him: "My sheep hear my voice, and I know them, and they follow me: and I give unto them eternal life; and they shall never perish, neither shall any man pluck them out of my hand" (10:27–28).

The real essence of this eternal life is the true knowledge of God: "This is life eternal, that they might know thee, the only true God, and Jesus Christ, whom thou hast sent" (John 17:3). It is the fruit of grace, for "as sin hath reigned unto death, even so might grace reign through righteousness unto eternal life by Jesus Christ our Lord" (Rom. 5:21). It is the gift of God: "For the wages of sin is death; but the gift of God is eternal life through Jesus Christ our Lord" (6:23). The apostle John testifies that he and the rest of the apostles have been witnesses of this eternal life in the face of our Lord Jesus Christ: "For the life was manifested, and we have seen it, and bear witness, and show unto you that eternal life, which was with the Father, and was manifested unto us" (1 John 1:2).

This eternal life is in the Son of God and through him is given unto us. For,

11. This is the record, that God hath given to us eternal life, and this life is in his Son.
12. He that hath the Son hath life; and he that hath not the Son of God hath not life.
13. These things have I written unto you that believe on the name of the Son of God; that ye may know that ye have eternal life, and that ye may believe on the name of the Son of God. (1 John 5:11–13)

In fact, Christ is that life, as he testifies of himself in John 14:6, "I am the way, the truth, and the life." And the apostle writes: "And we know that the Son of God is come, and hath given us an understanding, that we may know him that is true, and we are in him that is true, even in his Son Jesus Christ. This is the true God, and eternal life" (1 John 5:20).

Very often, therefore, the Bible speaks of the life eternal that is mentioned in the last article of the apostolic confession.

What is life? And what is life eternal? These questions we must answer very briefly in the light of the word of God.

Scripture offers us no definition of life. The nearest approach to a definition is found in John 17:3, where it is said that life eternal is the true knowledge of God in Jesus Christ. Yet the word of God frequently suggests something of the true nature of life.

First of all, we may say that life is a principle of free energy. Life is action. To live is to act. Activity is the expression of life. The word of God speaks of him always as the living God, and presents him as active. God is the living God, in distinction from idols. The latter are altogether vanity. They can neither see, nor hear, nor speak. In them is no action whatsoever: "But the LORD is the true God, he is the living God, and an everlasting king: at his wrath the earth shall tremble, and the nations shall not be able to abide his indignation" (Jer. 10:10). At

Mount Sinai Israel recognized him as the living God, for they heard his voice and saw that God talked with man (Deut. 5:25). They had witnessed how he divided the waters of Jordan before their feet, and drove out for them the nations from the land he had promised them. And in all this they knew him as the living God (Josh. 3:10).

God has life in himself. And that surely means that he is infinite energy, pure activity. He never slumbers nor sleeps. He is eternally active with his whole being. He hears and sees, wills and knows, loves and hates. His holiness is not a cold virtue; it is a living flame, a consuming fire. His righteousness is not an attribute that occasionally reveals itself in action; it is an energetic, ever-active power. His mercy is ever fervent. His lovingkindness is forever ardent. All that is in God is eternally and infinitely active, for he is the living God.

And as life is energy and activity in God, so it is also in the creature. For God is the author of all life, and apart from him there is no life.

But we may say more of life.

Life is harmony and fellowship. Also in this respect God alone is the source of life, and he is the living God. For he is triune. He is one in being, in nature, in mind and will, in holiness and righteousness, in knowledge and wisdom, and in all his infinite perfections. And he is a personal God. The Scriptures reveal him to us as three in persons, Father, Son, and Holy Ghost. These divine persons subsist in the one divine being, and they stand in relation of perfect harmony and fellowship with one another. The Father knows and loves the Son in infinite perfection in the Spirit. The Son knows and loves the Father in the Spirit. The Spirit knows and loves the Father through the Son in himself, and he searches the depths of God. Thus the three persons of the holy Trinity live in eternal harmony and perfect fellowship with one another. There is no separation or disunity, no disharmony or conflict, in God. He is a covenantal God, and lives the life of perfect friendship.

With a reflection of that life, man was originally created. God formed him out of the dust of the ground, breathed into his nostrils the breath of life, made him an intellectual and willing creature, a being that was adapted to bear and to reflect the very image of God. And with this image of God he was endowed. He was created with perfect knowledge, in order that his mind might react in love upon the revelation of the mind of God. He was created with uprightness of will, in order that in all his willing life he might be in harmony with the will of God and have his delight in the keeping of his commandments. And he was created with spotless holiness, so that all his desires and inclinations were consecrated to the living God. Thus man was a reflection of the life that is in God. He was made a covenantal creature, and lived a covenantal life, in fellowship of friendship with the Most High.

But this life he lost. Man no longer lives, although he still moves and acts. He is dead. For he is alienated from the living God. He no longer stands in the fellowship of friendship with the Most High. His present existence, even though it continues forever, is not everlasting life, but perpetual death.

However, in Jesus Christ our Lord God realizes and reveals what the Bible calls life eternal. And this eternal life is an entirely new life. It is not only different from our present state, which is death, but it is also different from and higher than the state of Adam in paradise. The reason of this is that eternal life has its source and reaches us from the incarnated Son of God. That incarnation is the central realization of the heavenly tabernacle of God's eternal covenant of friendship. For it is the most intimate union between God and man. In Christ, the Son of God, the second person of the holy Trinity, God of God, the express image of his substance (Heb. 1:3), is revealed in human nature, lives in us and lives with us.

And Scripture reveals very clearly that eternal life is conditioned by and has its source in Christ, the Son of God in human nature. He is "the resurrection, and the life" (John 11:25). He is "the way, the truth, and the life" (14:6). In him "the life was manifested," and he is the revelation of that "eternal life, which was with the Father" (1 John 1:2). He "is the true God and eternal life" (5:20). Eternal life, therefore, is the knowledge of God and of Jesus Christ whom God hath sent (John 17:3). Eternal life, therefore, is that knowledge of and fellowship with God that is rooted in the incarnation and is bestowed upon us through the Spirit of the Son of God.

Moreover, eternal life is resurrection life. It lies on the other side of death. It is victory over death. It may safely be said that except through the deep and dark way of sin and death this higher goal of bliss that is called eternal life could never be attained. No, we cannot morbidly beautify and extol the fall of Adam, as in fact it has been done, as if it were a good in itself. On our part, there is nothing but sin and shame in that fall of our first father in paradise, a cause for deep humiliation and repentance. We wantonly despised the riches of the knowledge of God and trampled his covenant underfoot, choosing rather to be allied with the devil and to follow his lie than to walk in the light of God's blessed favor.

Nevertheless, on God's part, there is only the revelation of his marvelous wisdom and power in this fall of the first man Adam. For he chose this way because he had provided some better thing for us. Even though the guilt and responsibility of the fall remains wholly man's, it cannot be doubted for a moment that also the fall of Adam was quite according to the counsel of the Most High. His purpose must be realized, and sin and death are subservient to that purpose. That purpose was the realization of his everlasting covenant of friendship with his people in Christ Jesus our Lord. He alone can and does bring life out of death. And that life out of death is resurrection life. And that resurrection life is life eternal. The knowledge of God as the God of our salvation, unto whom we cry from the depths of sin and death, and the fellowship with him, that is eternal life.

In the state of righteousness in paradise man tasted the grace of God positively as his favor. He did not know the depth of that grace as it is revealed in redemption, even the forgiveness of sins. He knew and tasted that God is good, for he was encompassed with divine blessings, but the abundant mercy revealed in the wonder of deliverance whereby God saves us from the power of sin, the curse, and death, to raise us to the highest possible blessedness of heavenly glory in his tabernacle, this he could not possibly know. He certainly knew God in his great power, knowledge, and wisdom. For the things that are made loudly declare them unto him. But he could not possibly know the mighty power of God revealed in the resurrection of Jesus Christ from the dead and in his exaltation in heavenly places, far above all principality and power and might and dominion and every name that is named, not only in this world, but also in that which is to come.

Eternal life is resurrection life. It could not possibly be attained, except through the deep way of sin and death. Hence, it could not be attained except through the death and the resurrection of the Son of God. When God chose the deep way of sin and death, he made it at once impossible for man of himself to walk in that way so that he would reach life eternal. God himself must walk in that way. Only his Son could become the first begotten of the dead. Hence, he came to us in our guilt and damnation, in our misery and death, when he sent his Son in the likeness of sinful flesh, and for sin.

In that Son of God, the God of our salvation, the head of the church, walked in all the way of righteousness and justice, of wrath and death and hell, in order to atone for sin and obtain for us everlasting righteousness and life. He walked the way of death, and through death into the resurrection, and became the revelation of the God of our salvation in all the abundance of his power and might, of his wisdom and knowledge, of his righteousness and holiness, of the riches of his grace and mercy, and everlasting, unchangeable love. And when that God of our salvation, our Lord Jesus Christ, makes his dwelling with us, calls us out of darkness into the light of life, instructs us by his Spirit and word in the true knowledge of God as revealed in him, then we have eternal life.

That life is everlasting. It can never be lost. For it is rooted in the incarnation of the Son of God.

This eternal life believers now possess in principle. "He that believeth on the Son hath everlasting life" (John 3:36). For he is reborn through the Spirit of Christ. He is raised from the dead. In Christ he is set "in heavenly places" (Eph. 2:6). And of this new life he is conscious by faith. He feels in his heart the beginning of eternal joy when he lays hold on the mercy and grace of God in the forgiveness of sin; when he is assured that, though all things within and without testify against him, he is righteous before God; when the Spirit of adoption assures him of his sonship, and he cries, "Abba, Father"; when he hates sin, and has his delight in the precepts of his God, and longs for the final deliverance from the body of this death; when he looks forward in hope, rooted in the love of God that is shed abroad in his heart, to the final adoption and justification, and the redemption of his body. In all this he has and tastes the beginning of eternal life. And the believer will enjoy the blessedness and peace of it according as he earnestly walks in the way of sanctification, fights against sin, and has a delight in the keeping of the precepts of his God.

This beginning of eternal life which we now enjoy will be translated into the fullness of joy in the tabernacle of God with men. That beginning will advance into the state of spiritual perfection after death, when the earthly house of this tabernacle shall be dissolved, and we shall inherit the house of God eternal in the heavens. But it will not reach its final perfection of glory until all the saints in Christ, all the elect of God, shall have been gathered, our bodies shall have put off corruption and mortality and shall have put on incorruption and immortality, the new heavens and the new earth shall have been created, and the tabernacle of God shall be with men forever.

To be sure, that new creation itself will be beautiful and glorious: for all things therein will be united in Christ as their head. But nevertheless, the essence of all the blessedness and glory of that new world will be the perfected fellowship of friendship with the living God in Christ. Everywhere in that new world we shall see Christ, and in him the Father. We shall see him face to face. All our knowledge will then be theology in the highest sense of the word. This is life eternal, to know thee, and Jesus Christ whom thou hast sent.

Of that glory we can only form a faint conception as long as we are in this life. That final perfection belongs to the things which "eye hath not seen, nor ear heard, neither have entered into the heart of man" (1 Cor. 2:9). But when it shall be revealed, all of that eternal life will be concentrated upon the everlasting praise of God, of whom, and through whom, and unto whom are all things. To him will be the glory forever (Rom. 11:36).

APPENDICES

Appendix 1

CONCEIVED BY
THE HOLY GHOST

I n the Christmas season we are, of course, very strongly reminded of the article in the apostolic confession: "And in Jesus Christ our Lord, who was conceived by the Holy Ghost, born of the Virgin Mary." And it is to this truth that I want to call your special attention in the present sermon as well as in the next. And I wish to do so on the basis of the word of God as it is found in Luke 1:26–38,

26. And in the sixth month the angel Gabriel was sent from God unto a city of Galilee, named Nazareth,
27. To a virgin espoused to a man whose name was Joseph, of the house of David; and the virgin's name was Mary.
28. And the angel came in unto her, and said, Hail, thou that art highly favoured, the Lord is with thee: blessed art thou among women.
29. And when she saw him, she was troubled at his saying, and cast in her mind what manner of salutation this should be.
30. And the angel said unto her, Fear not, Mary: for thou hast found favour with God.
31. And, behold, thou shalt conceive in thy womb, and bring forth a son, and shalt call his name JESUS.
32. He shall be great, and shall be called the Son of the Highest: and the Lord God shall give unto him the throne of his father David:
33. And he shall reign over the house of Jacob for ever; and of his kingdom there shall be no end.
34. Then said Mary unto the angel, How shall this be, seeing I know not a man?

35. And the angel answered and said unto her, The Holy Ghost shall come upon thee, and the power of the Highest shall overshadow thee: therefore also that holy thing which shall be born of thee shall be called the Son of God.

36. And, behold, thy cousin Elisabeth, she hath also conceived a son in her old age: and this is the sixth month with her, who was called barren.

37. For with God nothing shall be impossible.

38. And Mary said, Behold the handmaid of the Lord; be it unto me according to thy word. And the angel departed from her.

It was the sixth month, according to the text: that is, after the visit of the same angel to Zacharias in the temple, at which occasion he announced the birth of John the Baptist. This time Gabriel is sent to Nazareth, a small town built on the western and northwestern slopes of a hollow in the rugged country of Galilee, midway between the Sea of Galilee and the Mediterranean. Nazareth was proverbially despised, for it was said that no good thing could come out of Nazareth. Yet in a sense, though Christ is born in Bethlehem, he would also come out of Nazareth and be called the Nazarene: for there lived the virgin that was to be most blessed among women. And thither the angel Gabriel now speeds to bring the most amazing message ever brought to any human being.

In the words of our text we find the truth that is expressed in the apostolic confession that Jesus is conceived by the Holy Ghost and born of the virgin Mary. It is very important that the truth of the virgin birth and the conception by the Holy Spirit be firmly maintained by the church of Jesus Christ in the world. The church must hold fast to the truth concerning the mystery of the incarnation. She lives not by human philosophy, but by faith in revelation. And by that faith she confesses that Christ assumed a real human nature, body and soul, from the flesh and blood of the virgin Mary, that in his human nature he is the seed of David, in every respect like unto his brethren, sin excepted. She confesses, moreover, that the human nature through the wonder of the incarnation did not merge with the divine, nor was ever separated from the divine nature, but is and remains forever united with Christ's deity in the unity of the person of the Son of God. And in the same faith she confesses that the incarnation is in no sense an act of man, but solely of God. Man did not reach out for God or develop to new heights of God-consciousness; but God came down to us, ever to remain with us and dwell with us.

The incarnation is the revelation of the living God, of the God of our salvation. The Creator himself most intimately united himself with the creature. The Lord became servant. The Eternal One came into time, the Infinite One into space. Great is the mystery of godliness: God is manifest in the flesh.

This truth is plainly revealed in the words of our text. Mary was a virgin. For thus we read in the text, that Gabriel was sent "to a virgin espoused to a man whose name was Joseph, of the house of David; and the virgin's name was Mary." There can be no doubt that also Mary was of David's house, even though in the text the reference seems to be to Joseph. However, it seems rather certain that the genealogy in Luke 3 is not that of Joseph, but of Mary, though the text says that Jesus was thought to be the son of Joseph and undoubtedly was legally registered as such. Moreover, also the genealogy that occurs in Matthew in my opinion, although it too is apparently of Joseph, is nevertheless that of Mary. Moreover, in the text we read that the angel says to Mary: "The Lord God shall give unto him the throne of his father David." Presently, when John the Baptist is born and Zacharias' tongue is loosed, he sings that God "hath raised up an horn of salvation for us in the house of his servant David" (Luke 1:69). And besides, in all Scripture Christ is declared to be of the seed of David, the Lion of Judah's tribe, the root and offspring of David (Rom. 1:3; 2 Tim. 2:8; Heb. 7:14). All this could hardly be if Jesus was of David only by the legal reckoning through Joseph.

And Mary was a virgin. This is emphasized in the text. She was a virgin espoused to Joseph, which means that their legal relationship was as sacred as that of marriage, although as yet they did not live in the marriage relationship. The virgin birth was necessary not because a virgin is holier than a married woman, but because according to Scripture Christ was not to be born by the will of man. Besides, the Son of God was to unite himself with the human nature from the virgin Mary that the indubitable sign might be created that in the fullness of time the Son of God had united himself with human nature.

This is according to Scripture. Even in the old dispensation the sign of the virgin that would conceive and bear a son was given: "Therefore the Lord himself shall give you a sign; Behold, a virgin shall conceive, and bear a son, and shall call his name Immanuel" (Isa. 7:14). It is true that those who deny the virgin birth of Christ point out that the Hebrew word used in the text for virgin may also refer to a young woman recently married. Fact is, however, first of all, that the word signifies the age of puberty, a person of marriageable age but not yet married, and secondly, that the text speaks definitely of a sign. Now a sign is a phenomenon that draws the attention of men by its extraordinary character, its being radically different from the facts of experience, a wonder of grace. But there certainly would be nothing extraordinary in the fact that a young woman would conceive and bear a son. We maintain, therefore, that the prophecy in Isaiah 7:14 ultimately looks forward to the wonder of the birth of our Lord from the virgin Mary.

This is, moreover, corroborated by the passage in Matthew 1:18–25. In the twenty-second and twenty-third verses we read: "Now all this was done, that it might be fulfilled which was spoken of the Lord by the prophet, saying, Behold, a virgin shall be with child, and shall bring forth a son, and they shall call his name Emmanuel, which being interpreted is, God with us." This is evidently a reference to Isaiah 7:14. And "all this was done" refers to what is narrated in the preceding verses. Joseph having noticed Mary's condition had been minded to leave his espoused wife secretly. But the Lord had revealed to him in a dream that she was quite innocent of the sin he had suspected her to have committed. And in a dream it was explained to Joseph that that "which is conceived in her is of the Holy Ghost" (v. 20). This passage, therefore, is not only in itself clear proof for the virgin birth of the Savior, but also corroborates the view that in Isaiah 7:14 this amazing wonder was predicted.

When the angel came in unto Mary, he greeted her with the words: "Hail, thou that art highly favoured, the Lord is with thee: blessed art thou among women" (Luke 1:28). We read further that Mary was greatly troubled at this saying. She did not seem to be troubled at the appearance of the angel, probably because the angel had hidden some of his heavenly glory, seeing that the amazing message which he was to bring was in itself sufficient cause to trouble the mind of the lowly virgin. It is evident that the saying of the angel that caused trouble in Mary's heart and mind served as an introduction to prepare Mary for what was to follow.

Mary was, indeed, the highly favored one of the Lord. And she was the most blessed among women. We must remember that ever since the fall the promise had been the comfort of the believing women, the promise of the seed of the woman that would crush the head of the serpent. In the hope of that promise the believing women had borne the sorrow of childbearing, always bringing forth the redeemed church with a view to him that was to come. And that is still the case in the new dispensation. Also now the covenantal women bring forth their children in the hope that they may add to the promised seed and to the multitude which no man can number and that shall once surround the throne of God in glory. But among all these Mary was the most blessed, for she was the mother of the Lord himself.

Now let us pay particular attention to the question which Mary asks after she had heard the amazing message of the angel: "How shall this be, seeing I know not a man?" (v. 34). The message of the angel is found in verses 30–33:

30. Fear not, Mary: for thou hast found favour with God.

31. And, behold, thou shalt conceive in thy womb, and bring forth a son, and shalt call his name JESUS.

32. He shall be great, and shall be called the Son of the Highest: and the Lord God shall give unto him the throne of his father David:

33. And he shall reign over the house of Jacob for ever; and of his kingdom there shall be no end.

It is after she heard that message that Mary asks the question, "How shall this be, seeing I know not a man?"

What induced Mary to ask this question? The mere fact that at the moment Mary was still a virgin would hardly seem sufficient to explain this. It is true, of course, that she was not yet married. But it is also a fact that she was espoused to a man named Joseph. She was, therefore, about to be married. How, then, could she be so absolutely certain that she would not know a man? Certainly, there was nothing in the words of the angel that would suggest this, far less raise it beyond a doubt that she would become pregnant without the normal intercourse to cause such a condition.

Why could she not interpret the words of the angel as meaning that she would get married to Joseph as soon as possible, and that then, in that normal way, she would become with child? Would not that have been the most natural conclusion for her to draw from the announcement of the angel, rather than at once think of the astounding possibility that she would conceive without knowing a man? Yet of this one thing she appears absolutely sure: she will not know a man. And because of this the words of the angel appear to her to be humanly impossible of realization. How must this certainty on the part of Mary be explained?

It seems to us that there can be only one answer to this question: there was no man for her to know. That is, there was no man left in the royal line of the promise that could beget the promised Messiah. That Davidic generation of royal seed that according to the promise was expected to bring forth the Christ had ended in a virgin. The realization of the promise had become an impossibility from a human point of view. Long before Gabriel visited Mary in Nazareth the glorious tree of David had been cut down to the ground and never had it flourished again since the Babylonian captivity. But at the moment of the annunciation all that was left of it was "a root out of a dry ground" (Isa. 53:2). There was no male descendant in the royal line of the generations of the promise. Only a virgin was left. And therefore, when the angel came to announce to her that she would become the mother of him that would reign over the house of Jacob forever, the question arose immediately: "How shall this be, seeing I know not a man?"

This explanation is based on the conviction that in Matthew 1:1, 17 the evangelist gives us very really the "book of the generation of Jesus Christ" (v. 1), that is: not the legal line of Christ's fathers according to the flesh, but the organic line. In other words, in this book of generations we have the genealogy not of Joseph, but of Mary. If this is true, the sixteenth verse of the first chapter of Matthew must mean that Jacob had no male children, that Mary was the only heir, and that when Joseph married Mary he was received and inscribed legally in the registers of generations that ran from David over Jacob to the mother of Jesus. In this legal sense Joseph was of the house and lineage of David.

Whether he was also of the generations of David in the organic sense is a question that depends on the other question, whether or not in the third chapter of the gospel according to Luke we have the genealogy of Joseph. There is good ground to believe that also in Luke we meet with the genealogy of Mary, although legally it is that of Joseph. However this may be, if our interpretation of Matthew 1:16 be correct, Joseph was not of that line of generations, that continued line of Davidic kings, that would culminate in the Messiah. Mary alone was left. It was not improbable that she often pondered this in her heart, even before the angel came to visit her with the amazing message, and that the question that had frequently troubled her soul arose to her mind at once as she listened to the angel's words: "But how shall this be? How shall the promise be fulfilled, seeing there is not a man, and I am the only one left in the royal generations of David?"

If this be true, the virgin birth is established without a doubt. The denial of the virgin birth of Christ usually implies or leads to a denial of the incarnation of the Son of God, the truth that Jesus Christ came into the flesh. There are those who claim that the Son of God could just as well unite himself with our nature as it is normally conceived and born from a human mother and by the will of man. To say the least, this proposition is very difficult to prove. In fact, it is impossible of proof. We know very little about the mystery of the conception and birth of a normal child, much less about the birth of the Son of God in the flesh. Even though we may not be able to demonstrate the truth of this proposition, we must rather assume on the basis of Scripture that the virgin birth of Christ was also essentially and ontologically necessary, that is, that the Son of God could assume the human nature only by way of elimination of the will of man.

But whether this be so or not, certain it is that God purposely creates the sign of the virgin birth to make known unto us that Jesus

Christ's coming into the flesh is his act exclusively, and that Christ is born not by the will of man, but by the conception of the Holy Spirit. God reveals himself where all human possibilities have come to an end. The incarnation does not take place until the generations from which he was to be born according to the promise have ended in a virgin, that is, until an impossible situation has been created, in order that he may be revealed as the Lord, who not only calls the things that are not as if they were, but who also quickens the dead. Only when we are forced to ask the question, "How shall this be?", does God give us the answer: What is impossible with men, is possible with God (Luke 18:27).

And thus in the virgin birth God is revealed as the God of our salvation, who is mighty to save, and who surely will save his people even unto the very end. And well may we sing with the psalmist of Psalm 77:

> O God, most holy are Thy ways,
> And who like Thee deserves my praise?
> Thou only doest wondrous things,
> The whole wide world Thy glory sings;
> Thy outstretched arm Thy people saved,
> Tho' sore distressed and long enslaved.[1]

And again:

> Thy way was in the sea, O God,
> Thro mighty waters, deep and broad;
> None understood but God alone,
> To man Thy footsteps were unknown;
> But safe Thy people Thou didst keep,
> Almighty Shepherd of Thy sheep.[2]

---

[1] No. 211:1, in *The Psalter*.

[2] No. 211:3, in *The Psalter*.

Appendix 2

THE POWER
OF HIS RESURRECTION

O n the third day he arose again from the dead!
Such is the confession of the church of all ages.

Of the fact of the resurrection of Jesus Christ our Lord there are abundant evidences and witnesses. There is abundant evidence of the fact that this resurrection is real, that is, that his body was transformed from death into life; as well as of the fact he is *risen*, that he did not simply return from the grave into our present mortal body, that he entered into the glory of immortality. He was buried in the likeness of sinful flesh, weak, mortal, and in dishonor. But he returned with the likeness of the heavenly, in power and glory.

A silent witness of this, on the morning of that memorable third day, was the empty grave which the women and some of the apostles visited and believed. No one was present at the moment of the resurrection. We do not even know at what exact moment the Lord arose. It is possible, indeed, that he was raised even before the earthquake occurred and the angel descended from heaven to open the grave for inspection. Surely, the Lord had no need of the rolling away of that stone in order to issue forth from the grave in his spiritual body. And, therefore, all we read in the gospel according to Matthew, is that the angel rolled away the stone from the grave and sat upon it evidently to guard the grave from mutilation and to present it to the witnesses that would presently follow for inspection.

That empty grave was, indeed, a silent witness of the resurrection of the Lord. There was the place where the Lord had lain and which the women were invited to behold. There, on that place, where the Lord had lain, they beheld the wonder of the linen clothes in which Jesus' body had been wrapped at the burial. And these clothes, evidently, were not neatly folded up as is often alleged, but they must have lain there undisturbed in the very shape they assumed when they had been wrapped around the body of Jesus. A silent witness, indeed, of the wonder of his real and spiritual resurrection. Jesus had indeed arisen in the body, but not in the corruptible, earthly, and natural, but in the incorruptible, spiritual, and heavenly body.

Then, too, there was the testimony of the angels, the first preachers of the gospel of the resurrection to the amazed women. They proclaimed: Why seek ye the living among the dead? He is not here, but is risen even as he said unto you (Luke 24:5–6).

And lastly, there are the several appearances of the Lord to the apostles. These appearances that occurred during that marvelous period between his resurrection and his ascension were, at least, ten in number. In them the Lord showed himself to the apostles, and once even to five hundred disciples at the same time, and in different forms. But they all witnessed of the fact that Jesus had really risen from the dead as well as of the fact that he had arisen to the glory of immortal, heavenly life.

The fact of the resurrection, therefore, is well established. And the apostles went forth into the world emphatically preaching the gospel of the resurrection of Christ. For if Christ were not raised, our faith would be in vain, we would still be in our sin, and we would of all men be the most miserable. But now Christ is risen and is become the first-fruits of them that slept (1 Cor. 15:17, 19–20).

What, then, is the significance of the resurrection of the Lord? What is its power? Of this power of the resurrection of Christ the apostle Paul speaks in Philippians 3:10, "That I may know him, and the power of his resurrection."

What does this mean? What is the power of his resurrection and what does it mean to know that power?

The power of the resurrection of our Lord Jesus Christ is, first of all, righteousness, righteousness for sinners such as we are, righteousness as a free gift of grace. It is a righteousness that is far greater than even the righteousness which was Adam's before his fall into sin and death. Adam's righteousness could be lost and was lost the moment he fell into sin; the righteousness that is in the power of the resurrection of our Lord Jesus Christ is everlasting, can never be lost. The righteousness which Adam possessed in his original state made him worthy before God of the earthy and mortal life he possessed already. He would not die as long as he remained in the state of righteousness. But the righteousness that is the power of the resurrection of Christ is far greater: it makes us worthy of eternal life and glory in the eternal tabernacle of God with men.

In other words, the power of his resurrection is the power of the perfect and eternal justification of the sinner by the sovereign and free grace of the God of our salvation. For, do not forget, that resurrection is a word of God. When God raised up the Lord Jesus Christ from the dead, the almighty and efficacious word proceeded out of the mouth of God by which the darkness of sin and guilt was pierced and removed forever, and his people were justified. For who is he that on the third day arose in his own power and was raised by God the Father from the dead? He is Jesus Christ the Lord. He is not a mere individual, but the one who from all eternity is ordained by God the Father as the head of the elect, of his body, the church. From them he is forever inseparable.

He is the one, too, that for them and in their stead, voluntarily took their place in the hour of judgment, bore for them the wrath of God, entered into deepest death and hell on the accursed tree. And bearing the load of their sin and guilt on his mighty shoulders, he removed it by willingly making a sacrifice of himself upon the altar of the love of God, thus making perfect satisfaction for sin. He finished all. And while still on the cross, shortly before he laid down his life for his sheep, he cried out: "It is finished!" (John 19:30).

To this outcry of the obedient servant of Jehovah on the cross of Calvary the resurrection of Christ is the response of the Father. That resurrection is the seal of God upon the perfect sacrifice of the Lord. Never could he have been found worthy of life and glory, had he not perfectly atoned for the sin of those whom the Father had given him. Hence, the power of his resurrection is the word of God that in him we are justified forever. For even as we were inseparable from him in his death, so we are in him in his resurrection. He "was delivered for," or on account of our transgressions. He "was raised again for", or on account of "our justification" (Rom. 4:25).

In the resurrection of Christ, at that very moment, the whole church, all the elect, all that believe in his name, were forever declared righteous before God, freely, unconditionally, of mere and sovereign grace. In that resurrection they have the adoption unto children of God and everlasting life and glory.

That is the power of his resurrection.

The resurrection is the word of God concerning our justification. As on the first day of creation week he spoke: "Let there be light" (Gen. 1:3); so on the day of the resurrection of our Lord Jesus Christ his word of power went forth: "Let there be righteousness." And as on that first creation day there was light, so on the resurrection morning there was righteousness for all his people.

But there is more.

The power of the resurrection of our Lord Jesus Christ is also the power of a new life. It is the power of resurrection life for the whole church. For the risen Lord lives. He lives with a life that was never before witnessed or experienced on the earth. It is a life, not natural but spiritual, not in weakness but in power, not in dishonor but in glory, not earthy but heavenly, not mortal but immortal. It is a life that is not and can never be subject unto death anymore, a life over which sin has not and cannot have dominion forever. Such is the life of our risen Lord.

And Christ was raised not as an individual, but as the head of the body, both in a legal and in an organic sense of the word. On the third day, the day of the resurrection of Jesus Christ our Lord, the whole church, all the elect, you and I that believe on his name, were raised from the dead, were translated, principally, from death into immortality. And even now he causes, by the Spirit that is given unto him, that life to flow into our hearts when he regenerates us and causes us to hear his word of life: "Awake thou that sleepest, and arise from the dead, and Christ shall give thee light" (Eph. 5:14).

Such is the power of his resurrection.

And, therefore, the power of his resurrection is also the power of a new hope, the hope of eternal life in body and soul, the hope of our final resurrection. For, as the apostle has it in 1 Corinthians 15:20, "But now is Christ risen from the dead, and become the firstfruits of them that slept." The resurrection of the Lord Jesus Christ is resurrection in and of the body. It is the complete victory over all death, also over the grave. On the resurrection morning a divine word pierces the darkness of our death and it shall never return. It will accomplish all it speaks. It speaks of glory, of heavenly glory in body and soul.

That glory is Christ's, but again it is his as the head of the body, his church. Christ was raised as the firstfruits. When the firstfruits of Israel were brought into the temple, the harvest stood already ripe on the fields ready to be gathered in. Hence, when Christ was raised as the firstfruits of them that slept, the dead in Christ are waiting to be gathered in the glorious resurrection. His resurrection is only the beginning; the resurrection of all his people, of you and me that believe on his name shall be the final culmination. "O death, where is thy sting? O grave, where is thy victory?...Thanks be to God, which giveth us the victory through our Lord Jesus Christ" (1 Cor. 15:55, 57)!

The resurrection of Jesus Christ our Lord is the power of a glorious hope!

Do you wonder that the apostle longs to know him and the power of his resurrection? Do you wonder that he counts all things but loss and considers them as dung for the excellency of Jesus Christ his Lord?

But what does it mean to know him and to know the power of his resurrection? It certainly does not refer to a mere natural knowledge of the facts of his resurrection. It does not mean a knowledge which one can acquire by the exercise of his mental faculty, by intellectual power or acumen. The apostle is not thinking of the doctrine of the resurrection of Jesus however important and necessary this may be in itself. There is a wide difference between knowing all about the truth of the resurrection of Jesus Christ the Lord and knowing the power of his resurrection. There is an essential difference between knowing all about the power of electricity and turning on the switch by which you flood your home with light. You may know all about the power of ether as an anesthetic, you may have witnessed its power as it was applied to the patient on the operating table. But there is a wide difference between that and inhaling it so that you are lost unto the world.

You may know all about the power of his resurrection, so that you are able even to write treatises and books on this sublime subject and become instrumental in enlightening others and applying unto them the power of his glorious resurrection. You may have witnessed the manifestation of this glorious power as it was applied, by the grace of God, to others who are saved from sin and shame, and who by the power of that resurrection passed through the valley of the shadow of death with a song of victory on their dying lips. But to know him and the power of his resurrection is something quite different.

It refers to the knowledge of experience.

It signifies nothing less than that this marvelous power of the resurrection of our Lord Jesus Christ, mightily, irresistibly took hold of your inmost heart and soul and vibrated through every fiber of your being. It means that you experienced that power, tasted it, were overcome by it. It means that, principally, all that is in you of death and shame, of filth and unrighteousness, of enmity and rebellion against the living God, of fear and unrest, of darkness and despair, of guilt for which you could never atone, of corruption that held you in eternal bonds, of the misery of hell and the slavery of the devil, was dispelled, broken, crushed by the power of the resurrection of Jesus Christ our Lord. And, on the other hand, it means that life and glory, righteousness and holiness, love and peace, hope and rest, light and liberty, the righteousness of the kingdom of heaven, flooded your inmost soul through the power of his resurrection!

Oh, do not make a mistake! Although, principally, we are raised from the dead, we are still in the body of this death; although, principally, we are renewed unto a new life, we are still in our old nature; although, principally, we are in heaven, we are still on the earth. Hence, the power of the resurrection of Jesus Christ always reveals itself, in this world, as a tension. It becomes manifest as a tension, or, if you will, as a fight of the new against the old, of the new man in Christ against the old man of sin, of immortality against mortality, of the heavenly against the earthy. For, never forget, we have but a small beginning of the new obedience.

Hence, while that power of the resurrection makes you cry out daily: "God be merciful to me a sinner" (Luke 18:13); it at the same time causes you to shout with joy: "Therefore being justified by faith, we have peace with God through our Lord Jesus Christ" (Rom 5:1).

It causes you at once to know that you are a damnable sinner before God and to taste the joy of being righteous before God through faith, without the works of the law, merely by grace. The power of his resurrection makes you lament with the apostle Paul: "O wretched man that I am! who shall deliver me from the body of this death?" (7:24); but at the same time causes you to give the otherwise impossible answer to this question: "I thank God through Jesus Christ our Lord" (v. 25).

To know the power of his resurrection is the consciousness that you are liberated from the law of sin and death. That power is able to lift you up far above the heights that surround this valley of misery and death and is strong to press from your lips the triumphant shout: "O death, where is thy sting? O grave, where is thy victory?...Thanks be to God, which giveth us the victory through our Lord Jesus Christ" (1 Cor. 15:55, 57)! It is righteousness and life, joy and hope, freedom and victory forevermore!

FROM THE SAME AUTHOR

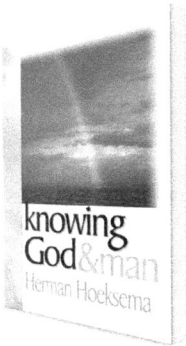

Knowing God and Man

God is God. This truth sets the tone for all thirteen chapters—six on God and seven on man. Each chapter on God directs the reader's attention to a different biblical aspect of the sovereign of the universe: God as God, as creator, as Lord, as good, as the living God, and as love. The seven chapters about man are clear explanations of man's covenantal relationship to God, his creation in the image of God, his fall, and his totally depraved nature, and they also direct the reader to the triune God and to Jesus Christ the redeemer.

For man, who is a rational, moral creature originally created after the image of God, this covenantal fellowship of the Trinity signifies that man lives only when this current of divine life energy of covenant friendship passes through him according to his measure and capacity as a creature, and when this current of life touches his inmost heart in divine love, and from his heart passes through his mind and will and all his being, filling him with light and joy, and with knowledge of God, truth, and righteousness.—Herman Hoeksema

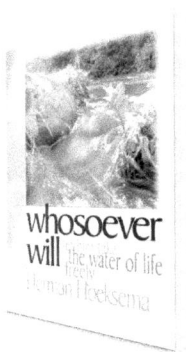

Whosoever Will

"And whosoever will, let him take the water of life freely" (Rev. 22:17). Hoeksema pastorally brings home to the believer the rich, personal meaning of these and similar biblical verses, explaining the doctrine of sovereign, particular grace regarding coming to faith in Jesus Christ.

We must come, then, to Christ, in order to drink the water of life, that is, to receive from him, and to appropriate unto ourselves all the spiritual blessings of grace, to obtain righteousness and life. Christ calls: 'Come unto me and drink'...He [Christ] is our righteousness. He is our complete redemption. And he imparts himself and all the blessings of salvation unto us through his Spirit. But this is done in such a way, that we receive and appropriate these blessings of salvation by a conscious and willing act on our part corresponding to Christ's act of imparting himself to us. This act on our part is expressed by the words: 'Come and drink!' The water of life, if I may retain the figure for a moment, is not poured down our throat without any act on our part, or even against our will. Even if such a thing were possible, we would never taste its pure and refreshing sweetness. But it is the will of God that we taste it, for we are saved to the glory of his grace in the Beloved. He wills that we taste his grace, that we consciously experience the wonder of his grace. We must come and drink the water of life! — Herman Hoeksema

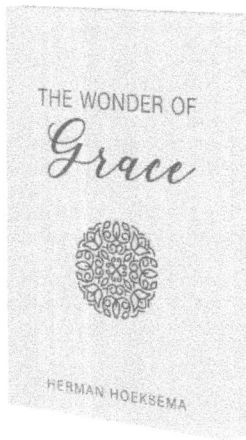

The Wonder of Grace

The author develops the concept of salvation by grace from the choosing of the believer by grace to the glorifying of the believer through grace. Each of the fifteen chapters is devoted to one aspect of the grace God bestows on the believer in the process of salvation. And as he progresses through the chapters, the reader will grow in the knowledge and confidence that salvation is by grace alone and that God is worthy of all praise and glory.

Only God can assure us of our salvation. On nothing less dare we base our assurance. But how does God speak to us? Always through the Scriptures. Apart from the Word of the gospel there is no Word of God to us. Hence, if we would make our calling and election sure, we must surely give diligence to read and study the Scriptures and to attend to the Word of God preached. But how do we know that God speaks to us personally? The answer is: he speaks to us by His Spirit, and thus applies the Word of the gospel to us personally, calling us evermore out of darkness to His marvelous light, and witnessing with our spirit that we are the sons of God (Rom. 8: 16). But here we must remember that this testimony of the Spirit that we are the sons of God is heard by us through the gospel only in the way of sanctification, the way of God's precepts, the way of repentance and conversion, the way in which the Spirit leads. In the way of sin and corruption, the way of the world and of the flesh, the Spirit does not witness with our spirit that we are children of God. On the contrary, in that way we grieve the Spirit; and we receive the testimony that we are still in our sins. If, then, we would make our calling and election sure, we must give diligence to walk in the way of light and righteousness, to fight the good fight of faith, according to the calling wherewith we are called. — Herman Hoeksema

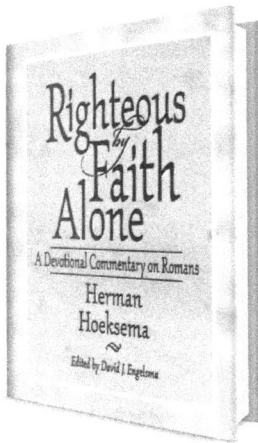

Righteous by Faith Alone: A Devotional Commentary on Romans

This exposition on what the author calls "one of the richest and most beautiful parts of the word of God" is clear in language, simple and warm in teaching, rich in practical application, and faithful to Scripture. This exposition is addressed not to scholars, but to the very same audience for whom the apostle wrote the epistle: the "beloved of God, called to be saints."

What does the Christian believe? Of what he is certain? In general, he is certain of this: God justifies the ungodly. This is basic in the life of the Christian. It is absolutely necessary that God justifies the ungodly if there is to be salvation. Yet this is impossible from every point of view. God cannot justify the ungodly. Not only is this impossible from God's point of view, it is also impossible insofar it comes to be a personal certainty in my mind. Everything in my experience testifies against this statement. My conscience testifies against the fact that I am justified. All the world testifies against me. You testify against me. I testify against you. The whole world stands before God and shouts against one another, 'You are damned.' The devil testifies again me. All my experience testifies against the fact that I am justified. My suffering, my pain, my troubles, my death: it all testifies against the fact that I am justified. Particularly my death testifies against it. One who is justified does not die. Saving faith is that I am certain, against all this testimony, that I am justified. The basis is the Word of God spoken in the resurrection. In the resurrection the Word of God comes to us and says, 'I justify the ungodly.' — Herman Hoeksema

Reformed Dogmatics
in 2 volumes

"There is a great deal of solid theology, and good theology, in this book...
[Hoeksema] always argues his own position with ability...This work...
represents his system of theology. He wrote it during the thirty years that he taught
in his own seminary while also serving as minister of a large congregation."
— *Christianity Today* (June 23, 1967)

All books available at **rfpa.org**,
or by calling the Reformed Free Publishing Association
at **616-457-5970** or emailing **mail@rfpa.org.**

Our Mission

To glorify God by making accessible to the broadest possible audience material that testifies to the truth of Scripture as understood and developed in the Reformed tradition.

Reformed Free Publishing Association
1894 Georgetown Center Drive
Jenison, MI 49428-7137
Website: rfpa.org
E-mail: mail@rfpa.org
Phone: 616-457-5970

www.ingramcontent.com/pod-product-compliance
Lightning Source LLC
Chambersburg PA
CBHW040406110426
42812CB00011B/2468